THE BEDFORD SERIES IN HISTORY AND CULTURE

D0342973

Notes on the State of Virginia

by Thomas Jefferson

WITH RELATED DOCUMENTS

Edited with an Introduction by

David Waldstreicher

University of Notre Dame

BEDFORD/ST. MARTIN'S   Boston   ♦   New York

*To Jacqueline Robinson, a great reader who makes
a revolutionary difference*

For Bedford/St. Martin's

Publisher for History: Patricia A. Rossi
Director of Development for History: Jane Knetzger
Developmental Editor: Molly E. Kalkstein
Editorial Assistant, Publishing Services: Maria Teresa Burwell
Senior Production Supervisor: Dennis J. Conroy
Production Associate: Christie Gross
Marketing Manager: Jenna Bookin Barry
Project Management: Books By Design, Inc.
Text Design: Claire Seng-Niemoeller
Indexer: Books By Design, Inc.
Cover Design: Billy Boardman
Cover Photo: Thomas Jefferson by Gilbert Stuart © Burstein Collection/CORBIS.
Composition: Stratford Publishing Services, Inc.
Printing and Binding: Haddon Craftsmen, an RR Donnelley & Sons Company

President: Charles H. Christensen
Editorial Director: Joan E. Feinberg
Director of Marketing: Karen R. Melton
Director of Editing, Design, and Production: Marcia Cohen
Manager, Publishing Services: Emily Berleth

Library of Congress Control Number: 2001097372

Copyright © 2002 by Bedford/St. Martin's

All rights reserved. No part of this book may be reproduced, stored in a retrieval
system, or transmitted in any form or by any means, electronic, mechanical,
photocopying, recording, or otherwise, except as may be expressly permitted by the
applicable copyright statutes or in writing by the Publisher.

Manufactured in the United States of America.

7   6
f   e   d   c   b

For information, write: Bedford/St. Martin's, 75 Arlington Street, Boston, MA 02116
(617-399-4000)

ISBN-10: 0-312-25713-9 (paperback)
          0-312-29428-X (hardcover)
ISBN-13: 978-0-312-25713-2 (paperback)
          978-0-312-29428-1 (hardcover)

Foreword

The Bedford Series in History and Culture is designed so that readers can study the past as historians do. The historian's first task is finding the evidence. Documents, letters, memoirs, interviews, pictures, movies, novels, or poems can provide facts and clues. Then the historian questions and compares the sources. There is more to do than in a courtroom, for hearsay evidence is welcome, and the historian is usually looking for answers beyond act and motive. Different views of an event may be as important as a single verdict. How a story is told may yield as much information as what it says.

Along the way the historian seeks help from other historians and perhaps from specialists in other disciplines. Finally, it is time to write, to decide on an interpretation and how to arrange the evidence for readers.

Each book in this series contains an important historical document or group of documents, each document a witness from the past and open to interpretation in different ways. The documents are combined with some element of historical narrative—an introduction or a biographical essay, for example—that provides students with an analysis of the primary source material and important background information about the world in which it was produced.

Each book in the series focuses on a specific topic within a specific historical period. Each provides a basis for lively thought and discussion about several aspects of the topic and the historian's role. Each is short enough (and inexpensive enough) to be a reasonable one-week assignment in a college course. Whether as classroom or personal reading, each book in the series provides firsthand experience of the challenge—and fun—of discovering, recreating, and interpreting the past.

Lynn Hunt
David W. Blight
Bonnie G. Smith
Natalie Zemon Davis
Ernest R. May

Preface

Thomas Jefferson's *Notes on the State of Virginia* (1785, 1787) is the only book published by one of America's greatest interpreters and statesmen. His most sustained explanations of American republican government, as well as his most developed arguments against slavery and in favor of racial hierarchy, can be found within the slim volume. Deeply aware of the controversial nature of these subjects in his time, Jefferson developed the work gradually, and only after a French bookseller threatened to go ahead with a French translation did he commit to publishing the volume, which appeared in the United States during the fateful year when the new Constitution was being considered by the states.

The *Notes* have been quoted and excerpted for more than two hundred years, but less often read as a whole. This book stresses the *Notes*'s importance as a public statement on the meaning of the American Revolution by a leader of the largest and most politically powerful of the new states. The Introduction presents the *Notes* as a response to Jefferson's, Virginia's, and America's revolutionary experiences. At a time of rapid change and real disorder, Jefferson imagined, and predicted, a new kind of order based on what he saw as the facts of Virginian, and American, life. The order Jefferson hoped to inspire proceeded from the natural world to the social world, seeking principles that would allow him to relate material realities to recent phenomena. A quintessential Enlightenment thinker, Jefferson placed nature inside of history, and history inside of nature. Natural history served as his paradigm, or organizing principle, for thinking about change in society. Natural history enabled him to speculate on old-world European history and make arguments about the American future.

Jefferson wrote about Virginia and America simultaneously. Events of the 1780s made it possible for Virginia, the largest and most populous state, to stand in for the new nation in ways that would not have been plausible or possible a few years later. Nevertheless, at every turn the *Notes* reveals itself as a quintessentially American document, and not least because Jefferson keeps returning to the presence of Native Americans and of African slaves. This is what made America most different, both to Europeans and, it seems, to the author of the Declaration of Independence himself. Although Jefferson at times seems to prefer to write about more easily resolved issues in the characterization of plants and animals, the culmination of his chapters regularly take up what he thinks of as the human *races* and how to understand them and their natures.

In writing about *nature* Jefferson sought an overall framework for addressing diversity and conflict in revolutionary America. In debating the "natures" of people of different races, Jefferson jumped into a contemporary debate over empires, nations, and justice. He insisted that the American Revolution was an important step toward meaningful human equality. At the same time, in comparing Africans and Native Americans to plants and animals, and placing them lower than Europeans and Americans in a hierarchy of developing civilizations, he helped open the door to modern scientific racism, the idea that some people, marked by race, are genetically inferior. It is this paradox that has given the text much of its continuing power and significance.

The other documents presented here illuminate the European and American political and intellectual contexts for Jefferson's composition of the *Notes* and their subsequent reception by Jefferson's contemporaries. There are many ways to approach such a complex document, a book that concerned itself, as Jefferson did, with the forms of government, diplomacy, environment, race relations, economics, manners, and local institutions. We tend to break these subjects into academic disciplines; eighteenth-century thinkers like Jefferson did not. Instead of choosing, this book seeks to understand how and why Jefferson made connections between, for example, race and nature, government and manners, landscape and institutions. It sees race relations as a connecting tissue, a problem Jefferson dealt with in ways that his contemporaries, and Americans ever since, have found both inspiring and horrifying.

Founding fathers like Jefferson have often been presented without their human failings or limitations. They get the credit for what is good about America. In response, it is easy to blame them for America's problems. Both approaches risk placing too much emphasis on powerful or representative individuals in history. When history is about celebrating or criticizing heroes and villains, it loses much of its power to explain the past, much less how we got from there to here. This book returns to the documents and the contexts within which those documents were written, seeking in them answers to questions that our contemporary focus on Jefferson's character may never yield.

ACKNOWLEDGMENTS

Pride of place must go to the University of Virginia, where I received a very fine undergraduate education and where I began to understand how much Jefferson could still matter. Later, Laura Wexler, a literary critic and historian of exceptional range and vision, guided me through the literature of the early American republic and helped me read the *Notes* with care. This book would not exist were it not for her remarkable generosity and mentorship.

The same must be said for David Brion Davis, for whose intellectual and cultural history course I first taught the text and discussed it with students. No one understands Jefferson, or his views on race and slavery, better than DBD, and I could not possibly enumerate the many ways in which my approach has been influenced by his example. I hope that his demand for rigor and carefulness in interpretation, as well as his achievements as an editor of exceptional documentary histories, have also had some fruits here.

Students at Bennington College, Yale University, and the University of Notre Dame shaped my appreciation of the *Notes* by asking good questions and by caring enough to read carefully. Katherine Kurzman and Molly Kalkstein of Bedford/St. Martin's deftly shepherded this volume toward production as did Nancy Benjamin of Books By Design. Joyce Appleby, Joseph J. Ellis, Barbara B. Oberg, Peter S. Onuf, John D. Saillant, and Ann Withington reviewed an early draft and provided exceptionally helpful suggestions on matters of fact, interpretation, and style. Their expertise, professionalism, and precision in response to my work reminded me how heavily and inevitably I have relied on a scholarly tradition of wrestling with Jefferson and his meaning. I therefore thank all the Jefferson scholars past and present, even the ones I disagree with implicitly and explicitly. As my grandmother, Minnie Sands Waldstreicher, used to say, it takes all kinds to make a world.

Finally, a big thank you to Jacqueline Robinson, whose support, understanding, and critical intelligence makes my world possible.

David Waldstreicher

Contents

PART ONE

Introduction: Nature, Race, and Revolution in Jefferson's America

Thomas Jefferson had a favorite story about Benjamin Franklin, fellow founder of the republic and the most famous American of his day. During the early 1780s, while serving as the new nation's minister to France, Franklin had a dinner party at his house. Half the guests at the table were American, the other half French. One of the French guests was the Abbé Guillaume-Thomas-François Raynal, who had written extensively about the failings of nature in America, as seen in the allegedly small size of American plants and animals. "During the dinner," Jefferson recalled, Raynal "got on his favorite theory of the degeneracy of animals, and even of man, in America, and urged it with his usual eloquence." Franklin then looked around and said, "Come, M[onsieur] l'Abbé, let us try this question by the fact before us. We are here one half Americans and one half French, and it happens that the Americans have placed themselves at one side of the table and our French friends on the other. Let both parties rise and we will see on which side nature has degenerated." The guests stood up. All the Americans at the dinner were tall; the French were much shorter, "and the Abbé himself, was a mere shrimp."[1]

The humor in the story lies in Franklin's half-serious resolution to a seemingly childish argument. Our specimens are bigger than

[1] Jefferson to Richard Walsh, Dec. 4, 1818, in *The Complete Thomas Jefferson,* ed. Saul K. Padover (New York, 1943), 894.

1

yours, says Franklin: we are bigger than you! Yet the humor can blind us to the real issues raised at Franklin's table. Abbé Raynal had downgraded American nature in part because of his outrage at the way that Spanish, French, and English colonialism in the Americas relied on war against Native Americans and enslavement of Africans. He depicted Native Americans as weak, backward, and innocent. He saw Europeans in America as bullies who returned to the violent, savage ways of their ancestors.[2] When Franklin brought Raynal's theory of history down to the impressive bodies of the Americans at his table, he changed the subject of the American story from the victimization of Indians and Africans to the achievements of accomplished white men like himself. He, Franklin, became the embodiment of America, and proof of its progress. He became *native*—not an expatriated, degenerated, Indian-fighting, slave-driving European, but a full grown man of the New World. He claimed the virtues of American nature for the new nation and threw off the blame for colonial sins.

Franklin had a great gift for the anecdote. His stories, however serious the implication, tend to be brief. Jefferson too was a storyteller. In many ways he was and remains America's greatest storyteller, the man who developed the ideas, the language, and even the narrative themes through which we still explain America to ourselves and to others. What is the Declaration of Independence if not a story about what England had done to the colonists and why the colonists had rebelled in response? (See Document 3.) Jefferson deeply believed his stories, at least in part because of his typically Enlightenment-era belief in reason, in the marshalling of fact, to overcome old superstitions. But Jefferson was more than a cold logician. To see only his logic, his faith in the new enlightened sciences, would be to miss the

[2]Antonello Gerbi, *The Dispute of the New World: The History of a Polemic, 1750–1900*, rev. ed. trans. Jeremy Moyle (Pittsburgh, 1973), 262. Raynal's *Histoire philosophique et politique des établissemens et du commerce des Européens dans les deux Indes* (1770) argued against the view that the New World was innocent, natural, or a source of hope for an ailing or corrupt European civilization, and portrayed Africans as victims of European greed. But Raynal, like others in France, left open the possibility that the North American colonies were an improvement over earlier, Spanish and French efforts. Eventually Raynal was in fact converted to a more positive view by the American Revolution and by Franklin's performances. Peter Gay, *The Enlightenment: An Interpretation. Volume II: The Science of Freedom* (New York, 1969), 414–15, 555–56. David Brion Davis, *The Problem of Slavery in Western Culture* (1966; repr. New York, 1988), 12–17, 417–21; David Brion Davis, *The Problem of Slavery in the Age of Revolution, 1770–1823* (Ithaca, N.Y., 1975), 23, 487; Anthony Pagden, *Lords of All the World: Ideologies of Empire in Spain, Britain and France, c.1500–c.1800* (New Haven, Conn., 1995), 3–4, 163–67.

romantic brilliance, as well as the darker side of his stories about America.[3]

In *Notes on the State of Virginia,* at a time of crisis in his home state and in the new republic as a whole, Jefferson brought the methods of late eighteenth-century natural history to bear on Virginian and American problems. The very methods that can make the book seem at first unappealing to us—its lists, its legalities, its dispassionate statements of fact that seem to break suddenly into passionate rhetoric—made it possible for Jefferson to tell his most ambitious and fully developed story. It is a story about nature in America that makes nature a "myth for all purposes," the best evidence for a revolutionary vision of the future.[4] It is a tale of American progress: of establishing political institutions on firm, republican, and even democratic grounds; of turning a colonial economy into a more self-sufficient national one by exploiting the great natural resources visible everywhere; and of doing both these things while dealing with the Native nations who had real power and real claims to both American nature and American identity. It is a story about black and white that sought to end slavery even while making the matter of race more black and white than before.

THOMAS JEFFERSON'S VIRGINIA

Born into the Virginia gentry, Thomas Jefferson would not at first seem to be a likely revolutionary, much less a critic of slavery. After all, his famous mountaintop estate, Monticello, was built by slaves. His historic role in the events of the American Revolution makes sense only in the light of the peculiar anxieties of his generation of Virginia planters.

[3]Robert A. Williams Jr., "Thomas Jefferson: Indigenous American Storyteller," in *Thomas Jefferson and the Changing West,* ed. James P. Ronda (Albuquerque, 1997), 43–74; Rhys Isaac, "Monticello Stories Old and New" in *Sally Hemings and Thomas Jefferson: History Memory, and Civic Culture,* ed. Jan Ellen Lewis and Peter S. Onuf (Charlottesville, Va., 1999), 114–26. For Jefferson's indebtedness to the eighteenth-century cult of sensibility, see especially Andrew Burstein, *The Inner Jefferson: Portrait of a Grieving Optimist* (Charlottesville, Va., 1995); Jay Fliegelman, *Declaring Independence: Jefferson, Natural Language, and the Culture of Performance* (Stanford, 1993).

[4]Robert A. Ferguson, *Law and Letters in American Culture* (Cambridge, Mass., 1984), 34–58; Charles A. Miller, *Jefferson and Nature: An Interpretation* (Baltimore, 1988), 251.

A decade before the Civil War, the deep South's statesmen would declare, "Cotton is King." This fact, they insisted, made slavery necessary to the American, and also the English, economy. Two centuries earlier, in Virginia, tobacco was king. As demand for tobacco increased in Europe, so did the value and population of Virginia until the colony outstripped all of the other mainland colonies in size and number.

Early in the seventeenth century, Virginia's leaders staved off disaster by learning to plant tobacco, but the crop required much attention and hard work. The only way to succeed in Virginia, it seemed, was by exploiting people who had been kidnapped or sold in Africa, people who had sold themselves as indentured servants, or people who had been convicted of crimes in Britain. Land may have been cheap, but good land became harder to find, and newer immigrants headed for the outer settlements, where they faced angry Native Americans. By the late seventeenth century, a Virginian social and political pattern had been established. Frontier planters called for defense, and sometimes war, against Indians, but found themselves relatively weak compared to the powerful patriarchs in the east. An opportunistic English gentleman, Nathaniel Bacon, took advantage of these divisions and led a rebellion in 1676, which brought white indentured servants and slaves together in defiance of local and imperial authority.[5]

The Virginia gentry restored order; not coincidentally, around this time they moved decisively "toward slavery," distinguishing European immigrants legally from African slaves, and encouraging whites with *headrights,* or promises of land. Virginia entered the eighteenth century as a microcosm of the colonial world: a land of unusual opportunities for some and special misery for others. The great planters consolidated their dominance of this society around the principles of *patriarchy,* or male dominance of the family and household consisting of women, children, and slaves. Ideally, the plantation was a self-sufficient world, the planter an independent man with the time to pursue leisure activities and even public service. The idea of self-sufficiency helped Virginia's leaders fashion a highly interdependent society in which marriages between families and the loaning of credit to friends and relatives for purchases of land and slaves solidified an elite

---

[5]Winthrop D. Jordan, *White over Black: American Attitudes toward the Negro, 1550–1812* (Chapel Hill, 1968), 71–83; Edmund S. Morgan, *American Slavery, American Freedom: The Ordeal of Colonial Virginia* (New York, 1975), 92–292.

group who otherwise tended to quite individualistically amass land and seek their own fortunes in the tobacco trade.[6]

Interlocking structures of authority in county and provincial government, the economy, and the official Anglican religious establishment supported an increasingly stable order in the early eighteenth century, much as in England itself during the same period. This political and social stability enabled white Virginians to meet a large part of the increasing world demand for tobacco. The Virginia provincial government even regulated the quality of tobacco so that barrels of the cured plant, stored at public warehouses, could serve as a medium of exchange in lieu of silver or paper money. During what later seemed to their children like a *golden age* (or the way things were meant to be), planters came to build more permanent, brick houses; bought more luxury goods for themselves and their families; and further developed the rituals of hospitality and fellowship, which marked them, they felt, not as just Virginian planters but as English gentlemen. By mid-century, Virginians had more ties with England than they did with any of the other, much closer North American and Caribbean colonies. They surveyed the landscape and dreamed of clearing great swamps and settling the Ohio River valley.[7]

Behind the brick facades, the lush curtains, and the new maps of a greater Virginia lay portents of crisis. Prices rose, fell, and fell again in the tobacco market. Planters became enmeshed in a "culture of debt" in which English and especially Scottish merchants sold them goods on credit, forcing them to take the risk that tobacco prices would fall by the time their crop came to market. Often they bought more land and slaves in desperate efforts to overcome past debts. Historians describe a persistent sense of "anxiety" in the personal papers of planters, which only increased as especially bad prices in the mid-1760s led to a calling in of debts. The very sources of wealth and stability—tobacco and slaves—had turned out to be sources of

---

[6]Rhys Isaac, *The Transformation of Virginia, 1740–1790* (Chapel Hill, 1982); Allan Kulikoff, *Tobacco and Slaves: The Development of Southern Cultures in the Chesapeake, 1680–1800* (Chapel Hill, 1986), 78–161; Kathleen M. Brown, *Good Wives, Nasty Wenches, and Anxious Patriarchs: Gender, Race and Power in Colonial Virginia* (Chapel Hill, 1996).

[7]Isaac, *Transformation of Virginia;* Richard L. Bushman, *The Refinement of America: Persons, Houses, Cities* (New York, 1992); Cary Carson, ed., *Of Consuming Interests: The Style of Life in the Eighteenth Century* (Charlottesville, Va., 1992); Charles Royster, *The Fabulous History of the Dismal Swamp Company: A Story of George Washington's Times* (New York, 1999).

vulnerability. Scottish *factors*, or storeowners associated with Glasgow firms, who were not themselves indebted to wealthy Virginians, cared little about the network of favors and dependencies that made it difficult for planters to call in their own debts and pay up. Even direct trade with English merchants became risky as international war drove up not only prices but also insurance rates on ships crossing the Atlantic. The growth of the tobacco trade had, in the end, not only made planters more rich, powerful, and numerous, it had also reinforced their dependence on overseas merchants and politicians and made them more colonial—less independent—even as their wealth and local power made them feel increasingly like equal members of a growing commercial empire.[8]

When the home government in London reacted to its own financial crisis after the Seven Years' War (1754–63) by passing legislation that favored British creditors over colonial debtors and declared settlement west of a "Proclamation" line agreed upon with several Indian nations to be illegal, men like Thomas Jefferson began to think in broad terms about what was happening to their world. The view from the mountaintop Jefferson planned to build on would remain a beautiful one, but it included portents of decline, scenes of loss, and even forebodings of disaster.

VIRGINIA'S JEFFERSON

Thomas Jefferson's father, Peter Jefferson, settled in the western county of Albemarle, a fact that shaped his son's outlook as much as did his infant memory of being carried to the new tract on a pillow by a slave. Peter Jefferson partook of the enthusiasm for available land, working as a surveyor and coauthoring an important map of Virginia in 1751, but he died in 1757, when his son was fourteen. Early on, Jefferson inherited his own estate, apparently without ever really coming

---

[8]T. H. Breen, *Tobacco Culture: The Mentality of the Great Tidewater Planters on the Eve of Revolution* (Princeton, N.J., 1985), 23; Jack P. Greene, "'Virtus et Libertas': Political Culture, Social Change, and the Origins of the American Revolution in Virginia, 1763–66," *Understanding the American Revolution: Issues and Actors* (Charlottesville, Va., 1995), 164–208; Jack P. Greene, "Society, Ideology, Politics: An Analysis of the Political Culture of Mid-Eighteenth Century Virginia," *Negotiated Authorities: Essays in Colonial Political and Constitutional History* (Charlottesville, Va., 1994), 259–318; Bruce A. Ragsdale, *A Planter's Republic: The Search for Economic Independence in Revolutionary Virginia* (Madison, Wisc., 1996), chaps. 1–3; Woody Holton, *Forced Founders: Indians, Debtors, Slaves, and the Making of the American Revolution in Virginia* (Chapel Hill, 1999), 3–38.

under the strong authority of a plantation patriarch (although he seems to have had real conflict with his mother, whom he avoided speaking of for most of his life). Three years later, Thomas Jefferson left for Williamsburg, capital of the colony and home of the College of William and Mary. He grew close to his instructor, a scientifically minded Scot named William Small, in the years before Small got into trouble with the rest of the faculty (all of whom were ministers). In 1762, young Jefferson stayed on to study law with George Wythe, a highly respected legal mind. Both Small and Wythe were good friends of the royal governor, Francis Fauquier. Jefferson had entered into the highest and most intellectually challenging circles of the province.[9]

He did so at an exciting time. Members of the House of Burgesses (Virginia's assembly or congress) like Jefferson's cousin, Richard Bland, began to speak and write about their rights in the British empire. Ideas about reforming Virginia society to eliminate debt and the sources of corruption from within began to circulate in response to such measures as the Currency Act of 1764, an English law that eliminated much of the flexibility in the various forms of money circulating in the colonies, a flexibility that planters had used to their advantage in paying debts. Virginians like Bland were in the forefront of efforts to articulate an American opposition within the political language of republicanism.

Republicanism, as colonists interpreted it in the mid-eighteenth century, was a theory of politics that explained the tendency for states and statesmen to become corrupt as countries developed and grew over time. Almost inevitably, in any kind of polity, power seduced leaders, and the powerful at court, or the metropolitan center of government, took advantage of citizens in the countryside. Republicanism became known as a "country" style of opposition to the innovations (and growth) of the British fiscal-military state managed from London. Even before the 1760s, colonists had found such ideas useful in claiming that their legislatures deserved more autonomy, at the expense of governors sent over by the king and his ministry.[10] More than a justification for decentralized government and low taxes, republicanism in the 1760s was a call to reform. It presumed that government should serve the interests of the majority of property holders. It demanded

---

[9]Dumas Malone, *Jefferson the Virginian* (Boston, 1948), 21–87; Fawn Brodie, *Thomas Jefferson: An Intimate History* (New York, 1974); Merrill D. Peterson, *Thomas Jefferson and the New Nation* (New York, 1970), 3–15.

[10]Bernard Bailyn, *The Ideological Origins of the American Revolution* (Cambridge, Mass., 1967); Greene, "'Virtus et Libertas,'"; Morgan, *American Slavery,* 369–87.

that citizens devote themselves to the public good, the preservation of propertied independence from the dangers posed by greedy insiders with access to power. Republicanism provided the theory that justified political actions like boycotts of English goods.

The republican themes of public debate in the early-to-mid 1760s—the need to consume fewer luxury goods like fine cloth, and to be politically vigilant and self-reliant—dovetailed with young Jefferson's own experience of hard study in his law books. In one of his first surviving letters, Jefferson described himself studying so hard and sleeping so deeply that he did not see a rat eating his own fashionable possessions, a pocketbook and silk garters. He felt different, he insisted, than the truly happy young people who could afford to "powder" and "embroider" their bodies and their talk at the fancy balls in town. The ambivalence in the letter is remarkable. Nineteen-year-old Thomas Jefferson was part of the fashionable gentry, yet he sought to keep a partial, critical distance from fashion and its excesses—even while being aware of the sacrifice at every moment.[11]

For the rest of his life, Jefferson would struggle with the contrast between his belief in hard work and self-sufficiency, and his desire to surround himself with the accouterments of European civilization which only tobacco and slavery could bring. He signed the first non-importation agreements, under which Virginians agreed not to buy certain European goods in protest against Parliament's taxes and restrictions on trade. Yet when the first "association" for nonimportation began to fail, he was quick to order silk stockings, letting a London merchant know to send him some as soon as the restrictions formally fell. His first publication was not a defense of Virginian independence but an advertisement placed in the September 14, 1769, issue of the *Virginia Gazette,* for Sandy, a fugitive mulatto shoemaker from his plantation (Figure 1). This skilled man, whom Jefferson called "artful and knavish," must have made boots for his other slaves and contributed to whatever possibility Jefferson might have imagined of not having to import clothing from England.[12]

Slaves were at the center of everything that was wonderful and worrisome in Jefferson's Virginia. They were expensive commodities who made goods and helped show them off. Often bought on credit, they were sources of debt who could work a planter out of debt. By

---

[11]Jefferson to John Page, Dec. 25, 1762, in *The Papers of Thomas Jefferson,* ed. Julian P. Boyd, Charles T. Cullen, and John Catanzariti (Princeton, N.J., 1950–), I, 4–5.

[12]Boyd, *Jefferson Papers,* I, 11, 33, 44. Jefferson sold Sandy in 1773 for 100 pounds.

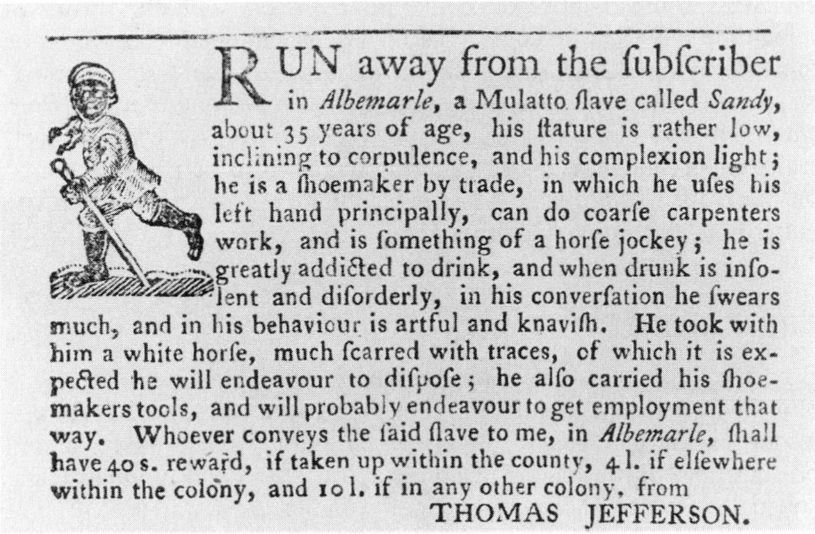

R UN away from the fubfcriber in *Albemarle*, a Mulatto flave called *Sandy*, about 35 years of age, his ftature is rather low, inclining to corpulence, and his complexion light; he is a fhoemaker by trade, in which he ufes his left hand principally, can do coarfe carpenters work, and is fomething of a horfe jockey; he is greatly addicted to drink, and when drunk is infolent and diforderly, in his converfation he fwears much, and in his behaviour is artful and knavifh. He took with him a white horfe, much fcarred with traces, of which it is expected he will endeavour to difpofe; he alfo carried his fhoemakers tools, and will probably endeavour to get employment that way. Whoever conveys the faid flave to me, in *Albemarle*, fhall have 40 s. reward, if taken up within the county, 4 l. if elfewhere within the colony, and 10 l. if in any other colony. from
THOMAS JEFFERSON.

Figure 1. Thomas Jefferson's advertisement for Sandy, a fugitive from one of his plantations, was placed in the *Virginia Gazette* (Williamsburg), September 14, 1769.
Virginia Historical Society, Richmond.

the early 1770s, Jefferson knew this as well as anyone. When his father-in-law, John Wayles, died in 1772 and left him 135 slaves and several plantations, Jefferson entered the top tier of planters, the wealthiest hundred men in the colony. Shortly before his death, though, John Wayles had imported 405 slaves from Africa, at a time when prices for tobacco plunged and buyers for slaves became hard to find. He had paid for the trans-Atlantic voyage on credit, and his son-in-law inherited these debts as well as others from the Wayles estate.[13]

At the same time, Jefferson inherited his wife's unacknowledged half-sisters and -brothers in slavery, the Hemings family. John Wayles, father of Martha Wayles Skelton Jefferson, had six children with Elizabeth Hemings, the daughter of an African slave and an English ship

[13]John Wayles to Jefferson, Oct. 20, 1772, *Virginia Gazette*, July 15, 1773, in *Jefferson Papers*, ed. Boyd, I, 95–96, 100; Lucia Stanton, "'Those Who Labor for My Happiness': Thomas Jefferson and His Slaves" in *Jeffersonian Legacies*, ed. Peter S. Onuf (Charlottesville, Va., 1993), 148; Malone, *Jefferson the Virginian*, 162ff; Jackson Turner Main, "The One Hundred," *William and Mary Quarterly*, 3d. Ser., 11 (1954), 377; Herbert E. Sloan, *Principle and Interest: Thomas Jefferson and the Problem of Debt* (New York, 1995), 14–23.

captain.[14] Thomas Jefferson could no more question this order of things directly than he could give up his plantations or his wife — or quickly pay his debts. This background, however, can help us understand the particular passion he brought to reforming Virginia from within. It also helps us make sense of his attitude toward slavery, which he pronounced unjust, continued to profit from, and yet blamed on the British as the epitome of everything that was wrong with the empire his generation had inherited.

VIRGINIA'S REVOLUTION

Even though Jefferson was a radical where it came to both the rights of ordinary citizens and the inherent injustice of slavery, he became a leader in Virginia and in America. His story about the past and present, told in the idioms of both natural rights and republicanism, suited the course of the American Revolution as it was seen by the men who dominated the movement.[15]

The resolutions Jefferson wrote for the citizens of his home county show how useful theories of natural rights could be. (See Document 1.) In their second and much more successful attempt at nonimportation, drafted in direct response to the Port Act of 1774 (which closed the port of Boston in punishment for the Boston Tea Party and

[14]Annette Gordon-Reed, *Thomas Jefferson and Sally Hemings: An American Controversy* (Charlottesville, Va., 1997), 1, 23, 128–30; Philip D. Morgan, "Interracial Sex in the British Chesapeake and the British Atlantic World, ca. 1700–1820" in *Sally Hemings and Thomas Jefferson,* 75–78.

[15]Some scholars of political and social thought have devoted close attention to Jefferson's attraction to natural rights as a theory of society and a first principle of politics, which they consider a harbinger of modern liberalism. Others stress Jefferson's adaptation of republicanism, which gave the patriots a language through which they could address corruption and the need for good citizens to band together to stave off the ever-present threats to liberty and good government. If Jefferson's vision of society exists anywhere fully formed, it is in the *Notes on the State of Virginia.* Yet, even there, Jefferson seems to combine natural rights (or liberal) and republican rhetoric. As a result, the most recent scholarship stresses the compatibility of natural rights and Jefferson's version of republicanism. For particularly useful entries into the debate, see Drew R. McCoy, *The Elusive Republic: Political Economy in Jeffersonian America* (Chapel Hill, 1980); Richard K. Matthews, *The Radical Politics of Thomas Jefferson* (Lawrence, Kans., 1984); Garrett Ward Sheldon, *The Political Philosophy of Thomas Jefferson* (Baltimore, 1991); Joyce Appleby, *Liberalism and Republicanism in the Historical Imagination* (Cambridge, Mass., 1992), 253–319; Michael P. Zuckert, *The Natural Rights Republic: Studies in the Foundation of the American Political Tradition* (Notre Dame, Ind., 1996), 13–89, 202–43; Thomas S. Engemann, ed., *Thomas Jefferson and the Politics of Nature* (Notre Dame, Ind., 2000).

affirmed the right of Parliament to control American trade), Jefferson and the Virginians linked *natural,* or God-given, rights to "legal rights" established by historical precedent. These rights derived from their "first settlement" and their continuing membership in the "British empire." Later that year, Jefferson went further. In *A Summary View of the Rights of British America* (1774), which he wrote as draft instructions to Virginia's delegates to the first Continental Congress, Jefferson told a story about preexisting rights of expatriation and compared the removal of Britons to America to the arrival of Saxons in Old England centuries before. Jefferson's use of natural-rights theory presumed a vision of history and a particular conception of colonial membership in the British empire. American freedom was not only natural, it was the same as English freedom, and it should include "free trade with all parts of the world." Jefferson cited seventeenth-century statutes affirming Virginians' privilege of making their own laws and insisted that the recent tendency for Parliament to "exercise authority over us . . . too plainly prove a deliberate and systematical plan of reducing us to slavery."[16]

Slavery? Why did Jefferson choose to compare British political and economic oppression with slavery? For a long time, slavery had meant the opposite of liberty, and it continued to mean that in the colonial world when colonists began to suspect, sometimes rightly, that some people in England regarded them as little different than their slaves — as distant objects, working for the profit of others. But Jefferson meant even more. In *A Summary View* he used the slave trade itself as a prime example of the king's tendency to veto laws made by colonial legislatures when asked to do so by self-interested Englishmen.

> For the most trifling reasons, and sometimes for no reason at all, his majesty has rejected laws of the most salutary tendency. The abolition of domestic slavery is the great object of desire in those colonies, where it was most unhappily introduced in their infant state. But previous to the enfranchisement of the slaves we have, it is necessary to exclude all further importations from Africa; yet our repeated attempts to effect this by prohibitions, and by imposing

---

[16]Thomas Jefferson, "A Summary View of the Rights of British America" (1774), in *Thomas Jefferson: Writings,* ed. Merrill Peterson (New York, 1984), 105–10; Sheldon, *Political Philosophy,* 46; H. Trevor Colbourn, *The Lamp of Experience: Whig History and the Intellectual Origins of the American Revolution* (Chapel Hill, 1961), 158–84; David N. Mayer, *The Constitutional Thought of Thomas Jefferson* (Charlottesville, Va., 1994), 11–52; Stephen A. Conrad, "Putting Rights Talk in its Place: *The Summary View* Revisited" in *Jeffersonian Legacies,* ed. Peter S. Onuf (Charlottesville, Va., 1993), 254–80.

duties which might amount to a prohibition, have been hitherto defeated by his majesty's negative: Thus preferring the immediate advantages of a few African corsairs to the lasting interests of the American states, and to the rights of human nature, deeply wounded by this infamous practice.[17]

Jefferson overstated his case. No majority championed the end of the slave trade, much less the abolition of slavery, in any colony in 1774. Virginia tobacco growers were at best divided over the matter, with larger, tidewater planters seeing slave imports as a source of debt, while smaller holders in the areas where labor was scarce wanted to keep the prices of slaves low by encouraging imports.[18] Virginians however, had periodically tried to tax slave imports and included them among the luxuries, the fruits of dependency, that they agreed to do without in 1774.

As a young member of the House of Burgesses, in 1769, Jefferson had tried to address the issue of slavery. His cousin Richard Bland put forward an antislavery proposal for him—and suffered real embarrassment in the process of even suggesting that the assembly should make it easier for individuals to free their own slaves. In his 1821 autobiography, Jefferson remembered this episode as an example of "the habitual belief" of his fellow planters "that it was our duty to be subordinate to the mother country in all matters of government." Only a few years later, though, more of the powerful Virginians had come to see it at least partly Jefferson's way. If tobacco had caused the imperial crisis—worsened by the shrinking of credit in 1772—then slavery was part of the problem. Along with efforts to control their own trade, to consume fewer luxuries, and to manufacture their own everyday goods, Virginia planters began to talk of growing wheat, a crop that (unlike tobacco) would not only feed them but also require fewer laborers.[19]

---

[17]Jefferson, "Summary View," 115–16. Jefferson changed the wording of "African corsairs" (or pirates) to "British corsairs" for the pamphlet edition. Boyd, *Jefferson Papers,* I, 130, 136 n.24.

[18]Decreased imports could also make surplus slaves into a source of profit for planters, which is precisely what occurred a few decades later. For arguments that reforming Virginians were never really serious about ending slavery (as opposed to ending the slave trade), see Robert McColley, *Slavery and Jeffersonian Virginia,* 2nd ed. (Urbana, Ill., 1973), 111–40; Paul Finkelman, *Slavery and the Founders: Race and Liberty in the Age of Jefferson* (Armonk, N.Y., 1996), 112–24; Joseph J. Ellis, *Founding Brothers: The Revolutionary Generation* (New York, 2000), 81–119.

[19]Thomas Jefferson, "Autobiography," *Thomas Jefferson: Writings,* ed. Merrill Peterson (New York, 1984), 5; Ragsdale, *Planters' Republic,* chap. 4; Holton, *Forced Founders,* 39–73.

These efforts at reform brought increasing numbers of Virginia landholders together in a broad social movement. The Continental Association of 1774, an intercolonial boycott of British goods, was a success in Virginia. Jefferson himself supported the most stringent resolutions. But the suspension of trade and the involvement of smaller planters in the boycott led to the closure of the county courts, which collected debts, and a controversy with the new governor, John Murray, the Earl of Dunmore. Dunmore had initially proven popular with Virginians for his willingness to lead a war against the Shawnees and Mingos who had skirmished with squatters in the west, but he had no intention of allowing debts to be unpaid. In April 1775, after the battles of Concord and Lexington began the American Revolution, Dunmore removed arms from the colony's storehouse, fled to the harbor, and soon threatened to free Virginia's slaves. He probably got the idea from the help some slaves had already offered and the increasing number who ran away from their masters early in 1775. After an initial naval attack from a ship off Hampton, Virginia, on October 27, 1775, Dunmore officially promised freedom to slaves who fled their masters to fight for England. (See Document 2.) He also sought alliances with the Native tribes he had so popularly fought a few years before.[20]

Events had further narrowed the distance between Jefferson's radical perspective and the needs and desires of his fellow Virginians. Elected to the Continental Congress, he was nominated to the committee to write a declaration of independence. John Adams of Massachusetts, long in the vanguard of the resistance, encouraged Jefferson himself to draft the document, arguing, as he recalled, "a Virginian ought to appear at the head of this business." Yet, the Declaration Jefferson wrote is not the same as the one Congress eventually passed, as Jefferson himself later observed. The finished Declaration generalizes British overtures to Native American and slave allies as "domestic insurrections," a term that might be said to euphemize a political struggle but one which nonetheless pointed out that the increasing numbers of slave runaways were, considered collectively, in rebellion.[21] (See Document 3.) For Jefferson, however, the culmination of

[20]Boyd, *Jefferson Papers,* I, 141–44; Benjamin Quarles, *The Negro in the American Revolution* (Chapel Hill, 1961); John E. Selby, *The Revolution in Virginia, 1775–1783* (Williamsburg, Va., 1988), 1–5, 41–79; Sylvia Frey, *Water from the Rock: Black Resistance in a Revolutionary Age* (Princeton, N.J., 1991), 55–56; Holton, *Forced Founders,* 133–63.
[21]John Adams to Timothy Pickering, Aug. 6, 1822, in Merrill D. Peterson, *Adams and Jefferson: A Revolutionary Dialogue* (Athens, Ga., 1976), 14; Jefferson, "Autobiography," 17–24; Sidney Kaplan, "The Domestic Insurrections of the Declaration of Independence," *Journal of Negro History* 62 (1976), 243–55.

the unnatural actions of the British king lay particularly in the king's "cruel war against human nature itself"—in slavery and the arming of slaves.

How could the Americans blame the king both for slavery and for liberating their slaves? The passage, struck out by Congress, has puzzled commentators, who generally agree that the passage made little sense and proceed to debate whether its antislavery, its blame of the king, or its outrage about armed slaves was the most hypocritical or inconsistent.[22] Jefferson would later blame the deletion of the paragraph on South Carolinians and Georgians who wanted to keep slavery and on northerners who had investments in the slave trade. Neither, he wrote, wanted the antislavery idea in the nation's founding document. Why then did Jefferson think such a passage belonged, if the colonies-turned-states had forged no consensus on the future of slavery? Revolutions create possibilities; they also lay open the logic of a situation. When Jefferson justified creating a new nation by calling the rebellion of slaves the quintessential British-inspired crime, he made sense in a Virginian context. (He had included similar language in his draft of a new constitution for Virginia a month before.) Dunmore's invitation to Africans made slaves national allies of the English. It made Americans a different nation: English no longer and now enemies of the English, the Africans, and the Indians.[23] In the moment of revolutionary excitement, Jefferson hoped that his constituents could free themselves from the corruptions of slavery, from the "savage" warfare that marked Virginia's history, and from England all at once. Returning to the state of nature, starting history all over again, the colonists might escape not only their own enslavement but possibly also their enslavement of others.

LAW AND WAR

To actually achieve American independence proved more difficult than declaring it, as Jefferson learned firsthand. Virginians earned a

[22]See, for example, Peterson, *New Nation,* 91–92; Garry Wills, *Inventing America: Jefferson's Declaration of Independence* (New York, 1978), 72–75; Joseph J. Ellis, *American Sphinx: The Character of Thomas Jefferson* (New York, 1996), 51–52; Pauline Maier, *American Scripture: Making the Declaration of Independence* (New York, 1997), 146–47.

[23]Boyd, *Jefferson Papers,* I, 338, 357, 378; John Chester Miller, *The Wolf by the Ears: Thomas Jefferson and the Problem of Slavery* (New York, 1977), 6–11; Peter S. Onuf, *Jefferson's Empire: The Language of American Nationhood* (Charlottesville, Va., 2000), 147–58.

reprieve by beating back Dunmore's attempt to subdue them in 1775–76. For several years, the theaters of war lay elsewhere. Jefferson returned home, served in the state's new House of Delegates, and pushed for the revision of the state's laws and its constitution, a subject he would take up at length in *Notes on the State of Virginia*. (See Document 12, Queries 13 and 14.) Jefferson saw independence not just as an outcome of Virginia's oppression by her "British brethren" but also as an opportunity to set his "country" on a future course. Although he would often insist on the need to be true to the will of the people as expressed in fundamental constitutions (even arguing that the Virginia Constitution of 1776 was actually illegal because it was not fashioned by a convention elected for that purpose), he also believed in the need to periodically rethink the fundamental laws.

Governmental principles and fundamental laws, for Jefferson, included not just the make-up of the branches of government or the qualifications for citizenship (he favored lowering the land-ownership requirement for voting) but also specifying the punishment of crimes, the laws of inheritance, the system of education, the relationship of church and state, the organization of the economy, and the question of slavery. He spelled out the implications of his set of reforms in the *Notes on the State of Virginia*. Government ought to promote the conditions under which a people might become and remain virtuous and thus be capable of republican self-government. Virginia's old aristocratic regime was vulnerable to this republican critique, especially after the American Revolution emboldened smaller farmers to insist on their own virtues as key participants in the boycotts and the armed struggle. The fact that some of the august Burgesses had confronted Lord Dunmore in June 1775, wearing the hunting shirts that were all the rage among backcountry militiamen, suggests that the Revolution had, from the beginning, the potential to overthrow not just the colonial order but the great planters' world. It is a measure of how much the revolution challenged the old order that Jefferson himself could be elected governor of the state in June 1779.[24]

Jefferson was thinking of his two years as governor when he began the English edition of the *Notes* with a preemptive self-criticism

[24]Peterson, *New Nation,* 97–158; Noble E. Cunningham Jr., *In Pursuit of Reason: The Life of Thomas Jefferson* (1987; repr. New York, 1988), 52–63; Jean Yarbrough, "Thomas Jefferson and Republicanism" in *Politics of Nature,* ed. Engemann, 59–80; Selby, *The Revolution,* 42, 120; Michael A. McDonnell and Woody Holton, "Patriot Versus Patriot: Social Conflict in Virginia and the Origins of the American Revolution," *Journal of American Studies* 34 (2000), 231–56.

concerning the limitations of his data about his home state: "The subjects are all treated imperfectly; some scarcely touched on. To apologize for this by developing the circumstances of the time and place of their composition, would be to open wounds which have already bled enough" (Document 12, "Advertisement"). Neither the very limited powers allowed him under the new constitution nor the military situation made the governorship easy. When the British, frustrated at Saratoga, turned back to a selective Southern strategy in 1780, Virginia's defenses, spread through various parts of the large territory and elsewhere in the Continental Army, proved both insufficiently flexible and too thin in number and supply. Jefferson worked hard to alleviate wartime shortages of clothing and food, but the state's tobacco economy emerged as a dangerous military weakness during an extended conflict. A surprise invasion by Benedict Arnold in January 1781, combined with Banastre Tarleton's cavalry raid on Charlottesville that May while Jefferson and the assembly's executive council met there in the waning days of his administration, led some skeptics to demand an investigation into the governor's conduct.[25]

Jefferson was quickly cleared of guilt, but he found the experience humiliating. Some of this bitterness finds its way into the *Notes,* when Jefferson indignantly exposes the debate, instigated by at least one of his opponents, over creating a military dictatorship to combat the crisis of 1781. (See Query 13.) Even before he was chased away from his mountaintop mansion by Tarleton, Jefferson had longed to return to thinking about the big picture, rather than attending to the small details of government. Sometime in 1780, he had received a questionnaire about the natural resources and institutions, circulated to all the governors of the new states, by François Marbois, head of the French delegation. (See Document 4.) Other governors found themselves too busy to reply, but Jefferson had a greater appreciation—and, perhaps, as a Virginian, a greater potential need—for future French aid. After a brief British invasion of coastal Portsmouth, Virginia, he had written to another French diplomat, D'Anmours, who had come a year earlier to strengthen French-American commercial ties. He asked D'Anmours to pass on to Marbois his thanks for the push back to his

[25]Peterson, *New Nation,* 166–235; John W. Shy, "British Strategy for Pacifying the Southern Colonies, 1778–1781" in *The Southern Experience in the American Revolution,* ed. Jeffrey J. Crow and Larry E. Tise (Chapel Hill, 1978), 155–73; Emory G. Evans, "Executive Leadership in Virginia 1776–1781: Henry, Jefferson, and Nelson" in *Sovereign States in an Age of Uncertainty,* ed. Ronald Hoffman and Peter J. Albert (Charlottesville, Va., 1981), 202–14; Jefferson to Benjamin Harrison, June 13, 1780, Jefferson to James Madison, July 26, 1780, *Papers of Thomas Jefferson,* III, 438, 507.

library and his research: "I am presently busily employed for Monsr. Marbois without his knowing it, and have to ackno[w]ledge to him the mysterious obligation for making me much better acquainted with my country than I ever was before." Exactly a month later, Arnold sailed up Chesapeake Bay, completely surprising the government at Richmond, and Jefferson had to flee with his family. He was probably working on the reply to Marbois when he was again almost captured by Tarleton's raid.[26]

THE FRENCH ALTERNATIVE

General George Washington's stunning victory at Yorktown on September 14, 1781, was an indirect result of Virginia's failures during the previous year: Lord Charles Cornwallis had begun to believe that he could roam the coast with impunity, only to be surprised by the joint efforts of a French fleet and the Continental army. Similarly, Jefferson's literary and philosophical triumph in the *Notes* was the unanticipated result of Virginia's military reversals, of the failure of Jefferson's revolutionary republicanism to put Virginia's own house in order, and of the stimulation of the French.

In 1781, the French were more than intellectual sparring partners. They were key allies in the Revolutionary War. Jefferson believed as deeply as anyone in what one historian has called the "French alternative" in early U.S. history. The English had proven themselves a power-hungry, corrupt nation, in Jefferson's view. Wedded to mercantilism, an economic policy under which each nation sought to control the flow of material resources and people to its own advantage at the expense of competing empires and colonized lands, the English would always be an adversary, even in peacetime. But the French, by intervening on the side of the United States, had shown that they favored the emergence of Britain's former colony as a counterweight to British dominance in North America and the Caribbean. They might even be persuaded to give up the old mercantilist system, in favor of international free trade.[27]

Although Jefferson liked to contrast scientific research with political drudgery, he effectively combined them in turning the information gathering of commercially minded French diplomats into the occasion

[26]Doron S. Ben-Atar, *The Origins of Jeffersonian Commercial Policy and Diplomacy* (London, 1993), 33; Jefferson to D'Anmours, Nov. 30, 1780, *Papers of Thomas Jefferson*, IV, 167–68; Selby, *The Revolution*, 221–23.
[27]Ben-Atar, *Origins*, 66–84.

for a treatise on the prospects of Virginia and America. The work itself, as it evolved during the early 1780s, reflected the local, federal, and international dimensions of Jefferson's statesmanship and of American politics itself as it emerged during these critical years. Jefferson at first refused a diplomatic posting, citing his exhaustion and frustration at the demands of public service in a letter to his friend James Monroe. (See Document 6.) After the illness and death of his wife in 1782, Jefferson threw himself into public work, accepting an assignment as a negotiator of peace with England, although the Treaty of Paris arrived before he could cross the Atlantic. He served in the Continental Congress, where he took a particular interest in the organization of the western territories. In the summer of 1784, he boarded a ship for France as one of the new ministers charged with getting loans and creating a new treaty of alliance and trade between the two nations.[28]

NOTES ON THE STATE OF VIRGINIA

From Manuscript to Book

Jefferson brought a revised draft of his answers to Marbois with him on his journey to France. Over the previous two and a half years he had shown parts of the work to French and American friends; by late 1784, the manuscript had tripled in size. Before he left the United States, Jefferson looked into getting a small edition printed in Philadelphia, but he discovered that it would be cheaper to do so in Paris. He had two hundred copies printed there, in English, but after he received them on May 10, 1785, he sent them only to a few dozen people.[29]

That Jefferson did not immediately seek extensive distribution for his work does not mean that he did not see the book as important or that he never really intended to publish it, as some scholars assume. On the contrary, the controversial nature of the project led him to proceed with caution. Despite victory and independence, America's reputation had not advanced in Europe. The new nation struggled to pay massive debts. Controversies over jurisdiction and taxation within and

---

[28]Marie Kimball, *Jefferson: War and Peace, 1776 to 1784* (New York, 1948), 270–74, 290–95; Malone, *Jefferson the Virginian,* 421; Ellis, *American Sphinx,* 44–90.

[29]Jefferson to Charles Thomson, May 21, 1784, Jefferson to James Madison, May 11, 1785, Jefferson to Louis Guillaume Otto, May 28, 1785, *Papers of Thomas Jefferson,* VII, 282, VIII, 147–48, 169–70.

between the states made it very difficult to establish economic as well as political independence from England. "We are diverted with the European accounts of the anarchy and opposition to government in America. Nothing can be more untrue than these relations," wrote Jefferson to a French admirer and author, François Jean Marquis de Chastellux.[30] By the end of 1784, Jefferson found it less easy to wave off such stories about a disorderly, declining new republic. (See Document 5.) The *Notes,* like his diplomacy, might serve the American cause by putting forth a vision of future prosperity. The pressing need for American voices abroad suggested the importance of publication and distribution.

Two factors, however, pushed in another direction. First, Jefferson regarded the *Notes* as somewhat fragmentary and, at best, a work in progress (which helps explain his choice of title). Only the United States' need for informed, supportive voices abroad led him to enlarge both the work and its audience. Second, and more important, was that in writing for a European audience he had included passages on the Virginia Constitution and on slavery that might be very controversial at home. He could not merely edit out these passages because they were central to the work as a whole and to his program for progress. He wrote gingerly to James Madison and Monroe in the spring of 1785, revealing both his fears and ambitions for the book: "I wish to put it into the hands of the young men at the [C]ollege [of William and Mary], as well on account of the political as physical parts. But there are sentiments on some subjects which I apprehend might be displeasing to the country perhaps to the assembly or to some who lead it." Madison agreed and prevailed on Jefferson to send copies to sympathetic William and Mary faculty who would distribute copies very carefully. Others received copies with inscriptions asking them not to lend or give the work to anyone they could not trust to keep it out of publishers' hands.[31]

In the end, however, the work was too interesting to too many people to remain so carefully distributed. The English version printed in Paris soon fell into the hands of a French book dealer who

[30]Jefferson to Chastellux, Jan. 16, 1784, *Papers of Thomas Jefferson,* V, 466.

[31]Douglas L. Wilson, "Jefferson and the Republic of Letters" in Onuf, ed., *Jeffersonian Legacies,* 53–57; Ellis, *American Sphinx,* 86–87; Jefferson to James Madison, May 11, 1785, Jefferson to James Monroe, June 17, 1785, *Papers of Thomas Jefferson,* VIII, 147–48, 229; Coolie Verner, "Mr. Jefferson Distributes His Notes: A Preliminary Checklist of the First Edition," *Bulletin of the New York Public Library* 56:4 (April 1952), 159–86.

threatened to publish a French edition. Jefferson then worked with André Morellet, quickly turning out their own authorized translation in 1786.[32] No law prevented a retranslation back from the French to the English, however, so, when London bookseller John Stockdale proposed an authorized English edition, Jefferson quickly agreed. Even before its appearance in 1787, excerpts appeared in the American press. The following year, a pirated American edition appeared in Philadelphia.[33] For better or worse, the new world of free trade and French connections, which Jefferson envisioned, had produced one of its first fruits—his book.

Nature

The inability to be heard on their own terms in the metropolitan centers of Europe illustrates the still all-too-colonial situation Jefferson and his constituents faced in the early 1780s as they tried to establish the United States economically and politically with the older nations of the western world. (The difficulty of getting a book published cheaply in the new nation may have served Jefferson as another reminder.) It was not enough, however, to tell a pro-American story in print. Jefferson believed in the rules of science; he associated fact-based knowledge with progress. In the long run, the best way to demonstrate the promise of America was to prove it scientifically, according to the intellectual rules for discussing nations and their prospects.

Marbois's request opened up the possibility of making a contribution to international science and to American nationhood at the same time. As his fellow scientist and politician Benjamin Rush would write in 1791, "Natural history is the foundation of all useful and practical knowledge." The study of nature could contain history because nature could be seen to be changing over time. When human actions counted as part of natural history, nature's close study led to lessons about human possibilities. At a time when those possibilities in America were open to question, a precise ordering of American natural history,

[32]Jefferson later distanced himself from this version, which he called "a different book and not mine," partly because Morellet shaped the material on slaves and slavery into a separate chapter. Dorothy Medlin, "Thomas Jefferson, André Morellet, and the French Version of *Notes on the State of Virginia*," *William and Mary Quarterly*, 3d. Ser., 35 (1978), 85–99; Jefferson to C.W.F. Dumas, Feb. 2, 1786, Jefferson to James Madison, Feb. 8, 1786, *Papers of Thomas Jefferson*, IX, 243–44, 264–65.

[33]Jefferson to George Wythe, Aug. 13, 1786, John Stockdale to Jefferson, Nov. 20, 1786, Joel Barlow to Jefferson, June 15, 1787, *Papers of Thomas Jefferson*, X, 243, 290n, 545–46, XI, 473, 595n.

from an American viewpoint, could answer those who doubted the future prospects of the United States.[34]

The *Notes* place ancient and recent Virginia history inside of natural history. Jefferson took the liberty of rearranging Marbois's queries so that, instead of starting with the unresolved problem of government in the new republic, as Marbois had, Jefferson begins with the most striking—and impressive—features of American nature. Virginia is a huge mass of land, larger on its own than England itself. (See Query 1.) The map that Jefferson included in the 1787 edition of the *Notes* draws the eye toward Virginia's many rivers, which create "channels of extensive communication" with the territory beyond. (See Figure 2.) Jefferson gave Virginia the broadest possible definition—all the way to the Missouri River!—even as Virginia gave up its western claims to the authority of the federal republic. What might seem to be grave problems in a European commercial context—the lack of cities and the dispersal of the population across wide spaces—are described as natural advantages. (See Queries 2 and 3.)

Jefferson shared a peculiarly Potomac-centered view of American development with George Washington and other founders of this country who would soon plant a capital city on the banks of that river. Jefferson and Washington, both eager speculators in western lands, tended to see untouched nature as both a beautiful thing and an economic opportunity. In Jefferson's hands, the existence of phenomenal natural resources suggests that recent economic and political setbacks are merely temporary. The story told here is one of progress from the wildness of nature to the calm of human settlement. This story fit very nicely with contemporary theories about the stages of human civilization, from "savage" hunting to settled agriculture. The shock of the strange, such as the mountains that might seem to obstruct the passage of goods and people, turns to the "sublime," as in the comfort of an especially good view, much as the American Revolution resolves itself in the establishment of governments based on more just foundations and the reform of society.[35] (See Figure 3.)

---

[34]Edward T. Martin, *Thomas Jefferson: Scientist* (New York, 1952); Christopher Looby, "The Constitution of Nature: Taxonomy as Politics in Jefferson, Peale, and Bartram," *Early American Literature* 22 (1987), 252–74 (Rush quoted at 252); Paul Semonin, "'Nature's Nation': Natural History as Nationalism in the New Republic," *Northwest Review* 30 (1992), 6–47.

[35]Miller, *Jefferson and Nature*, 138–39; Roy Porter, *The Creation of the Modern World: The Untold Story of the British Enlightenment* (New York, 2000), 250–57; Harold Hellenbrand, "Roads to Happiness: Rhetorical and Philosophical Designs in Jefferson's *Notes on the State of Virginia*," *Early American Literature* 20 (1985), 3–23; John Seelye, *Beautiful Machine: Rivers and the Republican Plan, 1755–1825* (New York, 1991).

Figure 2. Jefferson designed this "Map of the Country between Albemarle Sound and Lake Erie, Comprehending the Whole of Virginia, Maryland, Delaware, and Pensylvania, with parts of several other of the United States of America" for the 1787 edition of *Notes on the State of Virginia.* Benjamin Franklin Collection, Yale University Library.

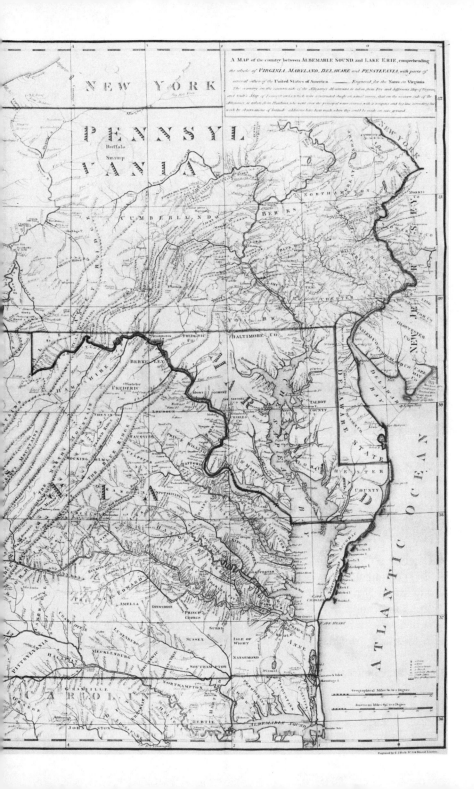

Figure 3. The Natural Bridge, from Marquis de Chastellux, *Voyages de M. le Marquis de Chastellux dans l'Amerique* (Paris, 1786). Jefferson had purchased the property on which the bridge rested, and took Chastellux there. Later the bridge would become a popular tourist destination.
Benjamin Franklin Collection, Yale University Library.

Once the context of New World nature as wondrous resource has been reestablished, Jefferson turns Marbois's seemingly innocuous query about "Mines and other subterranean riches," "its Trees Plants Fruits and other natural Riches" into a full-scale assault on established European views of the Americas. (See Document 4.) At the beginning of colonization during the sixteenth and early seventeenth centuries, Europeans crossed the ocean to find gold. They only later settled for the cash crops that could be drawn from the land with the help of conquered Indians and, then, African slaves. By the eighteenth century, to the leading intellectuals of countries like France the dominant facts of new-world history appeared to be the facts of life in the West Indies plantations, whose sugar sweetened their tables, and the southern staple colonies, whose grains fed the slaves. Modern economic historians tend to agree: Staple crops drove the development of the North American colonies. Even the colonies that did not themselves have many slaves supplied the staple colonies with grain and shipping services.[36] Jefferson's new world looks very different. It is almost less a farm than a garden. Natural "productions" include a wide variety of plants and animals, which are listed with great care.

Jefferson emphasizes the great number of useful plants, but he is not interested only in numbers. Size matters as well, which is why he argues about bones and the sizes of bones. Here he takes on the great French naturalist Georges LeClerc, Count Buffon, whose dozens of volumes on natural history had set the agenda for comparing the new world with the old. Jefferson did not rush to publish the *Notes* in part because it took several years for him to gather actual specimens, some of which he took to France with him, to refute Buffon's claim that American animals were smaller than those of Europe and Asia. Jefferson deeply respected Buffon, and hoped his fossils and skeletons would convince the naturalist that he had been wrong about American nature. He saw as more dangerous Buffon's disciple, the Abbé Raynal, who extrapolated the seeming "degeneracy" of new-world animals to make conclusions about degeneracy of new-world people. (See Document 8.)

The amount of time and money Jefferson put into collecting and sending cougar skins, elk horns, and entire moose carcasses across the Atlantic suggests the importance of this debate among participants in the international republic of letters. (See Document 11.) The scientific trump card, as the first readers were quick to notice, was the size of the mammoth, which Buffon had doubted. Yet Jefferson cites not just testimony about the size of bones, but, first, the oratory of Native Americans on the subject. His argument for the superiority of American nature also enlisted Native Americans and their achievements as evidence. He had to do both not only because of the undeniable presence of Indians in the landscape but also because Buffon and Raynal and the other natural historians of the era had based their

[36]John J. McCusker and Russell R. Menard, *The Economy of British America, 1607–1789* (Chapel Hill, 1985); Barbara L. Solow, "Slavery and Colonization" in *Slavery and the Atlantic System,* ed. Barbara L. Solow (New York, 1991), 21–42; Bernard Bailyn, "Slavery and Population Growth in Colonial New England" in *Engines of Enterprise: An Economic History of New England,* ed. Peter Temin (Cambridge, Mass., 2000), 253–60.

conclusions about the new world on what they could learn about Indians and what they knew about settlers' behavior toward them. Jefferson sought to beat the European defenders of the Native Americans—and defamers of New World nature—at their own game, to establish his own, alternative theory about the way nature had worked to create differences between the old and new worlds, and then to interpret the political meaning of those facts of natural history. He came to rely on the category of species: inherent traits subject to the influences of history. Jefferson's elevation of species over climate as a causal factor in history enables him to make a partial defense of the Indians' nature against European condescension. This defense parallels, and leads into, Jefferson's defense of the other Americans—the colonizers—against the accusations of Raynal.

Native Genius

The future of Virginia and America could not be secured without resolving the question of Native Americans. The very events that culminated in the revolution in Virginia had in fact been catalyzed by the land speculations of great planters like Jefferson and the frontier skirmishes provoked by land-hungry settlers, facts that the British used to their advantage in seeking Native allies during the war. Some Indian nations had nonetheless taken the side of the rebels (which did not always save them from further patriot encroachments on their land). As governor of Virginia, Jefferson enthusiastically pursued war against the Native Americans in the Ohio River valley, perhaps even at the price of protecting the state's Atlantic coast, while at the same time cultivating relations with Native American allies like the Kaskaskia chief Jean Baptiste DuCoigne. (See Document 5.) In his 1781 letter to DuCoigne, Jefferson depicted the not-yet-victorious colonists as fellow Americans—as similar to Indian warriors fighting for their own independence against hostile invaders.[37]

Jefferson was in a rhetorical bind when it came to Native Americans if some of their own attributes—reverence for nature, courage in the face of oppression, ownership of the land they lived on—were precisely those he wanted and needed to claim for Americans as opposed to the British. Moreover, as he wrote to Benjamin Hawkins in 1786, Americans' lack of attention to the rights of Native Americans

[37] Holton, *Forced Founders;* Jefferson to George Rogers Clark, Jan. 29, Dec. 25, 1780, *Papers of Thomas Jefferson,* III, 273–77, IV, 233–38; Onuf, *Jefferson's Empire,* 18–21; Anthony F. C. Wallace, *Thomas Jefferson and the Indians: The Tragic Story of the First Americans* (Cambridge, Mass., 1999), 21–74.

remained "a principal source of dishonor to the American character" in the eyes of the world. Natural history provides Jefferson with a way out of these dilemmas. In nature, Jefferson found "enlightened" justifications for "civilizing" the Indians by taking still more of their land. The appeal to DuCoigne that Natives can, if they were willing to embrace commercial agriculture, meld with Europeans to become a new "American" race, is genuine, but Jefferson had already assumed the inevitability of this progress from Native to American dominance over the land.[38]

In the *Notes,* Indians have the admirable qualities of natural beings, but they are primitive. Their virtues—especially those of male warriors—are precisely what leads to their passing. Thus Jefferson gets to have it both ways. With the story of Chief Logan, he explains how the mistakes of "bad" whites have victimized "good" Indians into doing what comes naturally: taking the warpath and losing, leading to the end of the male line. Native Americans have courage and military prowess, but the fact that their women work in the fields makes them aristocratic barbarians and justifies the overturning of their modes of agriculture, the products of which ("Indian corn," for example) Jefferson has already claimed, in his lists, for Virginia.

Even as he narrates the disappearance of Logan's family line, a story that might otherwise have confirmed Raynal's argument about Native bodily inferiority, Jefferson uses Logan as proof of the possibility of American "genius." His willingness to admit of genius in Native Americans provides evidence of Jefferson's lack of hatred for Indians to his European readers, even while his listing of their traits reinforces their status as a separate species, or race, and one that is disappearing fast (not unlike the mammoth). Their bones, too, are subjects of American science and can be claimed by Jefferson to give the land history, its proof of antiquity, a noble heritage. Such stories end with praise of Indian oratory—a cultural artifact that can be preserved, in print—and with Jefferson himself as the collector of Native American words, bones, and things; the teller of their tragic tale; and the keeper of the American museum.[39]

---

[38] Jefferson to Benjamin Hawkins, Aug. 13, 1786, *Papers of Thomas Jefferson,* X, 240; Bernard W. Sheehan, *Seeds of Extinction: Jeffersonian Philanthropy and the American Indian* (Chapel Hill, 1973); Daniel H. Usner Jr., "Iroquois Livelihood and Jeffersonian Agrarianism: Reaching behind the Models and Metaphors" in *Native Americans and the Early Republic,* ed. Frederick E. Hoxie, Ronald Hoffman, and Peter J. Albert (Charlottesville, Va., 1999), 200–25.

[39] Eventually, Jefferson displayed so many Native artifacts in the entrance to his mountaintop mansion that it came to be known as "Indian Hall." Jack McLaughlin, *Jefferson and Monticello: The Biography of a Builder* (New York, 1988), 358–59.

In Query 11, Jefferson gives another backhanded compliment to the natural virtues of Native Americans when describing their mode of politics as prepolitical, as antedating the invention of government and laws as Europeans know them.

Very possibly there may have been anciently three different stocks, each of which multiplying in a long course of time, had separated into so many little societies. This practice results from the circumstance of their having never submitted themselves to any laws, any coercive power, any shadow of government. Their only controls are their manners, and that moral sense of right and wrong, which, like the sense of tasting and feeling, in every man makes a part of his nature.

For Jefferson, this is the best place to be: Government, as Thomas Paine had put it in *Common Sense* (1776), was the "badge of lost innocence," not something to be wept over when one had a chance to begin again. For the Native Americans, however, this "innocent" situation, which renders them noble and independent, makes them also hopelessly primitive, even antique. Ironically, this is precisely what critics of America said they had done with their revolution: split into lawless, unorganized, anarchic small republics. Native American republicanism is to be praised, and even claimed as a legacy, but not supported on its own terms.[40]

Native Americans' very abilities, in the end, prove the impossibility of peaceful coexistence in the new republic. Natives may be admirable as individuals, but as nations they exist at an earlier stage of civilization. The Indians, at their most pure, remain in a state of nature, that is, in civilization's beginnings, not in civilization. They do not have monuments, the classical ruins after which Jefferson modeled Virginia's state buildings and his own Monticello. They have "mounds," which, however much they reverence them, are to be considered in the same manner as mammoth bones: facts of dead nature, not living history. They are America's ancients, a pure species whose languages and burial grounds can be dug up to become the raw materials for an American science—and perhaps for the next American literary and scientific genius. Here Jefferson did much more

---

[40]Thomas Paine, *Common Sense and Related Writings,* ed. Thomas P. Slaughter (Boston, 2000), 75; Robert F. Berkhofer Jr., *The White Man's Indian* (New York, 1978); Onuf, *Jefferson's Empire,* 23–41; Catherine A. Holland, *The Body Politic: Foundings, Citizenship, and Difference in the American Political Imagination* (New York, 2001), 29–35.

than twist romantic French views of Native Americans. He also told stories for America, reassuring stories for an age in which many actual Indians joined together across nations, took up tomahawks, refused European goods and religion, and gave their own meanings to a pan-Indian racial identity.[41]

Captive Nations

Native American strength and the need to justify American actions led Jefferson to his mixed portrait of Native cultures. Similarly, Jefferson's ample and yet seemingly contradictory passages on slavery and African Americans' nature in the *Notes* make sense when we consider not only Jefferson's deep personal investment in the institution of slavery and his earlier criticisms of it but also the events of the American Revolution. Hundreds of slaves enlisted formally (and many more informally) under Lord Dunmore, and thousands ran away. Jefferson himself lost thirty slaves when Lord Cornwallis swept through one of his plantations.[42]

Many African Americans showed themselves willing and able to take chances to seize freedom. The events of the war years forced Jefferson to consider Africans in America as a captive nation. In the *Notes,* he repeatedly acknowledges the justice of the African Americans' struggle for freedom, although only barely suggesting that they themselves are struggling in any meaningful sense, much less that slaves' efforts to become free had in fact played an important role in the events of the revolution in Virginia. He reminds readers, with some exaggeration, that Virginians had tried to limit the slave trade in colonial days; he makes slave emancipation the logical end of the revision of the laws of the state, and even a marker of progress.

> The spirit of the master is abating, that of the slave rising from the dust, his condition mollifying, the way I hope preparing, under the

[41] Gordon Sayre, "The Mound Builders and the Imagination of American Antiquity in Jefferson, Bartram, and Chateaubriand," *Early American Literature* 33 (1998), 225–49; Gregory Evans Dowd, *A Spirited Resistance: The North American Indian Struggle for Unity, 1745–1815* (Baltimore, 1992). According to Anthony F. C. Wallace, Jefferson systematically underestimated the numbers of Native Americans on his charts, in part by counting only warriors. Wallace, *Jefferson and the Indians,* 83–84, 90.

[42] Benjamin Quarles, "The Revolutionary War as a Black Declaration of Independence" in *Slavery and Freedom in the Age of the American Revolution,* ed. Ira Berlin and Ronald Hoffman (Urbana, Ill., 1983), 283–304; Frey, *Water from the Rock,* 45–80; Jefferson to Alexander McCaul, April 19, 1786, *Papers of Thomas Jefferson,* IX, 389.

auspices of heaven, for a total emancipation, and that this is disposed, in the order of events, to be with the consent of the masters, rather than by their extirpation.

This, however, is the *last* word, and it comes after a passionate denunciation of the way slavery itself theoretically destroys the bonds that should unite people in any society.

> And with what execration should the statesman be loaded, who permitting one–half the citizens thus to trample on the rights of the other, transforms those into despots, and these into enemies, destroys the morals of the one part, and the amor patriae of the other. For if a slave can have a country in this world, it must be any other in preference to that in which he is born to live and labour for another.... And can the liberties of a nation be thought secure when we have removed their only firm basis, a conviction in the minds if the people that these liberties are of the gift of God?

Jefferson, speaking more theoretically and about the effects of slavery on the master class and on Virginia as a whole, admits that freed slaves could possibly become citizens. However, in putting justice on the side of Africans, he also makes them "natural enemies," citizens of another country. Therefore, Africans should be colonized elsewhere, placed "beyond the reach of mixture."[43] They should repeat American history somewhere else, and thus simultaneously free themselves and free America from the corruptions introduced by oppressive colonial practices.

From Climate to Race

In the eighteenth century, as in the nineteenth and twentieth centuries, those who insisted on inherent racial differences usually have done so to justify existing inequalities as the natural state of things. If he opposed slavery and decided to say so clearly in the *Notes,* why did Jefferson go to even greater lengths to describe racial differences as a fundamental feature of life in Virginia and America? (See Query 14.) One reason is that neither antislavery nor colonization were supported by a majority of Virginians. In the *Notes,* racism serves as a compensa-

---

[43] Jordan, *White over Black,* 546–69; Onuf, *Jefferson's Empire,* 147–88.

tion for the failure to do justice.[44] Jefferson knew better; his understanding of the law of nations, and his arguments justifying the revolution, meant that African Americans deserved their liberty too, and yet
that seemed to be politically impossible. He needed another reason
to explain why things were the way they were, a reason that would
not make Americans of European ancestry look bad at a time when
they desperately needed the good opinion of Europeans. He wanted
a story about African Americans that would emphasize not what
the colonists had done to them or the history they shared with
colonists but rather what American revolutionaries had in common
with Europeans.

Buffon had argued that differences between Africans and Europeans—including skin color—were a product of climate. His disciple
Raynal had run with that theory to develop his argument that all
people in the New World degenerated because of the bad atmosphere.
The heat of the New World had earlier been used to justify enslavement on the grounds that only tropical peoples could work in the
American sun. For the French naturalists, New World weather
explained not slavery but why African slaves and Native Americans
did not multiply or become civilized by European standards. Racial differences were real, but they were not absolute because they were
largely products of climate.[45]

Jefferson had his own reasons not to accept this climate theory of
racial differences. In the *Notes,* he went so far as to suggest that with
more settlement, the weather in America was getting better all the
time. (See Query 7.) Jefferson argued, instead, that skin color, "the
first difference which strikes us," was a mark of natural inferiority.
Like the West Indian planter Edward Long, who had published a *History of Jamaica* in 1774, Jefferson sets out to prove racial inferiority
with a set of physical observations, but he culminates the argument by
returning to the problem of genius. Great philosophers like David
Hume and Immanuel Kant had already argued that the lack of great
writers, and even literacy, proved blacks inherently primitive. In

[44]Miller, *The Wolf,* 38. The uses to which Native and African Americans have put
racial theories, and the ways many different kinds of Americans have rejected racial distinctions or sought to give them positive meanings, is only just beginning to draw scholarly attention. See Mia Bay, *The White Image in the Black Mind: African-American Ideas
about White People, 1830–1925* (New York, 2000); Scott Malcolmson, *One Drop of
Blood: The American Misadventure of Race* (New York, 2000).

[45]Roxann Wheeler, *The Complexion of Race: Categories of Difference in Eighteenth-
Century British Culture* (Philadelphia, 2000), 5, 21–28.

response, critics of African bondage, like Benjamin Rush and Abbé Raynal, held up slave and former slave poets and writers like Phillis Wheatley and Ignatius Sancho to argue against racial justifications for slavery. When Jefferson wrote in his original manuscript that, unlike the Anglo-American Franklin and the Native American Logan, no African had excelled "in any art, in any science," a phrase which literally echoed Raynal's accusations of American inferiority, he put himself, as a white American, in the position of judging the primitives rather than being judged to be like one. Doing so reinforced his claims about American prospects while simultaneously supporting his argument that Africans were not, and could not be, American citizens. Race, as nature, separated white from black, even if natural rights meant that slavery should end.[46]

The Vision

Jefferson's American story could then move, in the last several queries, to the creation and maintenance of a rural nation, one that would be more republican than the colonies could ever be. In Queries 14 and 18 ("Laws" and "Manners"), the subject of slavery intrudes on Jefferson's explanations of Virginia society. He could not complete his vision for reform without exorcising the influence of slavery on Virginia customs. With the queries on religion and manners, Jefferson reaches a prophetic height, insisting that if the new republic does not purify itself by enacting religious freedom and some kind of emancipation scheme, all will indeed "be going down hill," as revolutionary enthusiasm and republican purity must.

Law, expressed in fundamental constitutions, is the means to independence and economic self-sufficiency, which in turn creates the conditions for republican government. In Jefferson's democratic agrarian vision, a society of self-sufficient farmers stands the best chance of avoiding "dependance." (See Query 18.) During the mid-1780s, the

[46]Thomas Jefferson, *Notes on the State of Virginia,* manuscript, Coolidge Collection, Massachusetts Historical Society; Henry Louis Gates Jr., "Phyllis Wheatley and the 'Nature of the Negro'," *Figures In Black: Words, Signs, and the "Racial" Self* (New York, 1987), 18–19, 67; Miller, *The Wolf,* 51–52; Alexander Boulton, "The American Paradox: Jeffersonian Equality and Racial Science," *American Quarterly* 47 (1995), 467–92; James Oakes, "Why Slaves Can't Read: The Political Significance of Jefferson's Racism" in *Thomas Jefferson and the Education of a Citizen,* ed. James Gilreath (Washington, D.C., 1999), 177–92; James W. Caesar, "Natural Rights and Scientific Racism" in *Politics of Nature,* ed. Engemann, 165–90. Earlier scholars emphasized the "tentative" nature of Jefferson's "hypothesis" of black inferiority: compare Dumas Malone, *Jefferson and the Rights of Man* (Boston, 1951), 100; Daniel Boorstin, *The Lost World of Thomas Jefferson* (1948; repr. Boston, 1960), 92–105; Peterson, *New Nation,* 264.

British strategy of unloading manufactured goods relatively cheaply to recapture the American market, combined with revolutionary war debts, caused the American economy to hit rock bottom, as cash flowed out of the country. Some proposed manufacturing as the solution to the problem of American dependence on European, especially British, imports. For Jefferson, however, such industries themselves led to poverty and dependency, as only countries with overpopulated cities, as he saw in Europe, could manufacture goods cheaply enough to market them abroad. Instead of turning to manufactures, Americans should become the world's breadbasket.[47] This meant pushing for free trade and western expansion. In Query 22, Jefferson describes how, "with such a country before us," Americans' "interest will be to throw open the doors of commerce, and to knock off all its shackles, giving perfect freedom to all persons for the vent [sale] of whatever they may choose to bring into our ports, and asking the same in theirs."

American commercial "slavery" to the British returns to the forefront, and African American racial slavery recedes to the background. How can slaves be so present and then so absent from Jefferson's picture of a land of farms? Slaves come back only as proof of agricultural wealth, at the end of Query 22, where he notes that the doubling of wealth every twenty years in this agricultural country is due not just to expansion but to "the multiplication of our slaves." Here is where Jefferson's willingness to wrestle at such length with slaves as a "race" and as a captive nation in the earlier queries has its payoff for promoters of the early American nation. It is very difficult to think of another group as a distinct race, as an enemy nation, and simultaneously as a domestic labor force.[48] Intentionally or not, by stressing the concepts of race and nation, Jefferson distracts himself, and the reader, from slaves as workers and as members of plantation families.

Naturalizing race allows Jefferson's Virginia story to end as a story of whitening America and turning all the citizens there into self-sufficient, property-owning farmers. The implications may be disturbing, but they are nonetheless clear. As Joseph J. Ellis has recently stated, "the intensity of [Jefferson]'s political radicalism, in short, was inextricably tied to the intensity of his white racism."[49] His vision of an

[47]McCoy, *Elusive Republic*, 90–135; Ben-Atar, *Origins*, 35–67.

[48]Robert John Ackermann, *Heterogeneities: Race, Gender, Class, Nation, and State* (Amherst, Mass., 1996); Patrick Wolfe, "Land, Labor and Difference: Elementary Structures of Race," *American Historical Review* 106 (2001), 867, 880.

[49]Joseph J. Ellis, "Why Jefferson Lives: A Meditation on the Man and the Myth" in Garry Wills et al., *Thomas Jefferson: Genius of Liberty* (New York, 2000), 166.

America of, by, and for white yeoman farmers denied the fact that Africans and Native American Indians tilled American soil. This is why he must advocate the removal of Africans and the assimilation of the Natives before he can make his foundational statements of democratic agrarianism: "those who labour in the earth are the chosen people of God" and "the most virtuous and independent citizens."

THE STRANGE HISTORY OF A BOOK

Stories and books are one thing; politics, although it may deal in stories and in books, is another. Jefferson turned out to be right in suspecting that his natural history would cause controversy on the western side of the Atlantic. His fellow American statesmen and scientists praised him effusively for refuting Buffon. But what struck most Americans who read the book during Jefferson's lifetime, as during ours, was Jefferson's stand on slavery and race. John Adams, a longtime critic of slavery, wrote Jefferson that "the passages upon slavery, are worth Diamonds." David Ramsay, a South Carolina slaveholder who had been born in Pennsylvania, objected that he had "depressed the negroes too low." [50]

Jefferson, as we have seen, had already feared that his attack on slavery would "revolt the minds of our countrymen against reformation" of slavery and the state constitution. Trends in the mid-1780s seemed to be heading in two directions, both against slavery and against tampering with the institution where it was most firmly established, south of the Potomac. Jefferson himself almost managed to get an antislavery passage into Congress's Ordinance of 1784, which mapped out western territories for new states. Massachusetts, Vermont, Connecticut, Rhode Island, and Pennsylvania had all abolished slavery or passed laws for gradual emancipation. The Northwest Ordinance of 1787 appeared to ban slavery from those future states. [51] Jefferson wrote confidently to the English radical Richard Price that "in a few years there will be no slaves Northward of Maryland." (See Document 9.) He was beginning to be struck by these regional differ-

[50]John Adams to Jefferson, May 22, 1785, quoted in John Ferling, *Setting the World Ablaze: Washington, Adams, Jefferson and the American Revolution* (New York, 2000), 285; David Ramsay to Jefferson, May 3, 1786, *Papers of Thomas Jefferson*, IX, 441.

[51]Jefferson to James Monroe, June 17, 1785, Jefferson to James Madison, May 11, 1785, Nov. 15, 1785, Jan. 25, 1786, *Papers of Thomas Jefferson*, VII, 229, VIII, 38, 194–95; Miller, *The Wolf*, 23–30; Finkelman, *Slavery and the Founders*, 34–56; Gary B. Nash, *Race and Revolution* (Madison, Wisc., 1991), 3–50.

ences, which seemed to have something to do with climate. (See Document 8.)

After *Notes* was published in Philadelphia in 1788, the reaction in America confirmed Jefferson's developing sense that slavery was too hot an issue to be addressed in the new national political arena, in part because of the quick advance of antislavery sentiment in the North. His book, in fact, became part of the debate itself. When a group of Quaker antislavery activists petitioned Congress to end slavery in 1790, South Carolina representatives Richard Jackson and William Loughton Smith read aloud from the floor of Congress the passages from the *Notes* about racial inferiority and the impossibility of whites and blacks living side by side in America. A year later, Benjamin Banneker, the African American mathematician and astronomer, wrote Jefferson a quite critical letter and enclosed the almanac he had calculated. (See Document 13.) Banneker inaugurated a tradition of arguing with Jefferson, which free African American activists in the North carried down to the Civil War and beyond. Their very existence, their ability to make the argument for their own equality, seemed to defy Jefferson's racial categories.[52]

During the rest of Jefferson's life, both his antislavery and his racist arguments got him in trouble all over the political spectrum. By 1796, South Carolina's William Loughton Smith was a political opponent, attacking him as a presidential candidate, for having condescended to answer Banneker's letter. During Jefferson's successful campaigns for the presidency in 1800 and 1804, northern Federalists attacked him for his slaveholding and his anti–African American prejudice as evidenced in *Notes on the State of Virginia*. Others, north and south, depicted him as dangerously antislavery, citing passages from the *Notes*. Both his antislavery and proslavery critics found uses for the story, well publicized in 1802, of his affair with Sally Hemings.[53]

[52]Ellis, *Founding Brothers*, 99–100; Richard Newman, Patrick Rael, and Philip Lapsansky, "Introduction," *Pamphlets of Protest: An Anthology of Early African American Protest Literature* (New York, 2001), 22; Bay, *White Image*, 17, 62, 79–80; David Walker, *Appeal to the Coloured Citizens of the World*, ed. Peter P. Hinks (University Park, Penn., 1999), 12, 14, 16–18, 28–30.

[53]Miller, *The Wolf*, 78; McColley, *Slavery*, 125–27; Jordan, *White over Black*, 442; Clement Clarke Moore, *Observations upon Certain Passages in Mr. Jefferson's Notes on Virginia, Which Appear to Have a Tendency to Subvert Religion, and Establish a False Philosophy* (New York, 1804), 19–28.

HEMINGSES, JEFFERSONS, AND HISTORY

The legend of "black Sal," despite the skepticism of Jefferson's defenders over the years, has turned out to be substantially correct, although we may never know as much as we would like to know about the nature of the human relationship between Hemings and Jefferson or its duration after Hemings arrived in France, with Jefferson's daughter Maria (Polly), in 1787. It seems likely, from recent research into the timing of Hemings's pregnancies, that Jefferson fathered all six of her children. In the light of today's scientific revelations (belief in the Hemings-Jefferson liaison was confirmed in the eyes of most scholars and the Thomas Jefferson Memorial Foundation in 1998 by DNA tests that matched descendants of the Jefferson and Hemings families), it is perhaps even inevitable that we see Jefferson as even more of a hypocrite, or even more tragically trapped by slavery's history.[54] Yet we should also remember the racial assumptions of the Jefferson critics who first spread the story. We may not wish to embrace their version of the story so quickly because, in accusing Jefferson of hypocrisy, they accepted the terms of Jefferson's own racism and encouraged his defenders to do the same.

For a long time, historians dismissed the Hemings's family's insistence that they were descendants of Jefferson in part because of the unsavory reputation of James Thomson Callendar, the journalist who first published the story in 1802. Callendar, a radical democrat from Ireland, had been encouraged by Jefferson as a political ally, and even went to jail during the Alien and Sedition Acts crisis of 1798–99, when journalists allied with the Jeffersonian opposition were prosecuted. Unrewarded financially by the victorious Jeffersonians in 1800–01, Callendar allied himself with the Federalists and became a professional scourge of the president and his administration. Callendar not only owed his sense of betrayal to the Jeffersonian battle of tyranny against liberty, he shared Jefferson's own racist presumptions and much of his language. Callendar labelled Sally "black," equating her skin color with race, and race with slavery. Defenders of Jefferson subsequently insisted that because of Jefferson's stated dislike of slaves' black skin in the *Notes,* he could never have engaged in a

---

[54]Fraser D. Neiman, "Coincidence or Causal Connection? The Relationship between Thomas Jefferson's Visits to Monticello and Sally Hemings's Conceptions," *William and Mary Quarterly,* 3d Ser., 57 (Jan. 2000), 198–210. For an update on the controversy, including a review of work published by those critical of the Thomas Jefferson Memorial Foundation, see Alexander O. Boulton, "The Monticello Mystery: Case Continued," *William and Mary Quarterly,* 3d Ser., 58 (Oct. 2001), 1039–46.

romance with a black woman. For almost two hundred years, Jefferson's *Notes* has provided both a source for accusing Jefferson of hypocrisy and an alibi for those who found his racist expressions far more natural than his relationship with Hemings.[55]

The real Sally Hemings, according to former Monticello slave Isaac Jefferson, was "mighty near white." She was also the half-sister of Martha Wayles, Jefferson's wife, who died in 1782. Perhaps Sally Hemings's apparent or near whiteness, as well as a possible resemblance to his wife, permitted Jefferson to put her, and her children, in still another category: neither white nor black but rather the less spoken of in-between that is the actual history of race in the Americas.[56] Perhaps Jefferson himself was of two minds about the matter. It may have suited him to think of Hemings as black by public, legal definition, but as something else in private. Her legal blackness certainly allowed him to leave their relationship, and his relationship to her children, ambiguous (to us, maddeningly so). In defining Hemings as black, we, like those who dismissed the Hemings story, risk echoing Jefferson's own racism—a focus on skin color that provided a rationale for his essentially political insistence that Africans could not become citizens, but that they had to remain slaves while in America. Knowing that slavery was wrong, Jefferson ascribed to race what should have been ascribed to slavery and to history—to America's revolutionary history and to his own family's history. Only by doing so could he deny the rights of Africans, and of his slave kin.

Jefferson's legacy of liberty and slavery is as complex and contradictory as that of the nation he helped found. During the years which followed the *Notes* he helped introduce the idea of banning slavery from the new western states. He also created an empire for slavery by successfully pushing American expansion west of the Appalachians after the Louisiana Purchase of 1803. He argued repeatedly and publicly against slavery, but he also put black inferiority on a scientific basis and, in doing so, helped lay the groundwork for the modern, scientific racism, which would prove so useful to proslavery advocates in the antebellum period.

[55]Jordan, *White over Black,* 464–69; Miller, *The Wolf,* 148–76; Michael Durey, *"With the Hammer of Truth": James Thomson Callendar and America's Early National Heroes* (Charlottesville, Va., 1990), 138; Gordon-Reed, *American Controversy,* 59–77, 134–36.

[56]Stanton, "'Those Who Labor,'" 152; Winthrop D. Jordan, "Hemings and Jefferson: Redux" in *Sally Hemings and Thomas Jefferson,* ed. Lewis and Onuf, 35–51; Gary B. Nash, "The Hidden History of Mestizo America," *Journal of American History* 82 (1995), 941–64.

Yet early proslavery theorists remained wary of Jefferson's anti-slavery credentials, and for good reason. Abolitionists kept his anti-slavery words from the *Notes* in public long enough for them to be quoted by the antislavery moderate Abraham Lincoln, in his debate at Galesburg, Illinois, with Stephen Douglas in 1858. Douglas had said that "the signers of the Declaration of Independence never dreamed of the Negro when they were writing that document. They referred to white men, to men of European birth and European descent, when they declared the equality of all men." Lincoln responded, "that while Mr. Jefferson was the owner of slaves, as he undoubtedly was, he, speaking on this very subject, used the strong language that he trembled for his country when he remembered that God is just. I will offer the highest premium in my power to Judge Douglas, if he will show that he, in all his life, has ever uttered a sentiment akin to that sentiment of Jefferson's."[57] The debate about Jefferson's real meaning had merged with the debate about the meaning of America.

Jefferson tried to write slavery and race out of the new American story but found that his personal, intellectual, and political lives made them his own story. In the twenty-first century, we are still learning the same lessons. For these reasons, our own stories about Jefferson, his words and his deeds, have to be reconsidered whenever we take another look at America's revolutionary history.

---

[57] James Oakes, *Slavery and Freedom: An Interpretation of the Old South* (New York, 1990), 86–87; Finkelman, *Slavery and the Founders,* 110; Harold Holzer, ed., *The Lincoln-Douglas Debates: The First Complete, Unexpurgated Text* (New York, 1993), 247, 253.

A NOTE ABOUT THE TEXTS

Most of the brief documents written by or to Thomas Jefferson that are included here are taken from the definitive versions in Julian P. Boyd, Charles T. Cullen, and John Catanzariti, eds., *The Papers of Thomas Jefferson* (Princeton, N.J.: Princeton University Press, 1950–). The series has been published chronologically through 1793 and is heading toward completion under the editorship of Barbara B. Oberg.

The first edition of *Notes on the State of Virginia* appeared in Paris in a small printing of 200 in 1784. A revised French edition appeared in 1786, and another English version in 1787, printed by John Stockdale in London. This book is based on the Stockdale text and on an edition published in Richmond, Virginia, by J. W. Randolph in 1853, based on Stockdale, which modernized punctuation. Quotations and expressions from non-English languages have been translated where Jefferson did not provide his own translation; a few are omitted entirely, where the meaning is obvious from the context. These are indicated by ellipses. Spelling has been modernized in some cases. Many of Jefferson's scholarly and discursive footnotes have been replaced. Some of the longer tables have been summarized. I have included photographs of several of these from the Stockdale edition to give the reader a sense of how this information would have appeared visually to contemporaries.

This book also omits the appendices that Jefferson first added with the Stockdale edition. These included commentaries on scientific matters by Jefferson's friend Charles Thomson, a "Draught of a Fundamental Constitution for the Commonwealth of Virginia," and the "Act for Establishing Religious Freedom," which Jefferson discusses in Document 12, Query 17. In 1800, Jefferson published a pamphlet responding to criticisms of his account of Chief Logan, *Relative to the Murder of Logan's Family.* This was subsequently included as a fourth appendix in later editions of the *Notes.* All four appendixes appear in what is still the standard scholarly edition: *Notes on the State of Virginia,* edited with an introduction and notes by William Peden (Chapel Hill: University of North Carolina Press, for the Institute of Early American History and Culture, 1954). Peden's volume also includes some of Jefferson's post-1787 revisions, which he apparently intended to include in another revised edition.

PART TWO

The Documents

1

THOMAS JEFFERSON

Resolutions of the Freeholders of Albemarle County

July 26, 1774

Thomas Jefferson drafted the document assented to by the freeholders, *or voting citizens, of his home county of Albemarle in the wake of the Boston Port Act. The language is vintage Jefferson and parallels the argument presented in* A Summary View of the Rights of British America. *Parliament's actions are illegitimate with respect to both traditional British liberties and natural rights.*

The nonimportation movement of 1774 in Virginia boycotted taxed articles but also extended to clothing, as part of the effort to punish England economically and to make the colony more self-sufficient. The Virginians went further and, after a strategic delay, banned exports, including tobacco, in an effort to raise prices in Europe and gain greater control over the trade.

[26 JULY 1774]

At a meeting of the freeholders of the county of Albemarle, assembled in their collective body, at the courthouse of the said county, on the 26th day of July, 1774,

Resolved, that the inhabitants of the several states of British America are subject to the laws which they adopted at their first settlement, and to such others as have been since made by their respective legislatures, duly constituted and appointed with their own consent; that no other legislature whatever may rightfully exercise authority over them, and that these privileges they hold as the common rights of mankind, confirmed by the political constitutions they have respectively assumed, and also by several charters of compact from the crown.

Julian P. Boyd, Charles T. Cullen, and John Catanzariti, eds., *The Papers of Thomas Jefferson* (Princeton, N.J.: Princeton University Press, 1950–), I, 117–18.

Resolved, that these their natural and legal rights have in frequent instances been invaded by the parliament of Great Britain, and particularly that they were so by an act lately passed to take away the trade of the inhabitants of the town of Boston, in the province of Massachusetts Bay, that all such assumptions of unlawful power are dangerous to the rights of the British empire in general, and should be considered as its common cause, and that we will ever be ready to join with our fellow subjects, in every part of the same, in exerting all those rightful powers, which God has given us, for the re-establishing and guaranteeing such their constitutional rights, when, where, and by whomsoever invaded.

It is the opinion of this meeting, that the most eligible means of effecting these purposes will be to put an immediate stop to all imports from Great Britain (cotton, oznabrigs,[1] striped duffil,[2] medicines, gunpowder, lead, books and printed papers, the necessary tools and implements for the handycraft arts and manufactures excepted for a limited time) and to all exports thereto after the 1st day of October, which shall be in the year of our Lord, 1775; and immediately to discontinue all commercial intercourse with every part of the British empire which shall not in like manner break off their commerce with Great Britain.

It is the opinion of this meeting, that we immediately cease to import all commodities from every part of the world which are subjected by the British parliament to the payment of duties in America.

It is the opinion of this meeting that these measures should be pursued until a repeal be obtained of the act for blocking up the harbour of Boston, of the acts prohibiting or restraining internal manufactures in America, of the acts imposing on any commodities duties to be paid in America, and of the acts laying restrictions on the American trade; and that on such repeal it will be reasonable to grant to our brethren of Great Britain such privileges in commerce as may amply compensate their fraternal assistance, past and future.

Resolved, however, that this meeting do submit these their opinions to the convention of deputies from the several counties of this colony, appointed to be held at Williamsburg on the 1st day of August next, and also to the general congress of deputies from the several American states, when and wheresoever held; and that they will concur in these or any other measures which such convention or such congress

[1] oznabrigs: coarse linens.
[2] striped duffil: another cloth.

shall adopt as most expedient for the American good. And we do appoint THOMAS JEFFERSON and JOHN WALKER our deputies to act for this county at the said convention, and instruct them to conform themselves to these our resolutions and opinions.

2

LORD DUNMORE

Proclamation of Freedom to Slaves and Servants
November 1775

Dunmore's carefully worded proclamation of November 1775 freed only the slaves of rebel masters, and only those who actually joined the British forces. Dunmore did not want to encourage wholesale slave rebellion; that would have angered loyal Virginian slaveholders. He did want to make the rebels as vulnerable as possible, however. This vulnerability, especially given the large number of southern slaves (in some places, more than half of the population), contributed to the crown's southern strategy for winning the war. It certainly helped make the American Revolution a bloody, destructive contest in places like South Carolina and Georgia. It also helped propel slaveholders like Jefferson into the conviction that their whole way of life could be at stake in the imperial controversy.

PROCLAMATION BY THE GOVERNOUR OF VIRGINIA.
By his Excellency the Right Honourable JOHN, *Earl of* DUNMORE, *His Majesty's Lieutenant and Governour-General of the Colony and Dominion of* VIRGINIA, *and Vice-Admiral of the same.*

A PROCLAMATION.

As I have ever entertained hopes that an accommodation might have taken place between *Great Britain* and this Colony, without being compelled by my duty to this most disagreeable, but now absolutely

Peter Force, ed., *American Archives,* 4th Ser., III (Washington, D.C.: M. St. Clair and Peter Force, 1840), 1385.

necessary step, rendered so by a body of armed men, unlawfully assembled, firing on His Majesty's Tenders;[1] and the formation of an Army, and that Army now on their march to attack His Majesty's Troops, and destroy the well-disposed subjects of this Colony: To defeat such treasonable purposes, and that all such traitors and their abettors may be brought to justice, and that the peace and good order of this Colony may be again restored, which the ordinary course of the civil law is unable to effect, I have thought fit to issue this my Proclamation, hereby declaring, that until the aforesaid good purposes can be obtained, I do, in virtue of the power and authority to me given by His Majesty, determine to execute martial law, and cause the same to be executed throughout this Colony. And to the end that peace and good order may the sooner be restored, I do require every person capable of bearing arms to resort to His Majesty's standard, or be looked upon as traitors to His Majesty's crown and Government, and thereby become liable to the penalty the law inflicts upon such offences—such as forfeiture of life, confiscation of lands, &c., &c.; and I do hereby further declare all indented servants, Negroes, or others, (appertaining to Rebels,) free, that are able and willing to bear arms, they joining His Majesty's Troops, as soon as may be, for the more speedily reducing this Colony to a proper sense of their duty to His Majesty's crown and dignity. I do further order and require all His Majesty's liege[2] subjects to retain their quit-rents,[3] or any other taxes due, or that may become due, in their own custody, till such time as peace may be again restored to this, at present, most unhappy Country, or demanded of them for their former salutary purposes, by officers properly authorized to receive the same.

Given under my hand, on board the Ship *William,* off *Norfolk,* the 7th day of *November,* in the sixteenth year of His Majesty's reign.

DUNMORE.

GOD *Save the King.*

---

[1]Tenders: boats sent out from a larger ship.
[2]liege: owing allegiance to.
[3]quit-rents: small amounts paid to the owner, usually of land, instead of services owed by the renter.

The Declaration of Independence:
Thomas Jefferson's Draft with Congress's Changes
July 4, 1776

In his later life, Jefferson was justifiably proud of the Declaration of Independence, even preferring his original draft to the significantly revised version Congress passed on July 4, 1776—later known as Independence Day. He carefully preserved his drafts and included this carefully marked version in the manuscript of his autobiography in 1821, noting that "the sentiments of men are known not only by what they receive but what they reject also." He indicated Congress's deletions with underlining and Congress's additions by arrows and corresponding text in the margins. (The additions are indicated here underneath the text, as footnotes.) The two versions of the final paragraph, which contains a lengthy deletion and addition, are set side by side, with Jefferson's version on the left.

The changes made by Congress were both stylistic and substantive, and they invite important questions about the philosophical and political logic of the American Revolution. Had Jefferson composed a masterful "expression of the American mind" at the time of its national emergence? John Adams thought so. In 1821, in the wake of the controversy about admitting Missouri to the union as a slave state, Jefferson was not so sure, because his original inclusion of an antislavery paragraph, which depicted the slave trade and the arming of slaves as the culmination of the king's tyrannies, had been struck out, replaced only by an ambiguous passage about the excitement of "domestic insurrections among us." The loss of the passage on slavery seemed like a great historical watershed. He blamed not his fellow Virginians but rather deep Southerners and New England slave traders: "the clause . . . reprobating the enslaving the inhabitants of Africa, was struck out in complaisance to South Carolina & Georgia, who had never attempted to restrain the importation of slaves, and who on the contrary still wished to continue it. Our Northern brethren also I believe felt a little tender under those censures; for tho' their people have very few slaves themselves yet they have been pretty considerable carriers of them to others."

Julian P. Boyd, Charles T. Cullen, and John Catanzariti, eds., *The Papers of Thomas Jefferson* (Princeton, N.J.: Princeton University Press, 1950–), I, 315–19.

The Declaration is printed here in both versions, much as Jefferson indicated in his autobiography: "The parts struck out by Congress shall be distinguished by a black line drawn under them," and the parts inserted by Congress are placed in brackets, or in a footnote (with footnote symbols *, †, ‡, §, ||, etc.), or (at the end) in a parallel column.

A Declaration by the representatives of the United states of America, in General[1] Congress assembled

When in the course of human events it becomes necessary for one people to dissolve the political bands which have connected them with another, and to assume among the powers of the earth the separate & equal station to which the laws of nature and of nature's god entitle them, a decent respect to the opinions of mankind requires that they should declare the causes which impel them to the separation.

We hold these truths to be self evident: that all men are created equal; that they are endowed by their creator with* inherent and inalienable rights; that among these are life, liberty & the pursuit of happiness: that to secure these rights, governments are instituted among men, deriving their just powers from the consent of the governed; that whenever any form of government becomes destructive of these ends, it is the right of the people to alter or to abolish it, & to institute new government, laying it's foundation on such principles, & organising it's Powers in such form, as to them shall seem most likely to effect their safety & happiness. Prudence indeed will dictate that governments long established should not be changed for light & transient causes; and accordingly all experience hath shewn that mankind are more disposed to suffer while evils are sufferable than to right themselves by abolishing the forms to which they are accustomed. But when a long train of abuses & usurpations[2] [begun at a distinguished period and] pursuing invariably the same object, evinces a design to reduce them under absolute despotism it is their right, it is their duty to throw off such government, & to provide new guards for their future security. Such has been the patient sufferance of these colonies; & such is now the necessity which constrains them to [expunge]† their former systems of government. The history of the

[1]General: Continental Congress.
*certain
[2]usurpations: unjustified subversive actions.
†alter

present king of Great Britain is a history of [unremitting]* injuries & usurpations, [among which appears no solitary fact to contradict the uniform tenor of the rest but all have]† in direct object the establishment of an absolute tyranny over these states. To prove this let facts be submitted to a candid world [for the truth of which we pledge a faith yet unsullied by falsehood.]

He has refused his assent to laws the most wholsome & necessary for the public good.

He has forbidden his governors to pass laws of immediate & pressing importance, unless suspended in their operation till his assent should be obtained; & when so suspended, he has utterly neglected to attend to them.

He has refused to pass other laws for the accommodation of large districts of people, unless those people would relinquish the right of representation in the legislature, a right inestimable to them, & formidable to tyrants only.

He has called together legislative bodies at places unusual, uncomfortable, and distant from the depository of their public records, for the sole purpose of fatiguing them into compliance with his measures.

He has dissolved representative houses repeated [& continually] for opposing with manly firmness his invasions on the rights of the people.

He has refused for a long time after such dissolutions to cause others to be elected, whereby the legislative powers, incapable of annihilation, have returned to the people at large for their exercise, the state remaining in the mean time exposed to all the dangers of invasion from without & convulsions within.

He has endeavored to prevent the population of these states; for that purpose obstructing the laws for naturalization of foreigners, refusing to pass others to encourage their migrations hither, & raising the conditions of new appropriations of lands.

He has† [suffered] the administration of justice [totally to cease in some of these states]§ refusing his assent to laws for establishing judiciary powers.

He has made [our] judges dependant on his will alone, for the tenure of their offices, & the amount & payment of their salaries.

*repeated
†all having
‡obstructed
§by

He has erected a multitude of new offices [by a self assumed power] and sent hither swarms of new officers to harrass our people and eat out their substance.

He has kept among us in times of peace standing armies [and ships of war] without the consent of our legislatures.

He has affected to render the military independant of, & superior to the civil power.

He has combined with others to subject us to a jurisdiction foreign to our constitutions & unacknowleged by our laws, giving his assent to their acts of pretended legislation for quartering large bodies of armed troops among us; for protecting them by a mock-trial from punishment for any murders which they should commit on the inhabitants of these states; for cutting off our trade with all parts of the world; for imposing taxes on us without our consent; for depriving us* of the benefits of trial by jury; for transporting us beyond seas to be tried for pretended offences; for abolishing the free system of English laws in a neighboring province, establishing therein an arbitrary government, and enlarging it's boundaries, so as to render it at once an example and fit instrument for introducing the same absolute rule into these† [states]; for taking away our charters, abolishing our most valuable laws, and altering fundamentally the forms of our governments; for suspending our own legislatures, & declaring themselves invested with power to legislate for us in all cases whatsoever.

He has abdicated government here‡ [withdrawing his governors, and declaring us out of his allegiance & protection].

He has plundered our seas, ravaged our coasts, burnt our towns, & destroyed the lives of our people.

He is at this time transporting large armies of foreign mercenaries to compleat the works of death, desolation & tyranny already begun with circumstances of cruelty and perfidy§ unworthy the head of a civilized nation.

He has constrained our fellow citizens taken captive on the high seas to bear arms against their country, to become the executioners of their friends & brethren, or to fall themselves by their hands.

He has‖ endeavored to bring on the inhabitants of our frontiers the merciless Indian savages, whose known rule of warfare is an undistinguished destruction of all ages, sexes, & conditions [of existence.]

---

*in many cases
†colonies
‡by declaring us out of his protection & waging war against us.
§scarcely paralleled in the most barbarous ages, & totally
‖excited domestic resurrections amongst us, & has

[He has incited treasonable insurrections of our fellow-citizens, with the allurements of forfeiture & confiscation of our property.

He has waged cruel war against human nature itself, violating it's most sacred rights of life and liberty in the persons of a distant people who never offended him, captivating & carrying them into slavery in another hemisphere or to incur miserable death in their transportation thither. This piratical warfare, the opprobrium of *infidel*[3] powers, is the warfare of the *Christian* king of Great Britain. Determined to keep open a market where *Men* should be bought & sold, he has prostituted his negative for suppressing every legislative attempt to prohibit or to restrain this execrable commerce. And that this assemblage of horrors might want no fact of distinguished die, he is now exciting those very people to rise in arms among us, and to purchase that liberty of which he has deprived them, by murdering the people on whom he also obtruded them: thus paying off former crimes committed against the *Liberties* of one people, with crimes which he urges them to commit against the *lives* of another.]

In every stage of these oppressions we have petitioned for redress in the most humble terms: our repeated petitions have been answered only by repeated injuries. A prince whose character is thus marked by every act which may define a tyrant is unfit to be the ruler of a* people [who mean to be free. Future ages will scarcely believe that the hardiness of one man adventured, within the short compass of twelve years only, to lay a foundation so broad & so undisguised for tyranny over a people fostered & fixed in principles of freedom.]

Nor have we been wanting in attentions to our British brethren. We have warned them from time to time of attempts by their legislature to extend[†] [a] jurisdiction over[‡] [these our states.] We have reminded them of the circumstances of our emigration & settlement here, [no one of which could warrant so strange a pretension: that these were effected at the expence of our own blood & treasure, unassisted by the wealth or the strength of Great Britain: that in constituting indeed our several forms of government, we had adopted one common king, thereby laying a foundation for perpetual league & amity with them: but that submission to their parliament was no part of our constitution, nor ever in idea, if history may be credited: and,]

[3]*infidel:* pagan or unbelieving.
*free
†an unwarrantable
‡us

we* appealed to their native justice and magnanimity† [as well as to] the ties of our common kindred to disavow these usurpations which‡ [were likely to] interrupt our connection and correspondence. They too have been deaf to the voice of justice & of consanguinity, [and when occasions have been given them, by the regular course of their laws, of removing from their councils the disturbers of our harmony, they have, by their free election, re-established them in power. At this very time too they are permitting their chief magistrate to send over not only soldiers of our common blood, but Scotch & foreign mercenaries to invade & destroy us. These facts have given the last stab to agonizing affection, and manly spirit bids us to renounce for ever these unfeeling brethren. We must endeavor to forget our former love for them, and to hold them as we hold the rest of mankind enemies in war, in peace friends. We might have been a free and a great people together; but a communication of grandeur & of freedom it seems is below their dignity. Be it so, since they will have it. The road to happiness & to glory is open to us too. We will tread it apart from them, and]§ acquiesce in the necessity which denounces our [eternal] separation‖ [!]

We therefore the representatives of the United states of America in General Congress assembled do in the name, & by the authority of the good people of these [states reject & renounce all allegiance & subjection to the kings of Great Britain & all others who may hereafter claim by, through or under them: we utterly dissolve all political connection which may heretofore have subsisted between us & the people or parliament of Great Britain: & finally we do assert &

We therefore the representatives of the United states of American in General Congress assembled, appealing to the supreme judge of the world for the rectitude of our intentions, do in the name, & by the authority of the good people of these colonies, solemnly publish & declare that these United colonies are & of right ought to be free & independant states; that they are absolved from all allegiance to the British crown, and that all political connection between

---

*have
†and we have conjured them by
‡would inevitably
§we must therefore
‖and hold them as we hold the rest of mankind, enemies in war, in peace friends.

declare these colonies to be free & independant states,] & that as free & independant states, they have full power to levy war, conclude peace, contract alliances, establish commerce, & to do all other acts & things which independant states may of right do.

And for the support of this declaration we mutually pledge to each other our lives, our fortunes & our sacred honour.

them & the state of Great Britain is, & ought to be, totally dissolved; & that as free & independant states they have full power to levy war, conclude peace, contract alliances, establish commerce & to do all other acts & things which independant states may of right do.

And for the support of this declaration, with a firm reliance on the protection of divine providence we mutually pledge to each other our lives, our fortunes & our sacred honour.

4

FRANÇOIS MARBOIS

Queries Concerning Virginia

November 1780

François Marbois served as secretary to the French minister to America, the Count de la Luzerne. The French government had asked him to collect information on the new republic; in 1778, France and the United States had signed a Treaty of Amity and Commerce, committing the French to the American cause. Marbois intended to convey this list of questions to informed men in each of the new states. He originally asked Joseph Jones, a member of the Virginia Assembly. Jones in turn asked Jefferson, who he believed had more extensive knowledge of their home state.

Julian P. Boyd, Charles T. Cullen, and John Catanzariti, eds., *The Papers of Thomas Jefferson* (Princeton, N.J.: Princeton University Press, 1950–), IV, 166.

[BEFORE 30 NOVEMBER 1780]

Articles of which you are requested to give some details

1. The Charters of your State.
2. The present Constitution.
3. An exact description of its limits and boundaries.
4. The Memoirs published in its name, in the time of its being a Colony and the pamphlets relating to its interior or exterior affairs present or ancient.
5. The History of the State.
6. A notice of the Counties Cities Townships Villages Rivers Rivulets and how far they are navagible. Cascades Caverns Mountains Productions Trees Plants Fruits and other natural Riches.
7. The number of its Inhabitants.
8. The different Religions received in that State.
9. The Colleges and public establishments. The Roads Buildings &c.
10. The Administration of Justice and a description of the Laws.
11. The particular Customs and manners that may happen to be received in that State.
12. The present State of Manufactures Commerce interior and exterior Trade.
13. A notice of the best Sea Ports of the State and how big are the vessels they can receive.
14. A notice of the commercial productions particular to that State and of those objects which the Inhabitants are obliged to get from Europe and from other parts of the World.
15. The weight measures and the currency of the hard money. Some details relating to the exchange with Europe.
16. The public income and expences.
17. The measures taken with regard of the Estates and Possessions of the Rebels commonly called Tories.
18. The condition of the Regular Troops and the Militia and their pay.
19. The marine and Navigation.
20. A notice of the Mines and other subterranean riches.
21. Some Samples of these Mines and of the extraordinary Stones. In short a notice of all what can increase the progress of human Knowledge.
22. A description of the Indians established in the State before the European Settlements and of those who are still remaining. An indication of the Indian Monuments discovered in that State.

5

THOMAS JEFFERSON

Letter to Jean Baptiste DuCoigne, Kaskaskia Chief

June 1781

Jefferson wrote his letter to DuCoigne, a chief of the Kaskaskia nation of the Illinois country, in the style of the council oratory he would write of admiringly in the Notes on the State of Virginia. *In doing so, he meets the Natives in part on their own ground. He identifies the American cause with that of the friendly Indian nations in other ways: They share a common enemy, Britain, and they both seek independence. According to the conventions of diplomacy as it had been worked out over the past century and a half, European and Native allies affirmed each other as fictive kin: thus Jefferson addresses DuCoigne as "brother." The Kaskaskia chief played his part in this affirmation of mutuality by naming one of his sons after Jefferson. In doing so, he transferred the position of European "father" from the king of France to the governor of Virginia. The two leaders also exchanged ceremonial gifts; Jefferson gave the chief a special bronze medal, and DuCoigne presented Jefferson with several painted buffalo skins, which were later displayed at Monticello.*

It is clear from Jefferson's letter that, in his visit to Williamsburg, DuCoigne had raised the issue of goods and supplies. Native American leaders often made their loyalty conditional on the terms of their trade with, and gifts from, Europeans. Jefferson's apologies indicate the economically difficult position of Virginia and the other states during the Revolutionary War, but Jefferson suggests that the new American nation will be a different kind of brotherhood: The Americans will teach their ways to their Native allies.

Julian P. Boyd, Charles T. Cullen, and John Catanzariti, eds., *The Papers of Thomas Jefferson* (Princeton, N.J.: Princeton University Press, 1950–), VI, 60–63.

CHARLOTTESVILLE, [CA. 1] JUNE, 1781.

BROTHER JOHN BAPTIST DE COIGNE

I am very much pleased with the visit you have made us, and particularly that it has happened when the wise men from all parts of our country were assembled together in council, and had an opportunity of hearing the friendly discourse you held to me. We are all sensible of your friendship, and of the services you have rendered, and I now, for my countrymen, return you thanks, and, most particularly, for your assistance to the garrison which was besieged by the hostile Indians. I hope it will please the Great Being above to continue you long in life, in health and in friendship to us; and that your son will afterwards succeed you in wisdom, in good disposition, and in power over your people. I consider the name you have given as particularly honorable to me, but I value it the more as it proves your attachment to my country. We, like you, are Americans, born in the same land, and having the same interests. I have carefully attended to the figures represented on the skins, and to their explanation, and shall always keep them hanging on the walls in remembrance of you and your nation. I have joined with you sincerely in smoking the pipe of peace; it is a good old custom handed down by your ancestors, and as such I respect and join in it with reverence. I hope we shall long continue to smoke in friendship together. You find us, brother, engaged in war with a powerful nation. Our forefathers were Englishmen, inhabitants of a little island beyond the great water, and, being distressed for land, they came and settled here. As long as we were young and weak, the English whom we had left behind, made us carry all our wealth to their country, to enrich them; and, not satisfied with this, they at length began to say we were their slaves, and should do whatever they ordered us. We were now grown up and felt ourselves strong; we knew we were free as they were, that we came here of our own accord and not at their biddance, and were determined to be free as long as we should exist. For this reason they made war on us. They have now waged that war six years, and have not yet won more land from us than will serve to bury the warriors they have lost. Your old father, the King of France, has joined us in the war, and done many good things for us. We are bound forever to love him, and wish you to love him, brother, because he is a good and true friend to us. The Spaniards have also joined us, and other powerful nations are now entering into the war to punish the robberies and violences the English have committed on them. The English stand alone, without a friend to support them, hated by all mankind because they are proud and unjust. This quarrel, when it first began, was a family quarrel between us and the English, who were then our brothers. We, therefore, did not wish you to engage in it at all. We are strong enough of ourselves without wasting your blood in fighting our battles. The English, knowing this, have been always suing to the Indians to help them fight. We do not wish you to take up the hatchet. We love and esteem you. We wish you to multiply and be strong. The English, on the other hand, wish to set you and us to cutting one another's throats, that when we are dead they may take all our land. It is better for you not to join in this quarrel, unless the English have killed any of your warriors or done you any other injury. If they have, you have a right to go to war with them, and revenge the injury, and we have none to restrain you. Any free nation has a right to punish those who have done them an injury. I say the same, brother, as to the Indians who treat you ill. While I advise you, like an affectionate friend, to avoid unnecessary war, I do not assume the right of restraining you from punishing your enemies. If the English have injured you, as they have injured the French and Spaniards, do like them and join us in the war. General Clarke will receive you and show you the way to their towns. But if they have not injured you, it is better for you to lie still and be quiet. This is the advice which has been always given by the great council of the Americans. We must give the same, because we are but one of thirteen nations, who have agreed to act and speak together. These nations keep a council of wise men always sitting together, and each of us separately follow their advice. They have the care of all the people and the lands between the Ohio and Mississippi, and will see that no wrong be committed on them. The French settled at Kaskaskias, St. Vincennes, and the Cohos, are subject to that council, and they will punish them if they do you any injury. If you will make known to me any just cause of complaint against them, I will represent it to the great council at Philadelphia, and have justice done you.

Our good friend, your father, the King of France, does not lay any claim to them. Their misconduct should not be imputed to him. He gave them up to the English the last war, and we have taken them from the English. The Americans alone have a right to maintain justice in all the lands on this side the Mississippi, — on the other side the Spaniards rule. You complain, brother, of the want of goods for the use of your people. We know that your wants are great, notwithstanding we have done everything in our power to supply them, and have often grieved for you. The path from hence to Kaskaskias is long and dangerous; goods cannot be carried to you in that way. New Orleans has been the only place from which we could get goods for you. We have bought a great deal there; but I am afraid not so much of them have come to you as we intended. Some of them have been sold of necessity to buy provisions for our posts. Some have been embezzled by our own drunken and roguish people. Some have been taken by the Indians and many by the English.

The Spaniards, having now taken all the English posts on the Mississippi, have opened that channel free for our commerce, and are in hopes of getting goods for you from them. I will not boast to you, brother, as the English do, nor promise more than we shall be able to fulfil. I will tell you honestly, what indeed your own good sense will tell you, that a nation at war cannot buy so many goods as when in peace. We do not make so many things to send over the great waters to buy goods, as we made and shall make again in time of peace. When we buy those goods, the English take many of them, as they are coming to us over the great water. What we get in safe, are to be divided among many, because we have a great many soldiers, whom we must clothe. The remainder we send to our brothers the Indians, and in going, a great deal of it is stolen or lost. These are the plain reasons why you cannot get so much from us in war as in peace. But peace is not far off. The English cannot hold out long, because all the world is against them. When that takes place, brother, there will not be an Englishman left on this side the great water. What will those foolish nations then do, who have made us their enemies, sided with the English, and laughed at you for not being as wicked as themselves? They are clothed for a day, and will be naked forever after; while you, who have submitted to short inconvenience, will be well supplied through the rest of your lives. Their friends will be gone and their enemies left behind; but your friends will be here, and will make you strong against all your enemies. For the present you shall have a share of what little goods we can get. We will order some immediately up the Mississippi for you and for us. If they be little, you will submit to suffer a little as your brothers do for a short time. And when we shall have beaten our enemies and forced them to make peace, we will share more plentifully. General Clarke will furnish you with ammunition to serve till we can get some from New Orleans. I must recommend to you particular attention to him. He is our great, good, and trusty warrior; and we have put everything under his care beyond the Alleghanies. He will advise you in all difficulties, and redress your wrongs. Do what he tells you, and you will be sure to do right. You ask us to send schoolmasters to educate your son and the sons of your people. We desire above all things, brother, to instruct you in whatever we know ourselves. We wish to learn you all our arts and to make you wise and wealthy. As soon as there is peace we shall be able to send you the best of school-masters; but while the war is raging, I am afraid it will not be practicable. It shall be done, however, before your son is of an age to receive instruction.

This, brother, is what I had to say to you. Repeat it from me to all your people, and to our friends, the Kickapous, Piorias, Piankeshaws and Wyattanons. I will give you a commission to show them how much we esteem you. Hold fast the chain of friendship which binds us together, keep it bright as the sun, and let them, you and us, live together in perpetual love.

6

THOMAS JEFFERSON

Letter to James Monroe
May 20, 1782

In the spring of 1782, Jefferson refused election to the Virginia House of Delegates. His wife was gravely ill at the time. Yet, his letter to Monroe also suggests other political and personal reasons for his desire to retire from political service. He felt insufficiently appreciated for his service as governor during the Revolutionary War. The sting of suspicion, even after the investigation into his conduct had been terminated, still hung in the air. Given his wounded pride, Jefferson was shocked when John Tyler of the House of Delegates wrote to him that it was illegal to refuse election to the House, and that he hoped "the House may insist upon you to give attendance without incur[r]ing the censure of being seized." The desire to correct his fellow Virginians' mistaken application of republican doctrine motivated his theoretical musings in this letter, as well as his efforts to reform the laws and explain his proposals for reform in the Notes on the State of Virginia.

Julian P. Boyd, Charles T. Cullen, and John Catanzariti, eds., *The Papers of Thomas Jefferson* (Princeton, N.J.: Princeton University Press, 1950–), VI, 184–86.

MONTICELLO MAY 20. 1782.

DEAR SIR

I have been gratified with the receipt of your two favours of the 6th. and 11th. inst[ant]. It gives me pleasure that your county has been wise enough to enlist your talents into their service. I am much obliged by the kind wishes you express of seeing me also in Richmond, and am always mortified when any thing is expected from me which I cannot fulfill, and more especially if it relate to the public service. Before I ventured to declare to my countrymen my determination to retire from public employment I examined well my heart to know whether it were thoroughly cured of every principle of political ambition, whether no lurking particle remained which might leave me uneasy when reduced within the limits of mere private life. I became satisfied that every fibre of that passion was thoroughly eradicated. I examined also in other views my right to withdraw. I considered that I had been thirteen years engaged in public service, that during that time I had so totally abandoned all attention to my private affairs as to permit them to run into great disorder and ruin, that I had now a family advanced to years which require my attention and instruction, that to this was added the hopeful offspring of a deceased friend whose memory must be for ever dear to me who have no other reliance for being rendered useful to themselves and their country, that by a constant sacrifice of time, labour, loss, parental and friendly duties, I had been so far from gaining the affection of my countrymen which was the only reward I ever asked or could have felt, that I had even lost the small estimation I before possessed: that however I might have comforted myself under the disapprobation of the well-meaning but uninformed people yet that of their representatives was a shock on which I had not calculated: that this indeed had been followed by an exculpatory declaration, but in the mean time I had been suspected and suspended in the eyes of the world without the least hint then or afterwards made public which might restrain them from supposing I stood arraigned for treasons of the heart and not mere weaknesses of the head.[1] And I felt that these injuries, for such they have been since acknowledged, had inflicted a wound on my spirit which will only be cured by the all-healing grave. If reason and inclination unite in justifying my retirement, the laws of my country are equally in favor of it. Whether the state may command the political services of all it's mem-

---

[1]Jefferson refers to the House of Delegates' inquiry into his performance as Governor.

bers to an indefinite extent, or if these be among the rights never wholly ceded to the public power, is a question which I do not find expressly decided in England. Obiter dictums[2] on the subject I have indeed met with, but the complection of the times in which these have dropped would generally answer them, and besides that, this species of authority is not acknowleged in our profession. In this country however since the present government has been established the point has been settled by uniform, pointed, and multiplied precedents. Offices of every kind, and given by every power, have been daily and hourly declined and resigned from the declaration of independance to this moment. The General assembly has accepted these without discrimination of office, and without ever questioning them in point of right. If a difference between the office of a delegate and any other could ever have been supposed, yet in the case of Mr. Thompson Mason who declined the office of delegate and was permitted by the house so to do that supposition has been proved to be groundless. But indeed no such distinction of offices can be admitted; reason and the opinions of the lawyers putting all on a footing as to this question and giving to the delegate the aid of all the precedents of the refusal of other offices, the law then does not warrant the assumption of such a power by the state over it's members. For if it does where is that law? Nor yet does reason, for tho' I will admit that this does subject every individual if called on to an equal tour of political duty yet it can never go so far as to submit to it his whole existence. If we are made in some degree for others, yet in a greater are we made for ourselves. It were contrary to feeling and indeed ridiculous to suppose a man had less right in himself than one of his neighbors or all of them put together. This would be slavery and not that liberty which the bill of rights has made inviolable and for the preservation of which our government has been changed. Nothing could so completely divest us of that liberty as the establishment of the opinion that the state has a *perpetual* right to the services of all it's members. This to men of certain ways of thinking would be to annihilate the blessing of existence; to contradict the giver of life who gave it for happiness and not for wretchedness, and certainly to such it were better that they had never been born. However with these I may think public service and private misery inseparably linked together, I have not the vanity to count myself among those whom the state would think worth oppressing with perpetual service. I have received a sufficient memento to the contrary. I am

---

[2]obiter dictums: incidental statements or remarks.

persuaded that having hitherto dedicated to them the whole of the active and useful part of my life I shall be permitted to pass the rest in mental quiet. I hope too that I did not mistake the mode any more than the matter of right when I preferred a simple act of renunciation to the taking sanctuary under those many disqualifications (provided by the law for other purposes indeed but) which afford asylum also for rest to the wearied. I dare say you did not expect by the few words you dropped on the right of renunciation to expose yourself to the fatigue of so long a letter, but I wished you to see that if I had done wrong I had been betrayed by a semblance of right at least.

I take the liberty of inclosing to you a letter for Genl. Chattlux[3] for which you will readily find means of conveyance. But I meant to give you more trouble with the one to Pelham who lives in the neighborhood of Manchester and to ask the favor of you to send it by your servant express which I am in hopes may be done without absenting him from your person but during those hours in which you will be engaged in the house. I am anxious that it should be received immediately. Mrs. Jefferson has added another daughter to our family. She has been ever since and still continues very dangerously ill. It will give me great pleasure to see you here whenever you can favor us with your company. You will find me still busy but in lighter occupations. But in these and all others you will find me to retain a due sense of your friendship & to be with sincere esteem Dr Sir Your mo. ob. & mo. hble servt.

P.S. Did you ever receive a copy of the Parl. debates and Histor. Register with a letter left for you with Mr. Jas. Buchanan?

---

[3]Genl. Chattlux: Marquis de Chastellux.

7

THOMAS JEFFERSON

An Anonymous Letter for the European Newspapers

November 1784

Many of the letters and essays that appeared in eighteenth-century news-papers did so unsigned. This convention made it an ordinary occurrence for otherwise famous people to write anonymously, from a particular vantage point. Jefferson adopted this strategy in this letter, which he hoped to have published in the Dutch Leyden Gazette, *a newspaper widely circulated in France and England. The "officer" explicitly argues that the English are engaging in a propaganda war to make America look bad in the eyes of Europeans.*

As with the Declaration of Independence and the Notes on the State of Virginia, *Jefferson is writing for a European as well as an American audience. This piece shows the continuity of his efforts to think through the problem of England becoming an enemy, and how to show to the world that the breakaway colonies have a bright future, despite present-day problems.*

[BEFORE 20 NOV. 1784]

I am an officer lately returned from service and residence in the U.S. of America. I have fought and bled for that country because I thought it's cause just. From the moment of peace to that in which I left it, I have seen it enjoying all the happiness which easy government, order and industry are capable of giving to a people. On my return to my native country what has been my astonishment to find all the public papers of Europe filled with accounts of the anarchy and destractions supposed to exist in that country. I have received serious condolances from all my friends on the bitter fruits of so prosperous a war. These friends I know to be so well disposed towards America that they wished the reverse of what they repeated from the public papers.

Julian P. Boyd, Charles T. Cullen, and John Catanzariti, eds., *The Papers of Thomas Jefferson* (Princeton, N.J.: Princeton University Press, 1950–), VII, 540–43.

I have enquired into the source of all this misinformation and have found it not difficult to be traced. The printers on the Continent have not yet got into the habit of taking the American newspapers. Whatever they retail therefore on the subject of America, they take from the English. If your readers will reflect a moment they will recollect that every unfavourable account which they have seen of the transactions in America has been taken from the English papers only. Nothing is known in Europe of the situation of the U.S. since the acknowlegement of their independance but thro' the channel of these papers. But these papers have been under the influence of two ruling motives 1. deep-rooted hatred, springing from an unsuccesful attempt to injure; 2. a fear that their island will be depopulated by the emigration of it's inhabitants to America. Hence no paper comes out without a due charge of paragraphs manufactured by persons employed for that purpose. According to these, America is a scene of continued riot and anarchy. Wearied out with contention, it is on the verge of falling again into the lap of Gr. Br. for repose. It's citizens are groaning under the oppression of heavy taxes. They are flying for refuge to the frozen regions which still remain subject to G.B. Their assemblies and congresses are become odious, in one paragraph represented as tyrannising over their constituents and in another as possessing no power or influence at all, &c., &c. The truth is as follows without aggravation or diminution. There was a mutiny of 300 souldiers in Philadelphia soon after the peace; and Congress, thinking the executive of that state did not act with proper energy to suppress and punish it, they left that city in disgust. Yet in this mutiny there neither was blood shed nor a blow struck. There has lately been a riot in Charlestown, occasioned by the feuds between the whigs who had been driven from their country by the British while they possessed it, and the tories who were permitted to remain by the Americans when they recovered it. There were a few instances in other states where individuals disgusted with some articles in the peace undertook to call town meetings, published the resolves of the few citizens whom they could prevail on to meet as if they had been the resolves of the whole town, and endeavored unsuccessfully to engage the people in the execution of their private views. It is believed that these attempts have not been more than ten or a dozen thro' the whole 13 states, [and not one of them has been succesful: on the contrary where any illegal act has been committed by the demagogues they have been put under a due course of legal prosecution.] The British when they evacuated New York, having carried off, contrary to the express articles of the treaty of peace, a great deal of property belonging to the citizens of the U.S. and particularly to those of the state of Virginia, amounting as has been said to half a million of pounds sterling, the assembly of that state lately resolved that till satisfaction was made for this, the article respecting British debts ought not to be carried into full execution, submitting nevertheless this their opinion to Congress, and declaring that if they thought otherwise, all laws obstructing the recovery of debts should be immediately repealed. Yet even this was opposed by a respectable minority in their senate who entered a protest against it in strong terms. The protest as it stands in the record follows immediately the resolutions protested against and therefore does not recite them. The English papers publish the protest without the resolutions and thus lead Europe to believe that the resolutions had definitively decided against the paiment of British debts. Yet nothing is less true. This is a faithful history of the high sounded disturbances of America. Those who have visited that country since the peace will vouch that it is impossible for any governments to be more tranquil and orderly than they are. What were the mutiny of 300 souldiers in Philada., the riot of whigs and tories in Charlestown to the riots of London [under Ld. G. Gordon, and of London and the country in general in the late elections?] Where is there any country of equal extent with the U.S. in which fewer disturbances have happened in the same space of time? Where has there been an instance of an army disbanded as was that of America without receiving a shilling of the long arrearages due them or even having their accounts settled and yet disbanded peaceably? Instead of resorting as is too often the case with disbanded armies to beggary or robbery for a livelihood they returned every man to his home and resumed his axe and spade; and it is a fact as true as it is singular that on the disbanding of an army of 30,000 men in America there have been but two or three instances of any of those who composed it being brought to the bar of justice as criminals; and that you may travel from one end to the other of the continent without seeing a beggar. With respect to the people their confidence in their rulers in general is what common sense will tell us it must be, where they are of their own choice annually, unbribed by money, undebauched by feasting, and drunkenness. It would be difficult to find one man among them who would not consider a return under the dominion of Gr. Br. as the greatest of all possible miseries. Their taxes are light, as they should be with a people so lately wasted in the most cruel manner by war. They pay in proportion to their property from one half to one and a half per cent annually on it's whole value as estimated by their neighbors, the different states requiring more or less as they have been less or more ravaged by their enemies. Where any other taxes are imposed they are very trifling and are calculated chiefly to bring merchants into contribution with the farmers.

Against their emigration [to the remaining British dominions] the superior rigor of their climate, the inferiority of their soil, the nature their governments and their being actually inhabited by their most mortal enemies the tory refugees, will be an eternal security. During the course of the war the English papers were constantly filled with accounts of their great victories, their armies were daily gaining. Yet Europe saw that they were daily losing ground in America, and formed it's idea of the truth not from what it heard but from what it saw. They wisely considered an enlargement of territory on the one side and contraction of it on the other as the best indication on which side victory really was. It is hoped that Europe will be as wise and as just now; that they will not consider the fabricated papers of England as any evidence of truth; but that they will continue to judge of causes from effects. If the distractions of America were what these papers pretend, some great facts would burst out and lay their miseries open to the eyes of all the world: no such effects appear; therefore no such causes exist. If any such existed they would appear in the American newspapers which are as free as any on earth, but none such can be found in them. These are the testimonials to which I appeal for belief. To bring more home to every reader the reliance which may be put on the English papers let him examine, if a Frenchman, what account they give of the affairs of France, if a Dutchman, what of the United Netherlds.; if an Irishman, what of Ireland, &c. If he finds that those of his own country with which he happens to be acquainted are wickedly misrepresented, let him consider how much more likely to be so are those of a nation so hated as America. America was the great pillar on which British glory was raised; America has been the instrument for levelling that glory with the dust. A little ill humour therefore might have found excuse in our commiseration; but an apostasy from truth, under whatever misfortunes, calls up feelings of a very different order.

8

THOMAS JEFFERSON

Letter to the Marquis de Chastellux

June 7, 1785

Jefferson sent the first edition of the Notes on the State of Virginia *to a select group of friends, including the Marquis de Chastellux, a French nobleman and general who had visited him at Monticello during the spring of 1782. The careful strategy of dissemination had less to do with Jefferson's shyness or lack of confidence in the work than in his concern that the very arguments that might make America look good in Europe, might hurt him, and his proposals, in Virginia.*

In this letter, Jefferson explains his rationale and goals in arguing with Count Buffon and the French natural historians. Interestingly, he carefully limits his claims about African Americans, acknowledging that their seeming inferiority to Europeans and Indians might be a result of their oppression after all.

PARIS JUNE 7, 1785

DEAR SIR

I have been honoured with the receipt of your letter of the 2d. instant, and am to thank you, as I do sincerely for the partiality with which you receive the copy of the Notes on my country. As I can answer for the facts therein reported on my own observation, and have admitted none on the report of others which were not supported by evidence sufficient to command my own assent, I am not afraid that you should make any extracts you please for the Journal de physique which come within their plan of publication. The strictures on slavery and on the constitution of Virginia are not of that kind, and they are the parts which I do not wish to have made public, at least till I know whether their publication would do most harm or good. It is possible that in my own country these strictures might produce an irritation which would indispose the people towards the two great objects I have in view, that

Julian P. Boyd, Charles T. Cullen, and John Catanzariti, eds., *The Papers of Thomas Jefferson* (Princeton, N.J.: Princeton University Press, 1950–), VIII, 184–86.

is the emancipation of their slaves, and the settlement of their constitution on a firmer and more permanent basis. If I learn from thence, that they will not produce that effect, I have printed and reserved just copies enough to be able to give one to every young man at the College. It is to them I look, to the rising generation, and not to the one now in power for these great reformations. The other copy delivered at your hotel was for Monsr. de Buffon. I meant to ask the favour of you to have it sent to him, as I was ignorant how to do it. I have one also for Monsr. Daubenton:[1] but being utterly unknown to him I cannot take the liberty of presenting it till I can do it through some common acquaintance.

I will beg leave to say here a few words on the general question of the degeneracy of animals in America. 1. As to the degeneracy of the man of Europe transplanted to America, it is no part of Monsr. de Buffon's system. He goes indeed within one step of it, but he stops there. The Abbé Raynal alone has taken that step. Your knowlege of America enables you to judge this question, to say whether the lower class of people in America, are less informed and less susceptible of information than the lower class in Europe: and whether those in America who have received such an education as that country can give, are less improved by it than Europeans of the same degree of education. 2. As to the Aboriginal man of America, I know of no respectable evidence on which the opinion of his inferiority of genius has been founded but that of Don Ulloa. As to Robertson, he never was in America, he relates nothing on his own knowlege, he is a compiler only of the relations of others, and a mere translator of the opinions of Monsr. de Buffon. I should as soon therefore add the translators of Robertson to the witnesses of this fact, as himself. Paw, the beginner of this charge, was a compiler from the works of others; and of the most unlucky description; for he seems to have read the writings of travellers only to collect and republish their lies. It is really remarkeable that in three volumes 12mo. of small print it is scarcely possible to find one truth, and yet that the author should be able to produce authority for every fact he states, as he says he can. Don Ulloa's testimony is of the most respectable. He wrote of what he saw. But he saw the Indian of South America only, and that after he had passed through ten generations of slavery. It is very unfair, from this sample, to judge of the natural genius of this race of men: and after supposing that Don Ulloa had not sufficiently calculated the allowance which

[1]Louis Jean Marie D'Aubenton, a French naturalist and contributor to Buffon's mammoth *Natural History*.

should be made for this circumstance, we do him no injury in considering the picture he draws of the present Indians of S. America as no picture of what their ancestors were 300 years ago. It is in N. America we are to seek their original character: and I am safe in affirming that the proofs of genius given by the Indians of N. America, place them on a level with Whites in the same uncultivated state. The North of Europe furnishes subjects enough for comparison with them, and for a proof of their equality. I have seen some thousands myself, and conversed much with them, and have found in them a masculine, sound understanding. I have had much information from men who had lived among them, and whose veracity and good sense were so far known to me as to establish a reliance on their information. They have all agreed in bearing witness in favour of the genius of this people. As to their bodily strength, their manners rendering it disgraceful to labour, those muscles employed in labour will be weaker with them than with the European labourer: but those which are exerted in the chase and those faculties which are employed in the tracing an enemy or a wild beast, in contriving ambuscades[2] for him, and in carrying them through their execution, are much stronger than with us, because they are more exercised. I believe the Indian then to be in body and mind equal to the whiteman. I have supposed the blackman, in his present state, might not be so. But it would be hazardous to affirm that, equally cultivated for a few generations, he would not become so. 3. As to the inferiority of the other animals of America, without more facts I can add nothing to what I have said in my Notes. As to the theory of Monsr. de Buffon that heat is friendly and moisture adverse to the production of large animals, I am lately furnished with a fact by Doctr. Franklin which proves the air of London and of Paris to be more humid than that of Philadelphia, and so creates a suspicion that the opinion of the superior humidity of America may perhaps have been too hastily adopted. And supposing that fact admitted, I think the physical reasonings urged to shew that in a moist country animals must be small, and that in a hot one they must be large, are not built on the basis of experiment. These questions however cannot be decided ultimately at this day. More facts must be collected, and more time flow off, before the world will be ripe for decision. In the mean time doubt is wisdom.

I have been fully sensible of the anxieties of your situation, and that your attentions were wholly consecrated, where alone they were wholly due, to the succour of friendship and worth. However much I

[2]ambuscades: ambushes.

prize your society I wait with patience the moment when I can have it without taking what is due to another. In the mean time I am solaced with the hope of possessing your friendship, and that it is not ungrateful to you to receive assurances of that with which I have the honour to be Dear Sir Your most obedient and most humble servt.,

TH: JEFFERSON

9

THOMAS JEFFERSON

Letter to Richard Price

August 7, 1785

Richard Price was an English radical who had sided with the Americans during the Revolutionary War. He also opposed slavery. In his pamphlet of 1785, Observations on the Importance of the American Revolution, and the Means of Making It a Benefit to the World, *he used language similar to Jefferson's to argue that the American revolt against Britain's political enslavement meant that Americans must give up slavery, "for it is self-evident that if there are any men whom they have a right to enslave, there may be others who have had a right to hold them in slavery." Sending his pamphlet to Jefferson, Price observed that English supporters of American rights and prospects would be greatly embarrassed if the new states did not move quickly against slavery.*

In response, Jefferson, for the first time, depicts a sectional divergence on the slavery question. He does not, however, see Virginia as part of an unalterably "solid" south. Virginia is more likely to abolish slavery than its northward neighbor, Maryland. Jefferson puts his hope in the younger generation, acknowledging that slavery and the American revolutionary spirit do not — or should not — go together.

Julian P. Boyd, Charles T. Cullen, and John Catanzariti, eds., *The Papers of Thomas Jefferson* (Princeton, N.J.: Princeton University Press, 1950–), VIII, 356–57.

PARIS AUG. 7. 1785.

SIR

Your favor of July 2. came duly to hand. The concern you therein express as to the effect of your pamphlet in America, induces me to trouble you with some observations on that subject. From my acquaintance with that country I think I am able to judge with some degree of certainty of the manner in which it will have been received. Southward of the Chesapeak it will find but few readers concurring with it in sentiment on the subject of slavery. From the mouth to the head of the Chesapeak, the bulk of the people will approve it in theory, and it will find a respectable minority ready to adopt it in practice, a minority which for weight and worth of character preponderates against the greater number, who have not the courage to divest their families of a property which however keeps their consciences inquiet. Northward of the Chesapeak you may find here and there an opponent to your doctrine as you may find here and there a robber and a murderer, but in no greater number. In that part of America, there being but few slaves, they can easily disencumber themselves of them, and emancipation is put into such a train that in a few years there will be no slaves Northward of Maryland. In Maryland I do not find such a disposition to begin the redress of this enormity as in Virginia. This is the next state to which we may turn our eyes for the interesting spectacle of justice in conflict with avarice and oppression: a conflict wherein the sacred side is gaining daily recruits from the influx into office of young men grown and growing up. These have sucked in the principles of liberty as it were with their mother's milk, and it is to them I look with anxiety to turn the fate of this question. Be not therefore discouraged. What you have written will do a great deal of good: and could you still trouble yourself with our welfare, no man is more able to give aid to the labouring side. The college of William and Mary in Williamsburg, since the remodelling of it's plan, is the place where are collected together all the young men of Virginia under preparation for public life. They are there under the direction (most of them) of a Mr. Wythe one of the most virtuous of characters, and whose sentiments on the subject of slavery are unequivocal. I am satisfied if you could resolve to address an exhortation to those young men, with all that eloquence of which you are master, that it's influence on the future decision of this important question would be great, perhaps decisive. Thus you see that, so far from thinking you have cause to repent of what you have done, I wish you to do more, and wish it on an assurance of it's effect. The information I have received from America of the reception of your pamphlet in the different states agrees with the expectations I had formed. — Our country is getting into a ferment against yours, or rather have caught it from yours. God knows how this will end: but assuredly in one extreme or the other. There can be no medium between those who have loved so much. I think the decision is in your power as yet, but will not be so long. I pray you to be assured of the sincerity of the esteem & respect with which I have the honour to be Sir Your most obedt. humble servt.,

TH: JEFFERSON

P.S. I thank you for making me acquainted with Monsr. D'Ivernois.

10

THOMAS JEFFERSON

Letter to the Marquis de Chastellux

September 2, 1785

Jefferson's friend the Marquis de Chastellux wrote a book about his travels in America, including Virginia, in which he highly praised Jefferson. Chastellux's generalizations about the character of Americans, written very much in the spirit of the Notes on the State of Virginia, *moved Jefferson to think about differing American sectional types. Given the reflections on "Manners" he was writing in the* Notes *at this time, Jefferson's table of northern and southern character types suggests that he was beginning to think of slavery, and plantation life, as the South's distinctive characteristic. Jefferson nonetheless seems to prefer southern character, seeing his fellow Virginians as at least less devoted to their own financial interests than are northerners. In making such comparisons, Jefferson was participating in a process of defining North against South in order to explain the benefits or costs of slavery. This conversation would intensify in the years before the Civil War, when abolitionists and proslavery southerners both began to argue that there were actually two nations in America.*

Julian P. Boyd, Charles T. Cullen, and John Catanzariti, eds., *The Papers of Thomas Jefferson* (Princeton, N.J.: Princeton University Press, 1950–), VIII, 467–69.

PARIS SEP. 2. 1785.

DEAR SIR

You were so kind as to allow me a fortnight to read your journey through Virginia. But you should have thought of this indulgence while you were writing it, and have rendered it less interesting if you meant that your readers should have been longer engaged with it. In fact I devoured it at a single meal, and a second reading scarce allowed me sang froid[1] enough to mark a few errors in the names of persons and places which I note on a paper herein inclosed, with an inconsiderable error or two in facts which I have also noted because I supposed you wished to state them correctly. From this general approbation however you must allow me to except about a dozen pages in the earlier part of the book which I read with a continued blush from beginning to end, as it presented me a lively picture of what I wish to be, but am not. No, my dear Sir, the thousand millionth part of what you there say, is more than I deserve. It might perhaps have passed in Europe at the time you wrote it, and the exaggeration might not have been detected. But consider that the animal is now brought there, and that every one will take his dimensions for himself. The friendly complexion of your mind has betrayed you into a partiality of which the European spectator will be divested. Respect to yourself therefore will require indispensably that you expunge the whole of those pages except your own judicious observations interspersed among them on Animal and physical subjects. With respect to my countrymen there is surely nothing which can render them uneasy, in the observations made on them. They know that they are not perfect, and will be sensible that you have viewed them with a philanthropic eye. You say much good of them, and less ill than they are conscious may be said with truth. I have studied their character with attention. I have thought them, as you found them, aristocratical, pompous, clannish, indolent, hospitable, and I should have added, disinterested, but you say attached to their interest. This is the only trait in their character wherein our observations differ. I have always thought them so careless of their interests, so thoughtless in their expences and in all their transactions of business that I had placed it among the vices of their character, as indeed most virtues when carried beyond certain bounds degenerate into vices. I had even ascribed this to it's cause, to that warmth of their climate which unnerves and unmans both body and mind. While on

---

[1] sang froid: cold blood (a French expression).

this subject I will give you my idea of the characters of the several states.

In the North they are	In the South they are
cool	fiery
sober	Voluptuary[2]
laborious	indolent
persevering	unsteady
independant	independant
jealous of their own liberties, and just to those of others	zealous for their own liberties, but trampling on those of others
interested	generous
chicaning[3]	candid
superstitious and hypocritical in their religion	without attachment or pretentions to any religion but that of the heart.

These characteristics grow weaker and weaker by gradation from North to South and South to North, insomuch that an observing traveller, without the aid of the quadrant may always know his latitude by the character of the people among whom he finds himself. It is in Pennsylvania that the two characters seem to meet and blend and to form a people free from the extremes both of vice and virtue. Peculiar circumstances have given to New York the character which climate would have given had she been placed on the South instead of the North side of Pennsylvania. Perhaps too other circumstances may have occasioned in Virginia a transplantation of a particular vice foreign to it's climate. You could judge of this with more impartiality than I could, and the probability is that your estimate of them is the most just. I think it for their good that the vices of their character should be pointed out to them that they may amend them; for a malady of either body or mind once known is half cured.

I wish you would add to this piece your letter to Mr. Madison on the expediency of introducing the arts into America. I found in that a great deal of matter, very many observations, which would be useful to the legislators of America, and to the general mass of citizens. I

[2]Voluptuary: addicted to the gratification of the senses.
[3]chicaning: quibbling, usually for the purpose of getting a better deal.

read it with great pleasure and analysed it's contents that I might fix them in my own mind. I have the honor to be with very sincere esteem Dear Sir Your most obedient & most humble servt.,

TH: JEFFERSON

11

THOMAS JEFFERSON

Letter to Archibald Stuart

January 25, 1786

Jefferson's time in Paris confirmed his sense of the fragility of the new republic and the importance of his efforts to secure a republican government within the country, and the good opinion of Europeans without. He brought these themes together in this candid letter to fellow Virginian Archibald Stuart, who had served Jefferson's administration during the war.

Even after the publication in France of the Notes *on the State of Virginia, Jefferson continued his campaign to change the minds of Buffon and other French naturalists on the small size of animal life in the Americas. This letter exemplifies how politics and science mixed in Jefferson's practice of statesmanship and diplomacy.*

PARIS JAN. 25. 1786.

DEAR SIR

I have received your favor of the 17th. of October, which though you mention as the third you have written me, is the first which has come to hand. I sincerely thank you for the communications it contains. Nothing is so grateful to me at this distance as details both great and small of what is passing in my own country. Of the latter we receive little here, because they either escape my correspondents or are thought unworthy notice. This however is a very mistaken opinion, as

Julian P. Boyd, Charles T. Cullen, and John Catanzariti, eds., *The Papers of Thomas Jefferson* (Princeton, N.J.: Princeton University Press, 1950–), IX, 217–19.

every one may observe by recollecting that when he has been long absent from his neighborhood the small news of that is the most pleasing and occupies his first attention either when he meets with a person from thence, or returns thither himself. I still hope therefore that the letter in which you have been so good as to give me the minute occurrences in the neighborhood of Monticello may yet come to hand, and I venture to rely on the many proofs of friendship I have received from you, for a continuance of your favors. This will be the more meritorious as I have nothing to give you in exchange. The quiet of Europe at this moment furnishes little which can attract your notice, nor will that quiet be soon disturbed, at least for the current year. Perhaps it hangs on the life of the K.[1] of Prussia, and that hangs by a very slender thread. American reputation in Europe is not such as to be flattering to it's citizens. Two circumstances are particularly objected to us, the nonpaiment of our debts, and the want of energy in our government. These discourage a connection with us. I own it to be my opinion that good will arise from the destruction of our credit. I see nothing else which can restrain our disposition to luxury, and the loss of those manners which alone can preserve republican government. As it is impossible to prevent credit, the best way would be to cure it's ill effects by giving an instantaneous recovery to the creditor. This would be reducing purchases on credit to purchases for ready money. A man would then see a prison painted on every thing he wished but had not ready money to pay for.—I fear from an expression in your letter that the people of Kentucké[2] think of separating not only from Virginia (in which they are right) but also from the confederacy. I own I should think this a most calamitous event, and such an one as every good citizen on both sides should set himself against. Our present federal limits are not too large for good government, nor will the increase of votes in Congress produce any ill effect. On the contrary it will drown the little divisions at present existing there. Our confederacy must be viewed as the nest from which all America, North and South is to be peopled. We should take care too not to think it for the interest of that great continent to press too soon on the Spaniards. Those countries cannot be in better hands. My fear is that they are too feeble to hold them till our population can be sufficiently advanced to gain it from them piece by piece. The navigation of the Mississippi we must have. This is all we are as yet ready to receive. I

[1]K: king.
[2]Kentucké: the Kentucky territory.

have made acquaintance with a very sensible candid gentleman here who was in South America during the revolt which took place there while our revolution was working. He says that those disturbances (of which we scarcely heard any thing) cost on both sides an hundred thousand lives.—I have made a particular acquaintance here with Monsieur de Buffon, and have a great desire to give him the best idea I can of our elk. Perhaps your situation may enable you to aid me in this. Were it possible, you could not oblige me more than by sending me the horns, skeleton, and skin of an elk. The most desireable form of receiving them would be to have the skin slit from the under jaw along the belly to the tail, and down the thighs to the knee, to take the animal out, leaving the legs and hoofs, the bones of the head, and the horns attached to the skin. By sewing up the belly &c. and stuffing the skin it would present the form of the animal. However as an opportunity of doing this is scarcely to be expected, I shall be glad to receive them detached, packed in a box, and sent to Richmond to the care of Doctor Currie. Every thing of this kind is precious here, and to prevent my adding to your trouble I must close my letter with assurances of the esteem and attachment with which I am Dr. Sir your friend & servt.,   TH: JEFFERSON

P.S. I must add a prayer for some Paccan[3] nuts, 100. if possible, to be packed in a box of sand and sent me. They might come either directly or viâ N. York.

---

[3] Paccan: pecan.

NOTES

ON THE

STATE OF VIRGINIA.

WRITTEN BY

THOMAS JEFFERSON.

ILLUSTRATED WITH

A MAP, including the States of VIRGINIA, MARY-
LAND, DELAWARE and PENNSYLVANIA.

LONDON:

PRINTED FOR JOHN STOCKDALE, OPPOSITE
BURLINGTON-HOUSE, PICCADILLY.

M.DCC.LXXXVII.

12

THOMAS JEFFERSON

Notes on the State of Virginia

1781–1787

The first English edition of Notes on the State of Virginia *was also the first to be published under Jefferson's name. In the "Advertisement," he explains the origins of the book and alludes to the context of the Revolutionary War in Virginia.*

The Notes *are often seen as science interspersed with political commentary. Yet Jefferson made political points from the very beginning, in comparing Virginia's breadth to the small size of England. By using the rules of science, Jefferson hoped to rise above the kind of harsh diatribes he saw in contemporary newspapers. There was a time for passionate political rhetoric and a time for facts to be presented to "a candid world." The* Notes *represents the most extended attempt to explain and justify the American republican experiment in the years between independence and the ratification of the Constitution.*

Everything Jefferson later wrote would be measured against his opinions in the Notes, *during his lifetime and ever since. Ironically, he worried that his definitive statement would not be well received, in particular because of its honesty about Virginia's new constitutional government and the slavery question. In a sense, Jefferson predicted the power of his text, which would be taken to heart, quoted, loved, and reviled for two centuries and more.*

Thomas Jefferson, *Notes on the State of Virginia* (London: Printed for John Stockdale, 1787).

Opposite: **Figure 4.** *Notes on the State of Virginia,* title page from the edition published by John Stockdale in London, 1787.
Benjamin Franklin Collection, Yale University Library.

ADVERTISEMENT.

The following Notes were written in Virginia in the year 1781, and somewhat corrected and enlarged in the winter of 1782, in answer to Queries proposed to the Author, by a Foreigner of Distinction,[1] then residing among us. The subjects are all treated imperfectly; some scarcely touched on. To apologize for this by developing the circumstances of the time and place of their composition, would be to open wounds which have already bled enough. To these circumstances some of their imperfections may with truth be ascribed; the great mass to the want of information and want of talents in the writer. He had a few copies printed, which he gave among his friends; and a translation of them has been lately published in France, but with such alterations as the laws of the press in that country rendered necessary. They are now offered to the public in their original form and language.

Feb. 27, 1787.

QUERY I: BOUNDARIES OF VIRGINIA

An Exact Description of the Limits and Boundaries of the State of Virginia?

Virginia is bounded on the East by the Atlantic; on the North by a line of latitude, crossing the Eastern Shore through Watkins's Point, being about 37° 57′ North latitude; from thence by a straight line to Cinquac, near the mouth of Patowmac; thence by the Patowmac, which is common to Virginia and Maryland, to the first fountain of its Northern branch; thence by a meridian line, passing through that fountain till it intersects a line running East and West, in latitude 39° 43′ 42.4″, which divides Maryland from Pennsylvania, and which was marked by Messrs. Mason and Dixon; thence by that line, and a continuation of it westwardly to the completion of 5 degrees of longitude from the Eastern boundary of Pennsylvania, in the same latitude, and thence by a meridian line to the Ohio: on the West by the Ohio and Missisipi, to latitude 36° 30′ North; and on the South by the line of latitude last mentioned. By admeasurements through nearly the whole of this last line, and supplying the unmeasured parts from good data, the Atlantic and Missisipi, are found in this latitude to be 758 miles dis-

[1]Foreigner of Distinction: François Marbois.

tant, equal to 13° 38′ of longitude, reckoning 55 miles and 3144 feet to the degree. This being our comprehension of longitude, that of our latitude, taken between this and Mason and Dixon's line, is 3° 13′. 42.4″, equal to 223.3 miles, supposing a degree a great circle to be 69 m. 864 f., as computed by Cassini.[2] These boundaries include an area somewhat triangular, of 121,525 square miles, whereof 79,650 lie westward of the Alleghaney mountains, and 57,034 westward of the meridian of the mouth of the Great Kanhaway. This State is therefore one-third larger than the islands of Great Britain and Ireland, which are reckoned at 88,357 square miles.

These limits result from, 1. The ancient charters from the crown of England. 2. The grant of Maryland to the Lord Baltimore, and the subsequent determinations of the British Court as to the extent of that grant. 3. The grant of Pennsylvania to William Penn, and a compact between the General Assemblies of the Commonwealths of Virginia and Pennsylvania as to the extent of that grant. 4. The grant of Carolina, and actual location of its Northern boundary, by consent of both parties. 5. The treaty of Paris of 1763.[3] 6. The confirmation of the charters of the neighboring States by the Convention of Virginia at the time of constituting their Commonwealth. 7. The cession made by Virginia to Congress of all the lands to which they had title on the North side of the Ohio.

QUERY II: RIVERS

A Notice of Its Rivers, Rivulets, and How Far They Are Navigable?

An inspection of a map of Virginia, will give a better idea of the geography of its rivers than any description in writing. Their navigation may be imperfectly noted.

Roanoke, so far as it lies within this State, is no where navigable but for canoes, or light batteaux;[4] and, even for these, in such detached parcels as to have prevented the inhabitants from availing themselves of it at all.

James River, and its waters, afford navigation as follows.

---

[2]Cassini: Gian Domenico Cassini, an Italian astronomer who directed the Royal Observatory in Paris.

[3]The 1763 Treaty of Paris officially ended the Seven Years' War between England and France.

[4]batteaux: small boats.

The whole of *Elizabeth River,* the lowest of those which run into James River, is a harbor, and would contain upwards of 300 ships. The channel is from 150 to 200 fathom wide, and at common flood tide, affords 18 feet water to Norfolk. The Strafford, a 60 gun ship, went there, lightening herself to cross the bar at Sowell's Point. The Fier Rodrigue, pierced for 64 guns, and carrying 50, went there without lightening. Craney Island, at the mouth of this river, commands its channel tolerably well.

Nansemond River is navigable to Sleepy Hole for vessels of 250 tons; to Suffolk for those of 100 tons; and to Milner's for those of 25.

Pagan Creek affords 8 or 10 feet water to Smithfield, which admits vessels of 20 tons.

Chickahominy has at its mouth a bar, on which is only 12 feet water at common flood tide. Vessels passing that, may go 8 miles up the river; those of 10 feet draught may go 4 miles further; and those of 6 tons burthen, 20 miles further.

Appamattox may be navigated as far as Broadways, by any vessel which has crossed Harrison's Bar in James River; it keeps 8 or 9 feet water a mile or two higher up to Fisher's Bar, and 4 feet on that and upwards to Petersburgh, where all navigation ceases.

James River itself affords harbor for vessels of any size in Hampton Road, but not in safety through the whole winter; and there is navigable water for them as far as Mulberry Island. A 40 gun ship goes to James town, and, lightening herself, may pass to Harrison's Bar, on which there is only 15 feet water. Vessels of 250 tons may go to Warwick; those of 125 go to Rocket's, a mile below Richmond; from thence is about 7 feet water to Richmond; and about the centre of the town, 4 feet and a half, where the navigation is interrupted by falls, which, in a course of 6 miles, descend about 80 feet perpendicular; above these it is resumed in canoes and batteaux, and is prosecuted safely and advantageously to within 10 miles of the Blue Ridge; and even through the Blue Ridge a ton weight has been brought; and the expense would not be great, when compared with its object, to open a tolerable navigation up Jackson's River and Carpenter's Creek, to within 25 miles of Howard's Creek of Green briar, both of which have then water enough to float vessels into the Great Kanhaway. In some future state of population, I think it possible, that its navigation may also be made to interlock with that of the Patowmac, and through that to communicate by a short portage with the Ohio. It is to be noted, that this river is called in the maps *James River,* only to its confluence with the Rivanna; thence to the Blue Ridge it is called the Fluvanna; and thence to its source, Jackson's River. But, in common speech, it is called James River to its source.

The *Rivanna,* a branch of James River, is navigable for canoes and batteaux to its intersection with the Southwest mountains, which is about 22 miles; and may easily be opened to navigation through those mountains to its fork above Charlottesville.

York River, at York Town, affords the best harbor in the State for vessels of the largest size. The river there narrows to the width of a mile, and is contained within very high banks, close under which the vessels may ride. It holds 4 fathom water at high tide for 25 miles above York to the mouth of Poropotank, where the river is a mile and a half wide, and the channel only 75 fathom, and passing under a high bank. At the confluence of *Pamunkey* and *Mattapony,* it is reduced to 3 fathom depth, which continues up Pamunkey to Cumberland, where the width is 100 yards, and up Mattapony to within 2 miles of Frazer's Ferry, where it becomes 2½ fathom deep, and holds that about 5 miles. Pamunkey is then capable of navigation for loaded flats to Brockman's bridge, 50 miles above Hanover town, and Mattapony to Downer's bridge, 70 miles above its mouth.

Piankatank, the little rivers making out of *Mobjack bay,* and those of the *Eastern shore,* receive only very small vessels, and these can but enter them.

Rappahanock affords 4 fathom water to Hobb's Hole, and 2 fathom from thence to Fredericksburg.

Patowmac is 7½ miles wide at the mouth; 4½ at Nomony Bay; 3 at Aquia; 1½ at Hallooing point; 1¼ at Alexandria. Its soundings are, 7 fathom at the mouth; 5 at St. George's Island; 4½ at Lower Matchodic; 3 at Swan's Point, and thence up to Alexandria; thence 10 feet water to the falls, which are 13 miles above Alexandria. These falls are 15 miles in length, and of very great descent, and the navigation above them for batteaux and canoes, is so much interrupted as to be little used. It is, however, used in a small degree up the Cohongoronta branch as far as Fort Cumberland, which was at the mouth of Wills's Creek: and is capable, at no great expense, of being rendered very practicable. The Shenandoah branch interlocks with James River about the Blue Ridge, and may perhaps in future be opened.

The *Missisipi* will be one of the principal channels of future commerce for the country westward of the Alleghaney. From the mouth of this river to where it receives the Ohio, is 1000 miles by water, but only 500 by land, passing through the Chickasaw country. From the mouth of the Ohio to that of the Missouri, is 230 miles by water, and

140 by land. From thence to the mouth of the Illinois River, is about 25 miles. The Missisipi, below the mouth of the Missouri, is always muddy, and abounding with sand bars, which frequently change their places. However, it carries 15 feet water to the mouth of the Ohio, to which place it is from one and a half to two miles wide, and thence to Kaskaskia, from one mile to a mile and a quarter wide. Its current is so rapid, that it never can be stemmed by the force of the wind alone, acting on sails. Any vessel, however, navigated with oars, may come up at any time, and receive much aid from the wind. A batteau passes from the mouth of Ohio to the mouth of Missisipi in three weeks, and is from two to three months getting up again. During its floods, which are periodical, as those of the Nile, the largest vessels may pass down it if their steerage can be ensured. These floods begin in April, and the river returns into its banks early in August. The inundation extends further on the western than eastern side, covering the lands in some places for 50 miles from its banks. Above the mouth of the Missouri, it becomes much such a river as the Ohio, like it clear, and gentle in its current, not quite so wide, the period of its floods nearly the same, but not rising to so great an height. The streets of the village at Cohoes are not more than 10 feet above the ordinary level of the water, and yet were never overflowed. Its bed deepens every year. Cohoes, in the memory of many people now living, was insulated by every flood of the river. What was the Eastern channel has now become a lake, 9 miles in length and one in width, into which the river at this day never flows. This river yields turtle of a peculiar kind, perch, trout, gar, pike, mullets, herrings, carp, spatula fish of 50 lb weight, cat fish of an hundred pounds weight, buffalo fish, and sturgeon. Alligators or crocodiles have been seen as high up as the Acansas. It also abounds in herons, cranes, ducks, brant, geese and swans. Its passage is commanded by a fort established by this State, 5 miles below the mouth of Ohio, and 10 miles above the Carolina boundary.

The Missouri, since the treaty of Paris, the Illinois and Northern branches of the Ohio since the cession to Congress, are no longer within our limits. Yet having been so heretofore, and still opening to us channels of extensive communication with the Western and Northwestern country, they shall be noted in their order.

The *Missouri* is, in fact, the principal river, contributing more to the common stream than does the Missisipi, even after its junction with the Illinois. It is remarkably cold, muddy and rapid. Its overflowings are considerable. They happen during the months of June and July. Their commencement being so much later than those of the Missisipi, would induce a belief that the sources of the Missouri are northward of those of the Missisipi, unless we suppose that the cold increases again with the ascent of the land from the Missisipi westwardly. That this ascent is great, is proved by the rapidity of the river. Six miles above the mouth it is brought within the compass of a quarter of a mile's width: yet the Spanish merchants at Pancore, or St. Louis, say they go two thousand miles up it. It heads far westward of the Rio Norte, or North River. There is, in the villages of Kaskaskia, Cohoes and St. Vincennes, no inconsiderable quantity of plate, said to have been plundered during the last war by the Indians from the churches and private houses of Santa Fé, on the North River, and brought to these villages for sale. From the mouth of Ohio to Santa Fé are forty days journey, or about 1000 miles. What is the shortest distance between the navigable waters of the Missouri, and those of the North River, or how far this is navigable above Santa Fé, I could never learn. From Santa Fé to its mouth in the Gulf of Mexico is about 1200 miles. The road from New Orleans to Mexico crosses this river at the post of Rio Norte, 800 miles below Santa Fé: and from this post to New Orleans is about 1200 miles; thus making 2000 miles between Santa Fé and New Orleans, passing down the North River, Red River and Missisipi; whereas, it is 2230 through the Missouri and Missisipi. From the same post of Rio Norte, passing near the mines of La Sierra and Laiguana, which are between the North River and the River Salina to Sartilla, is 375 miles; and from thence, passing the mines of Charcas, Zacatecas and Potosi, to the City of Mexico is 375 miles; in all, 1550 miles from Santa Fé to the City of Mexico. From New Orleans to the City of Mexico is about 1950 miles: the roads, after setting out from the Red River, near Natchitoches, keeping generally parallel with the coast, and about 200 miles from it, till it enters the City of Mexico.

The *Illinois* is a fine river, clear, gentle, and without rapids; insomuch that it is navigable for batteaux to its source. From thence is a portage of 2 miles only to the Chickago, which affords a batteau navigation of 16 miles to its entrance into Lake Michigan. The Illinois, about 10 miles above its mouth, is 300 yards wide.

The *Kaskaskia* is 100 yards wide at its entrance into the Missisipi, and preserves that breadth to the Buffalo plains, 70 miles above. So far also it is navigable for loaded batteaux, and perhaps much further. It is not rapid.

The *Ohio* is the most beautiful river on earth. Its current gentle, waters clear, and bosom smooth and unbroken by rocks and rapids, a single instance only excepted. It is a quarter of a mile wide at Fort

Pitt; 500 yards at the mouth of the Great Kanhaway; 1 mile and 25 poles[5] at Louisville; quarter of a mile on the Rapids, 3 or 4 miles below Louisville; half a mile where the low country begins, which is 20 miles above Green River; one and a quarter at the receipt of the Tanissee; and a mile wide at the mouth. Its length, as measured according to its meanders by Captain Hutchings,[6] is as follows:

From Fort Pitt:

	Miles.		Miles.
To Log's Town	18½	Little Miami	126¼
Big Beaver Creek	10¾	Licking Creek	8
Little Beaver Creek	13½	Great Miami	26¾
Yellow Creek	11¾	Big Bones	32½
Two Creeks	21¾	Kentuckey	44¼
Long Reach	53¾	Rapids	77¼
End Long Reach	16½	Low country	155¾
Muskingum	25½	Buffalo River	64½
Little Kanhaway	12¼	Wabash	97¼
Hockhocking	16	Big Cave	42¾
Great Kanhaway	82½	Shawanee River	52½
Guiandot	43¾	Cherokee River	13
Sandy Creek	14½	Massac	11
Sioto	48¼	Missisipi	46
			1,188

In common Winter and Spring tides it affords 15 feet water to Louisville, 10 feet to La Tarte's Rapids, 40 miles above the mouth of the Great Kanhaway, and a sufficiency at all times for light batteaux and canoes to Fort Pitt. The Rapids are in latitude 38° 8'. The inundations of this river begin about the last of March, and subside in July. During these, a first rate man of war may be carried from Louisville to New Orleans, if the sudden turns of the river and the strength of its current will admit a safe steerage. The Rapids at Louisville descend about 30 feet in a length of a mile and a half. The bed of the river there is a solid rock, and is divided by an island into two branches, the Southern of which is about 200 yards wide, and is dry four months in the year. The bed of the Northern branch is worn into channels by the constant course of the water, and attrition of the pebble stones carried

[5] 16½ or 18 feet.
[6] Thomas Hutchins, *A Topographical Description of Virginia, Pennsylvania, Maryland, and North Carolina* (London, 1778).

on with that, so as to be passable for batteaux through the greater part of the year. Yet it is thought that the southern arm may be the most easily opened for constant navigation. The rise of the waters in these rapids does not exceed 10 or 12 feet. A part of this island is so high as to have been never overflowed, and to command the settlement at Louisville, which is opposite to it. The fort, however, is situated at the head of the falls. The ground on the South side rises very gradually.

The *Tanissee,* Cherokee or Hogohege River is 600 yards wide at its mouth, a quarter of a mile at the mouth of Holston, and 200 yards at Chotee, which is 20 miles above Holston, and 300 miles above the mouth of the Tanissee. This river crosses the Southern boundary of Virginia, 58 miles from the Missisipi. Its current is moderate. It is navigable for loaded boats of any burthen to the Muscleshoals, where the river passes through the Cumberland mountain. These shoals are 6 or 8 miles long, passable downwards for loaded canoes, but not upwards, unless there be a swell in the river. Above these the navigation for loaded canoes and batteaux continues to the Long island. This river has its inundations also. Above the Chickamogga towns is a whirlpool, called the Sucking–pot, which takes in trunks of trees or boats, and throws them out again half a mile below. It is avoided by keeping very close to the bank, on the South side. There are but a few miles portage between a branch of this river and the navigable waters of the River Mobile, which runs into the Gulf of Mexico.

Cumberland, or Shawanee river, intersects the boundary between Virginia and North Carolina, 67 miles from the Missisipi, and again 198 miles from the same river, a little above the entrance of Obey's River into the Cumberland. Its clear fork crosses the same boundary, about 300 miles from the Missisipi. Cumberland is a very gentle stream, navigable for loaded batteaux 800 miles, without interruption; then intervene some rapids of 15 miles in length, after which it is again navigable 70 miles upwards, which brings you within 10 miles of the Cumberland mountains. It is about 120 yards wide through its whole course, from the head of its navigation to its mouth.

The *Wabash* is a very beautiful river, 400 yards wide at the mouth, and 300 at St. Vincennes, which is a post 100 miles above the mouth, in a direct line. Within this space there are two small rapids, which give very little obstruction to the navigation. It is 400 yards wide at the mouth, and navigable 30 leagues upwards for canoes and small boats. From the mouth of Maple River to that of Eel River is about 80 miles in a direct line, the river continuing navigable, and from 100 to 200 yards in width. The Eel River is 150 yards wide, and affords at all times navigation for periaguas,[7] to within 18 miles of the Miami of the lake. The Wabash, from the mouth of Eel River to Little River, a distance of 50 miles direct, is interrupted with frequent rapids and shoals, which obstruct the navigation, except in a swell. Little River affords navigation during a swell to within 3 miles of the Miami, which thence affords a similar navigation into Lake Erie, 100 miles distant in a direct line. The Wabash overflows periodically in correspondence with the Ohio, and in some places 2 leagues from its banks.

Green River is navigable for loaded batteaux at all times 50 miles upwards; but it is then interrupted by impassable rapids, above which the navigation again commences, and continues good 30 or 40 miles to the mouth of Barren River.

Kentuckey River is 90 yards wide at the mouth, and also at Boonsborough, 80 miles above. It affords a navigation for loaded batteaux 180 miles in a direct line, in the winter tides.

The *Great Miami* of the Ohio is 200 yards wide at the mouth. At the Piccawee towns, 75 miles above, it is reduced to 30 yards; it is, nevertheless, navigable for loaded canoes 50 miles above these towns. The portage from its Western branch into the Miami of Lake Erie is 5 miles; that from its Eastern branch into Sandusky river is 9 miles.

Salt River is at all times navigable for loaded batteaux 70 or 80 miles. It is 80 yards wide at its mouth, and keeps that width to its fork, 25 miles above.

The *Little Miami* of the Ohio is 60 or 70 yards wide at its mouth, 60 miles to its source, and affords no navigation.

The *Sioto* is 250 yards wide at its mouth, which is in latitude 38° 22′ and at the Saltlick towns, 200 miles above the mouth, it is yet 100 yards wide. To these towns it is navigable for loaded batteaux, and its eastern branch affords navigation almost to its source.

Great Sandy River is about 60 yards wide, and navigable 60 miles for loaded batteaux.

Guiandot is about the width of the river last mentioned, but is more rapid. It may be navigated by canoes 60 miles.

The *Great Kanhaway* is a river of considerable note for the fertility of its lands, and still more, as leading towards the head waters of James River. Nevertheless, it is doubtful whether its great and numerous rapids will admit a navigation, but at an expense to which it will

---

[7]periaguas: Large, flat-bottomed canoes, sometimes with two masts, used with great proficiency by Pacific coast and Caribbean natives.

require ages to render its inhabitants equal. The great obstacles begin at what are called the great falls, 90 miles above the mouth, below which are only 5 or 6 rapids, and these passable, with some difficulty, even at low water. From the falls to the mouth of Greenbriar is 100 miles, and thence to the lead mines 120. It is 280 yards wide at its mouth.

Hock–hocking is 80 yards wide at its mouth, and yields navigation for loaded batteaux to the Press–place, 60 miles above its mouth.

The *Little Kanhaway* is 150 yards wide at the mouth. It yields a navigation of 10 miles only. Perhaps its Northern branch, called Junius's Creek, which interlocks with the Western of Monongahela, may one day admit a shorter passage from the latter into the Ohio.

The *Muskingum* is 280 yards wide at its mouth, and 200 yards at the lower Indian towns, 150 miles upwards. It is navigable for small batteaux to within one mile of a navigable part of Cayahoga River, which runs into Lake Erie.

At Fort Pitt the river Ohio loses its name, branching into the Monongahela and Alleghaney.

The *Monongahela* is 400 yards wide at its mouth. From thence is 12 or 15 miles to the mouth of Yohoganey, where it is 300 yards wide. Thence to Red Stone by water is 50 miles, by land 30. Then to the mouth of Cheat River by water 40 miles, by land 28, the width continuing at 300 yards, and the navigation good for boats. Thence the width is about 200 yards to the western fork, 50 miles higher, and the navigation frequently interrupted by rapids; which, however, with a swell of 2 or 3 feet become very passable for boats. It then admits light boats, except in dry seasons, 65 miles further to the head of Tygart's valley, presenting only some small rapids and falls of 1 or 2 feet perpendicular, and lessening in its width to 20 yards. The *Western fork* is navigable in the winter 10 or 15 miles towards the Northern of the Little Kanhaway, and will admit a good wagon road to it. The *Yohoganey* is the principal branch of this river. It passes through the Laurel Mountain, about 30 miles from its mouth; is so far from 300 to 150 yards wide, and the navigation much obstructed in dry weather by rapids and shoals. In its passage through the mountain it makes very great falls, admitting no navigation for 10 miles to the Turkey Foot. Thence to the great crossing, about 20 miles, it is again navigable, except in dry seasons, and at this place is 200 yards wide. The sources of this river are divided from those of the Patowmac by the Alleghaney Mountain. From the falls, where it intersects the Laurel Mountain, to Fort Cumberland, the head of the navigation on the

Patowmac, is 40 miles of very mountainous road. Wills's Creek, at the mouth of which was Fort Cumberland, is 30 or 40 yards wide, but affords no navigation as yet. *Cheat River,* another considerable branch of the Monongahela, is 200 yards wide at its mouth, and 100 yards at the Dunkard's settlement, 50 miles higher. It is navigable for boats, except in dry seasons. The boundary between Virginia and Pennsylvania crosses it about 3 or 4 miles above its mouth.

The *Alleghaney River,* with a slight swell, affords navigation for light batteaux to Venango, at the mouth of French Creek, where it is 200 yards wide; and it is practised even to Le Bœuf, from whence there is a portage of 15 miles to Presque Isle, on Lake Erié.

The country watered by the Missisipi and its Eastern branches, constitutes five-eighths of the United States, two of which five-eighths are occupied by the Ohio and its waters; the residuary streams which run into the Gulf of Mexico, the Atlantic, and the St. Laurence, water the remaining three-eighths.

Before we quit the subject of the western waters, we will take a view of their principal connections with the Atlantic. These are three; the Hudson's River, the Patowmac, and the Missisipi itself. Down the last will pass all heavy commodities. But the navigation through the Gulf of Mexico is so dangerous, and that up the Missisipi so difficult and tedious, that it is thought probable that European merchandise will not return through that channel. It is most likely that flour, timber, and other heavy articles will be floated on rafts, which will themselves be an article for sale as well as their loading, the navigators returning by land or in light batteaux. There will therefore be a competition between the Hudson and Patowmac rivers for the residue of the commerce of all the country westward of Lake Erié, on the waters of the lakes, of the Ohio, and upper parts of the Missisipi. To go to New York, that part of the trade which comes from the lakes or their waters must first be brought into Lake Erié. Between Lake Superior and its waters and Huron are the Rapids of St. Mary, which will permit boats to pass, but not larger vessels. Lakes Huron and Michigan afford communication with Lake Erié by vessels of 8 feet draught. That part of the trade which comes from the waters of the Missisipi must pass from them through some portage into the waters of the lakes. The portage from the Illinois River into a water of Michigan is of 1 mile only. From the Wabash, Miami, Muskingum, or Alleghaney, are portages into the waters of Lake Erié, of from 1 to 15 miles. When the commodities are brought into, and have passed through Lake Erié, there is between that and Ontario an interruption by the falls of

Niagara, where the portage is of 8 miles; and between Ontario and the Hudson's River are portages at the falls of Onondago, a little above Oswego, of a quarter of a mile; from Wood Creek to the Mohawks River 2 miles; at the little falls of the Mohawks River half a mile, and from Schenectady to Albany 16 miles. Besides the increase of expense occasioned by frequent change of carriage, there is an increased risk of pillage produced by committing merchandise to a greater number of hands successively. The Patowmac offers itself under the following circumstances. For the trade of the lakes and their waters westward of Lake Erié, when it shall have entered that lake, it must coast along its southern shore, on account of the number and excellence of its harbors, the northern, though shortest, having few harbors, and these unsafe. Having reached Cayahoga, to proceed on to New York it will have 825 miles and five portages; whereas it is but 425 miles to Alexandria, its emporium on the Patowmac, if it turns into the Cayahoga, and passes through that, Bigbeaver, Ohio, Yohoganey, (or Monongalia and Cheat) and Patowmac, and there are but two portages; the first of which between Cayahoga and Beaver may be removed by uniting the sources of these waters, which are lakes in the neighborhood of each other, and in a champaign country; the other from the waters of Ohio to Patowmac will be from 15 to 40 miles, according to the trouble which shall be taken to approach the two navigations. For the trade of the Ohio, or that which shall come into it from its own waters or the Missisipi, it is nearer through the Patowmac to Alexandria than to New York by 580 miles, and it is interrupted by one portage only. There is another circumstance of difference too. The lakes themselves never freeze, but the communications between them freeze, and the Hudson's River is itself shut up by the ice three months in the year; whereas the channel to the Chesapeake leads directly into a warmer climate. The Southern parts of it very rarely freeze at all, and whenever the Northern do, it is so near the sources of the rivers, that the frequent floods to which they are there liable break up the ice immediately, so that vessels may pass through the whole winter, subject only to accidental and short delays. Add to all this, that in case of a war with our neighbors, the Anglo-Americans or the Indians, the route to New York becomes a frontier through almost its whole length, and all commerce through it ceases from that moment.—But the channel to New York is already known to practice; whereas the upper waters of the Ohio and the Patowmac, and the great falls of the latter, are yet to be cleared of their fixed obstructions.

QUERY III: SEA PORTS

A Notice of the Best Sea Ports of the State, and How Big Are the Vessels They Can Receive?

Having no ports but our rivers and creeks, this query has been answered under the preceding one.

QUERY IV: MOUNTAINS

A Notice of Its Mountains?

For the particular geography of our mountains I must refer to Fry and Jefferson's map of Virginia, and to Evans's analysis of his map of America[8] for a more philosophical view of them than is to be found in any other work. It is worthy of notice, that our mountains are not solitary and scattered confusedly over the face of the country, but that they commence at about 150 miles from the sea-coast, are disposed in ridges one behind another, running nearly parallel with the sea-coast, though rather approaching it as they advance northeastwardly. To the southwest, as the tract of country between the sea-coast and the Missisipi becomes narrower, the mountains converge into a single ridge, which, as it approaches the Gulf of Mexico, subsides into plain country, and gives rise to some of the waters of that Gulf, and particularly to a river called the Apalachicola, probably from the Apalachies, an Indian nation formerly residing on it. Hence the mountains giving rise to that river, and seen from its various parts, were called the Apalachian mountains, being in fact the end or termination only of the great ridges passing through the continent. European geographers however extended the name northwardly as far as the mountains extended; some giving it, after their separation into different ridges, to the Blue Ridge, others to the North mountain, others to the Alleghaney, others to the Laurel ridge, as may be seen in their different maps. But the fact I believe is, that none of these ridges were ever known by that name to the inhabitants, either native or emigrant, but as they saw them so called in European maps. In the same direction generally are the veins of lime stone, coal and other minerals hitherto discovered; and so range the falls of our great rivers. But the courses

---

[8]Joshua Fry and Peter Jefferson, father of Thomas Jefferson, published a map of Virginia in 1751. Lewis Evans, *Geographical, Historical, Political, Philosophical, and Mechanical Essays: The First, Containing an Analysis of a General Map of the Middle British Colonies in America* (Philadelphia, 1755).

of the great rivers are at right angles with these. James and Patowmac penetrate through all the ridges of mountains eastward of the Alleghaney; that is broken by no watercourse. It is in fact the spine of the country between the Atlantic on one side, and the Missisipi and St. Laurence on the other. The passage of the Patowmac through the Blue Ridge is perhaps one of the most stupendous scenes in Nature. You stand on a very high point of land. On your right comes up the Shenandoah, having ranged along the foot of the mountain an hundred miles to seek a vent. On your left approaches the Patowmac, in quest of a passage also. In the moment of their junction they rush together against the mountain, rend it asunder, and pass off to the sea. The first glance of this scene hurries our senses into the opinion, that this earth has been created in time, that the mountains were formed first, that the rivers began to flow afterwards, that in this place particularly they have been dammed up by the Blue Ridge of mountains, and have formed an ocean which filled the whole valley; that continuing to rise they have at length broken over at this spot, and have torn the mountain down from its summit to its base. The piles of rock on each hand, but particularly on the Shenandoah, the evident marks of their disrupture and avulsion from their beds by the most powerful agents of nature, corroborate the impression. But the distant finishing which nature has given to the picture is of a very different character. It is a true contrast to the foreground. It is as placid and delightful as that is wild and tremendous. For the mountain being cloven asunder, she presents to your eye, through the cleft, a small catch of smooth blue horizon, at an infinite distance in the plain country, inviting you, as it were, from the riot and tumult roaring around, to pass through the breach and participate of the calm below. Here the eye ultimately composes itself; and that way too the road happens actually to lead. You cross the Patowmac above the junction, pass along its side through the base of the mountain for three miles, its terrible precipices hanging in fragments over you, and within about 20 miles reach Frederic town, and the fine country round that. This scene is worth a voyage across the Atlantic. Yet here, as in the neighborhood of the natural bridge, are people who have passed their lives within half dozen miles, and have never been to survey these monuments of a war between rivers and mountains, which must have shaken the earth itself to its centre.

The height of our mountains has not yet been estimated with any degree of exactness. The Alleghaney being the great ridge which divides the waters of the Atlantic from those of the Missisipi, its summit is doubtless more elevated above the ocean than that of any other mountain. But its relative height, compared with the base on which it stands, is not so great as that of some others, the country rising behind the successive ridges like the steps of stairs. The mountains of the Blue Ridge, and of these the Peaks of Otter, are thought to be of a greater height, measured from their base, than any others in our country, and perhaps in North America. From data, which may found a tolerable conjecture, we suppose the highest peak to be about 4000 feet perpendicular, which is not a fifth part of the height of the mountains of South America, nor one-third of the height which would be necessary in our latitude to preserve ice in the open air unmelted through the year. The ridge of mountains next beyond the Blue Ridge, called by us the North mountain, is of the greatest extent; for which reason they were named by the Indians the Endless mountains.

A substance supposed to be Pumice, found floating on the Missisipi, has induced a conjecture, that there is a volcano in some of its waters; and as these are mostly known to their sources, except the Missouri, our expectations of verifying the conjecture would of course be led to the mountains which divide the waters of the Mexican Gulf from those of the South Sea; but no volcano having ever yet been known at such a distance from the sea, we must rather suppose that this floating substance has been erroneously deemed Pumice.

QUERY V: CASCADES

Its Cascades and Caverns?

The only remarkable cascade in this country, is that of the Falling Spring in Augusta. It is a water of James River, where it is called Jackson's River, rising in the Warm Spring mountains, about 20 miles southwest of the warm spring, and flowing from that valley. About three quarters of a mile from its source, it falls over a rock 200 feet into the valley below. The sheet of water is broken in its breadth by the rock in two or three places, but not at all in its height. Between the sheet and rock at the bottom you may walk across dry. This cataract will bear no comparison with that of Niagara, as to the quantity of water composing it; the sheet being only 12 or 15 feet wide above, and somewhat more spread below; but it is half as high again, the latter being only 156 feet, according to the mensuration[9] made by order of

---

[9]mensuration: measurement.

M. Vaudreuil, Governor of Canada, and 130 according to a more recent account.

In the Lime Stone country there are many caverns of very considerable extent. The most noted is called Madison's Cave, and is on the North side of the Blue Ridge, near the intersection of the Rockingham and Augusta line with the south fork of the southern river of Shenandoah. It is in a hill of about 200 feet perpendicular height, the ascent of which on one side is so steep, that you may pitch a biscuit from its summit into the river which washes its base. The entrance of the cave is in this side about two-thirds of the way up. It extends into the earth about 300 feet, branching into subordinate caverns, sometimes ascending a little, but more generally descending, and at length terminates in two different places at basins of water of unknown extent, and which I should judge to be nearly on a level with the water of the river; however, I do not think they are formed by refluent water from that, because they are never turbid; because they do not rise and fall in correspondence with that in times of flood, or of drought, and because the water is always cool. It is probably one of the many reservoirs with which the interior parts of the earth are supposed to abound, and which yield supplies to the fountains of water, distinguished from others only by its being accessible. The vault of this cave is of solid limestone, from 20 to 40 or 50 feet high, through which water is continually percolating. This, tricking down the sides of the cave, has incrusted them over in the form of elegant drapery; and dripping from the top of the vault generates on that, and on the base below, stalactites of a conical form, some of which have met and formed massive columns.

Another of the these caves is near the North mountain, in the county of Frederick, on the lands of Mr. Zane. The entrance into this is on the top of an extensive ridge. You descend 30 or 40 feet, as into a well, from whence the cave then extends, nearly horizontally, 400 feet into the earth, preserving a breadth of from 20 to 50 feet, and a height of from 5 to 12 feet. After entering this cave a few feet, the mercury, which in the open air was at 50°, rose to 57° of Farenheit's thermometer, answering to 11° of Reaumur's, and it continued at that to the remotest parts of the cave. The uniform temperature of the cellars of the observatory of Paris, which are 90 feet deep, and of all subterranean cavities of any depth, where no chemical agents may be supposed to produce a factitious heat, has been found to be 10° of Reaumur, equal to 54½° of Farenheit. The temperature of the cave above mentioned so nearly corresponds with this, that the difference may be ascribed to a difference of instruments.

At the Panther Gap, in the ridge which divides the waters of the Cow and the Calf Pasture, is what is called the *Blowing Cave.* It is in the side of a hill, is of about 100 feet diameter, and emits constantly a current of air of such force, as to keep the weeds prostrate to the distance of 20 yards before it. This current is strongest in dry frosty weather, and in long spells of rain weakest. Regular inspirations and expirations of air, by caverns and fissures, have been probably enough accounted for, by supposing them combined with intermitting fountains; as they must of course inhale air while their reservoirs are emptying themselves, and again emit it while they are filling. But a constant issue of air, only varying in its force as the weather is dryer or damper, will require a new hypothesis. There is another Blowing Cave in the Cumberland Mountain, about a mile from where it crosses the Carolina line. All we know of this is, that it is not constant, and that a fountain of water issues from it.

The *Natural bridge,* the most sublime of Nature's works, though not comprehended under the present head, must not be pretermitted.[10] It is on the ascent of a hill, which seems to have been cloven through its length by some great convulsion. The fissure just at the bridge is, by some admeasurements, 270 feet deep, by others only 205. It is about 45 feet wide at the bottom, and 90 feet at the top; this of course determines the length of the bridge, and its height from the water. Its breadth in the middle is about 60 feet, but more at the ends, and the thickness of the mass at the summit of the arch about 40 feet. A part of this thickness is constituted by a coat of earth, which gives growth to many large trees. The residue, with the hill on both sides, is one solid rock of limestone. The arch approaches the semi-elliptical form; but the larger axis of the ellipsis, which would be the cord of the arch, is many times longer than the transverse. Though the sides of this bridge are provided in some parts with a parapet of fixed rocks, yet few men have resolution to walk to them and look over into the abyss. You involuntarily fall on your hands and feet, creep to the parapet and peep over it. Looking down from this height about a minute gave me a violent headache. If the view from the top be painful and intolerable, that from below is delightful in an equal extreme. It is impossible for the emotions arising from the sublime, to be felt beyond what they are here: so beautiful an arch, so elevated, so light, and springing as it were up to heaven, the rapture of the spectator is really indescribable! The fissure continuing narrow, deep, and straight

[10]pretermitted: omitted.

for a considerable distance above and below the bridge, opens a short but very pleasing view of the North mountain on one side, and Blue Ridge on the other, at the distance each of them of about five miles. This bridge is in the county of Rockbridge, to which it has given name, and affords a public and commodious passage over a valley, which cannot be crossed elsewhere for a considerable distance. The stream passing under it is called Cedar Creek. It is a water of James River, and sufficient in the dryest seasons to turn a grist mill, though its fountain is not more than two miles above.

QUERY VI: PRODUCTIONS MINERAL, VEGETABLE, AND ANIMAL

A Notice of the Mines and Other Subterraneous Riches; Its Trees, Plants, Fruits, &c.?

I knew a single instance of gold found in this State. It was interspersed in small specks through a lump of ore, of about four pounds weight, which yielded seventeen pennyweight of gold, of extraordinary ductility. This ore was found on the North side of Rappahanock, about four miles below the falls. I never heard of any other indication of gold in its neighborhood.

On the Great Kanhaway, opposite to the mouth of Cripple Creek, and about 25 miles from our Southern boundary, in the county of Montgomery, are mines of lead. The metal is mixed, sometimes with earth, and sometimes with rock, which requires the force of gunpowder to open it; and is accompanied with a portion of silver, too small to be worth separation under any process hitherto attempted there. The proportion yielded is from 50 to 80 lb of pure metal from 100 lb of washed ore. The most common is that of 60 to the 100 lb. The veins are at some times most flattering; at others they disappear suddenly and totally. They enter the side of the hill, and proceed horizontally. Two of them are wrought at present by the public, the best of which is 100 yards under the hill. These would employ about 50 laborers to advantage. We have not, however, more than 30 generally, and these cultivate their own corn. They have produced 60 tons of lead in the year; but the general quantity is from 20 to 25 tons. The present furnace is a mile from the ore bank, and on the opposite side of the river. The ore is first wagoned to the river, a quarter of a mile, then laden on board of canoes and carried across the river, which is there about 200 yards wide, and then again taken into wagons and carried to the furnace. This mode was originally adopted, that they might avail themselves of a good situation on a creek for a pounding mill; but it would be easy to have the furnace and pounding mill on the same side of the river, which would yield water, without any dam, by a canal of about half a mile in length. From the furnace the lead is transported 130 miles along a good road, leading through the peaks of Otter to Lynch's Ferry, or Winston's, on James River, from whence it is carried by water about the same distance to Westham. This land carriage may be greatly shortened by delivering the lead on James River, above the Blue ridge, from whence a ton weight has been brought on two canoes. The Great Kanhaway has considerable falls in the neighborhood of the mines. About seven miles below are three falls, of three or four feet perpendicular each; and three miles above is a rapid of three miles continuance, which has been compared in its descent to the great fall of James River. Yet it is the opinion that they may be laid open for useful navigation, so as to reduce very much the portage between the Kanhaway and James River.

A valuable lead mine is said to have been lately discovered in Cumberland, below the mouth of Red river. The greatest, however, known in the Western country are on the Missisipi, extending from the mouth of Rock river 150 miles upwards. These are not wrought, the lead used in that country being from the banks on the Spanish side of the Missisipi, opposite to Kaskaskia.

A mine of copper was once opened in the county of Amherst, on the North side of James River, and another in the opposite country, on the South side. However, either from bad management or the poverty of the veins, they were discontinued. We are told of a rich mine of native copper on the Ouabache, below the upper Wiaw.

The mines of iron worked at present are Callaway's, Ross's, and Ballendine's, on the South side of James River; Old's on the North side, in Albemarle; Miller's in Augusta, and Zane's, in Frederic. These two last are in the valley between the Blue Ridge and North mountain. Callaway's, Ross's, Miller's, and Zane's, make about 150 tons of bar iron each in the year. Ross's makes also about 1600 tons of pig iron annually; Ballendine's 1000; Callaway's, Millar's, and Zane's, about 600 each. Besides these, a forge of Mr. Hunter's, at Fredericksburgh, makes about 300 tons a year of bar iron, from pigs imported from Maryland; and Taylor's forge, on Neapsco of Patowmac, works in the same way, but to what extent I am not informed. The indications of iron in other places are numerous, and dispersed through all the middle country. The toughness of the cast iron of Ross's and Zane's furnaces is very remarkable. Pots and other utensils, cast thinner than usual, of this iron, may be safely thrown into or out of the wagons in which they are transported. Salt pans made of the same, and no longer wanted for that purpose, cannot be broken up, in order to be melted again, unless previously drilled in many parts.

In the Western country we are told of iron mines between the Muskingum and Ohio; of others on Kentucky, between the Cumberland and Barren Rivers, between Cumberland and Tanissee, on Reedy Creek, near the Long Island, and on Chestnut Creek, a branch of the Great Kanhaway, near where it crosses the Carolina line. What are called the iron banks, on the Missisipi, are believed, by a good judge, to have no iron in them. In general, from what is hitherto known of that country, it seems to want iron.

Considerable quantities of black lead are taken occasionally for use from Winterham, in the county of Amelia. I am not able, however, to give a particular state of the mine. There is no work established at it, those who want, going and procuring it for themselves.

The country on James river, from 15 to 20 miles above Richmond, and for several miles northward and southward, is replete with mineral coal of a very excellent quality. Being in the hands of many proprietors, pits have been opened, and before the interruption of our commerce, were worked to an extent equal to the demand.

In the western country coal is known to be in so many places, as to have induced an opinion that the whole tract between the Laurel mountain, Missisipi, and Ohio, yields coal. It is also known in many places on the North side of the Ohio. The coal at Pittsburg is of very superior quality. A bed of it at that place has been afire since the year 1765. Another coal hill on the Pike Run of Monongahela has been afire ten years; yet it has burnt away about twenty yards only.

I have known one instance of an Emerald found in this country. Amethysts have been frequent, and chrystals common; yet not in such numbers any of them as to be worth seeking.

There is very good marble, and in very great abundance, on James river, at the mouth of Rockfish. The samples I have seen, were some of them of a white as pure as one might expect to find on the surface of the earth; but most of them were variegated with red, blue and purple. None of it has been ever worked. It forms a very large precipice, which hangs over a navigable part of the river. It is said there is marble at Kentucky.

But one vein of lime stone is known below the Blue Ridge. Its first appearance in our country is in Prince William, two miles below the

Pignut Ridge of mountains; thence it passes on nearly parallel with that, and crosses the Rivanna about five miles below it, where it is called the Southwest Ridge. It then crosses Hardware, above the mouth of Hudson's Creek, James River at the mouth of Rockfish, at the marble quarry before spoken of, probably runs up that river to where it appears again at Ross's iron works, and so passes off southwestwardly by Flat Creek of Otter River. It is never more than one hundred yards wide. From the Blue Ridge westwardly, the whole country seems to be founded on a rock of limestone, besides infinite quantities on the surface, both loose and fixed. This is cut into beds, which range, as the mountains and sea-coast do, from southwest to northeast, the lamina of each bed declining from the horizon towards a parallelism with the axis of the earth. Being struck with this observation, I made, with a quadrant, a great number of trials on the angles of their declination, and found them to vary from 22° to 60°, but averaging all my trials, the result was within one-third of a degree of the elevation of the pole or latitude of the place, and much the greatest part of them taken separately were little different from that, by which it appears that these lamina are in the main parallel with the axis of the earth. In some instances, indeed, I found them perpendicular, and even reclining the other way; but these were extremely rare, and always attended with signs of convulsion, or other circumstances of singularity, which admitted a possibility of removal from their original position. These trials were made between Madison's Cave and the Patowmac. We hear of limestone on the Missisipi and Ohio, and in all the mountainous country between the eastern and western waters, not on the mountains themselves, but occupying the valleys between them.

Near the Eastern foot of the North Mountain are immense bodies of *Schist,* containing impressions of shells in a variety of forms. I have received petrified shells of very different kinds from the first sources of the Kentucky, which bear no resemblance to any I have ever seen on the tide-waters. It is said that shells are found in the Andes, in South America, 15,000 feet above the level of the ocean. This is considered by many, both of the learned and unlearned, as a proof of an universal deluge. To the many considerations opposing this opinion, the following may be added. The atmosphere, and all its contents, whether of water, air, or other matters, gravitate to the earth; that is to say, they have weight. Experience tells us that the weight of all those together never exceeds that of a column of mercury of 31 inches height, which is equal to one of rain water of 35 feet high. If the whole contents of the atmosphere then were water, instead of what they are, it would cover the globe but 35 feet deep; but as these waters as they fell would run into the seas, the superficial measure of which is to that of the dry parts of the globe as two to one, the seas would be raised only 52½ feet above their present level, and of course would overflow the lands to that height only. In Virginia this would be a very small proportion even of the champaign country, the banks of our tide-waters being frequently, if not generally, of a greater height. Deluges beyond this extent then, as for instance, to the North mountain or to Kentucky, seem out of the laws of nature. But within it they may have taken place to a greater or less degree, in proportion to the combination of natural causes which may be supposed to have produced them. History renders probable some instances of a partial deluge in the country lying round the Mediterranean sea. It has been often supposed, and is not unlikely, that that sea was once a lake.[11] While such, let us admit an extraordinary collection of the waters of the atmosphere from the other parts of the globe to have been discharged over that and the countries whose waters run into it. Or without supposing it a lake, admit such an extraordinary collection of the waters of the atmosphere, and an influx of waters from the Atlantic ocean, forced by long continued Western winds. That lake, or that sea, may thus have been so raised as to overflow the low lands adjacent to it, as those of Egypt and Armenia, which, according to a tradition of the Egyptians and Hebrews, were overflowed about 2300 years before the Christian era; those of Attica, said to have been overflowed in the time of Ogyges, about 500 years later; and those of Thessaly, in the time of Deucalion, still 300 years posterior. But such deluges as these will not account for the shells found in the higher lands. A second opinion has been entertained, which is, that in times anterior to the records, either of history or tradition, the bed of the ocean, the principal residence of the shelled tribe, has, by some great convulsion of Nature, been heaved to the heights at which we now find shells and other remains of marine animals. The favorers of this opinion do well to suppose the great events on which it rests to have taken place beyond all the eras of history; for within these certainly none such are to be found; and we may venture to say further, that no fact has taken place, either in our own days, or in the thousands of years recorded in history, which proves the existence of any natural agents, within or without the bowels of the earth, of force sufficient to heave, to the height of 15,000 feet, such masses as the Andes. The difference between the power

---

[11]Georges Louis LeClerc, Comte de Buffon, *Les Époques de la Nature,* II, 96, in *Histoire Naturelle Générale et Particulière* (44 vols., Paris, 1749–1804).

necessary to produce such an effect, and that which shuffled together the different parts of Calabria in our days, is so immense, that from the existence of the latter, we are not authorized to infer that of the former.

M. de Voltaire has suggested a third solution of this difficulty.[12] He cites an instance in Touraine, where, in the space of 80 years, a particular spot of earth had been twice metamorphosed into soft stone, which had become hard when employed in building. In this stone shells of various kinds were produced, discoverable at first only with the microscope, but afterwards growing with the stone. From this fact, I suppose he would have us infer, that besides the usual process for generating shells by the elaboration of earth and water in animal vessels, Nature may have provided an equivalent operation by passing the same materials through the pores of calcareous earths and stones; as we see calcareous drop stones generating every day by the percolation of water through limestone, and new marble forming in the quarries from which the old has been taken out; and it might be asked whether it is more difficult for Nature to shoot the calcareous juice into the form of a shell, then other juices into the forms of chrystals, plants, animals, according to the construction of the vessels through which they pass? There is a wonder somewhere. Is it greatest on this branch of the dilemma; on that which supposes the existence of a power, of which we have no evidence in any other case; or on the first, which requires us to believe the creation of a body of water, and its subsequent annihilation? The establishment of the instance cited by M. de Voltaire, of the growth of shells unattached to animal bodies, would have been that of his theory. But he has not established it. He has not even left it on ground so respectable as to have rendered it an object of enquiry to the literati of his own country. Abandoning this fact, therefore, the three hypotheses are equally unsatisfactory; and we must be contented to acknowledge that this great phenomenon is as yet unsolved. Ignorance is preferable to error; and he is less remote from the truth who believes nothing, than he who believes what is wrong.

There is great abundance (more especially when you approach the mountains) of stone, white, blue, brown, &c., fit for the chisel, good mill stone, such also as stands the fire, and slate stone. We are told of flint, fit for gun flints, on the Meherrin in Brunswic, on the Missisipi

---

[12]Voltaire, "Coquilles," *Questions sur L'Encyclopedie* in *Ouevres Complêtes* (58 vols., Paris, 1775–85), XXXIX, 147.

between the mouth of Ohio and Kaskaskia, and on others of the western waters. Isinglass or mica is in several places; load stone also, and an asbestos of a ligneous texture, is sometimes to be met with.

Marle[13] abounds generally. A clay, of which, like the Sturbridge in England, bricks are made, which will resist long the violent action of fire, has been found on Tuckahoe Creek of James River, and no doubt will be found in other places. Chalk is said to be in Botetourt and Bedford. In the latter county is some earth, believed to be gypseous. Ochres are found in various parts.

In the lime stone country are many caves, the earthy floors of which are impregnated with nitre.[14] On Rich Creek, a branch of the Great Kanhaway, about 60 miles below the lead mines, is a very large one, about 20 yards wide, and entering a hill a quarter or half a mile. The vault is of rock, from 9 to 15 or 20 feet above the floor. A Mr. Lynch, who gives me this account, undertook to extract the nitre. Besides a coat of the salt which had formed on the vault and floor, he found the earth highly impregnated to the depth of seven feet in some places, and generally of three, every bushel yielding on an average three pounds of nitre. Mr. Lynch having made about 1000 lb of the salt from it, consigned it to some others, who have since made 10,000 lb. They have done this by pursuing the cave into the hill, never trying a second time the earth they have once exhausted, to see how far or soon it receives another impregnation. At least fifty of these caves are worked on the Greenbriar. There are many of them known on Cumberland River.

The country westward of the Alleghaney abound with springs of common salt. The most remarkable we have heard of are at Bullet's Lick, the Big Bones, the Blue Licks, and on the North Fork of Holston. The area of Bullet's Lick is of many acres. Digging the earth to the depth of three feet, the water begins to boil up, and the deeper you go, and the drier the weather, the stronger is the brine. A thousand gallons of water yield from a bushel to a bushel and a half of salt, which is about 80 lb of water to 1 lb of salt; but of sea water 25 lb yield 1 lb of salt. So that sea water is more than three times as strong as that of these springs. A Salt Spring has been lately discovered at the Turkey Foot on Yohogany, by which river it is overflowed, except at very low water. Its merit is not yet known. Duning's Lick is also as yet untried, but it is supposed to be the best on this side the Ohio. The

---

[13] marle: soil heavy with clay, valuable as fertilizer.
[14] nitre: potassium nitrate, or saltpeter, used in gunpowder.

Salt Springs on the margin of the Onondago Lake are said to give a saline taste to the waters of the lake.

There are several Medicinal Springs, some of which are indubitably efficacious, while others seem to owe their reputation as much to fancy and change of air and regimen as to their real virtues. None of them having undergone a chemical analysis in skilful hands, nor been so far the subject of observations as to have produced a reduction into classes of the disorders which they relieve, it is in my power to give little more than an enumeration of them.

The most efficacious of these are two springs in Augusta, near the first sources of James River, where it is called Jackson's River. They rise near the foot of the ridge of mountains, generally called the Warm Spring Mountain, but in the maps Jackson's mountains. The one is distinguished by the name of the Warm Spring, and the other of the Hot Spring. The Warm Spring issues with a very bold stream, sufficient to work a grist mill, and to keep the waters of its basin, which is 30 feet in diameter, at the vital warmth, viz: 96° of Farenheit's thermometer. The matter with which these waters is allied is very volatile; its smell indicates it to be sulphureous, as also does the circumstance of its turning silver black. They relieve rheumatisms. Other complaints also of very different natures have been removed or lessened by them. It rains here four or five days in every week.

The *Hot spring* is about six miles from the Warm, is much smaller, and has been so hot as to have boiled an egg. Some believe its degree of heat to be lessened. It raises the mercury in Farenheit's thermometer to 112 degrees, which is fever heat. It sometimes relieves where the Warm Spring fails. A fountain of common water, issuing within a few inches of its margin, gives it a singular appearance. Comparing the temperature of these with that of the Hot Springs of Kamschatka, of which Krachininnikow gives an account,[15] the difference is very great, the latter raising the mercury to 200°, which is within 12° of boiling water. These springs are very much resorted to in spite of a total want of accommodation for the sick. Their waters are strongest in the hottest months, which occasions their being visited in July and August principally.

The Sweet Springs are in the county of Botetourt, at the Eastern foot of the Alleghaney, about 42 miles from the Warm Springs. They are still less known. Having been found to relieve cases in which the

[15]Etienne Petrovich Kracheninnikov, *Histoire de Kamtchatka et des Contrees Voisines* (Lyon, 1767).

others had been ineffectually tried, it is probable their composition is different. They are different also in their temperature, being as cold as common water: which is not mentioned, however, as a proof of a distinct impregnation. This is among the first sources of James river.

On Patowmac River, in Berkeley county, above the North mountain, are Medicinal Springs, much more frequented than those of Augusta. Their powers, however, are less, the waters weakly mineralized, and scarcely warm. They are more visited, because situated in a fertile, plentiful, and populous country, better provided with accommodations, always safe from the Indians, and nearest to the more populous states.

In Louisa county, on the head waters of the South Anna branch of York River, are springs of some medicinal virtue. They are not much used however. There is a weak chalybeate[16] at Richmond, and many others in various parts of the country, which are of too little worth, or too little note, to be enumerated after those before mentioned.

We are told of a Sulphur Spring on Howard's Creek of Greenbriar, and another at Boonsborough on Kentucky.

In the low grounds of the Great Kanhaway, 7 miles above the mouth of Elk River, and 67 above that of the Kanhaway itself, is a hole in the earth of the capacity of 30 or 40 gallons, from which issues constantly a gaseous stream so strong as to give to the sand about its orifice the motion which it has in a boiling spring. On presenting a lighted candle or torch within 18 inches of the hole, it flames up in a column of 18 inches diameter, and four or five feet height, which sometimes burns out within 20 minutes, and at other times has been known to continue three days, and then has been left still burning. The flame is unsteady, of the density of that of burning spirits, and smells like burning pit coal. Water sometimes collects in the basin, which is remarkably cold, and is kept in ebullition by the gas escaping through it. If the vapor be fired in that state, the water soon becomes so warm that the hand cannot bear it, and evaporates wholly in a short time. The circumjacent lands are the property of General Washington and of General Lewis.

There is a similar one on Sandy River, the flame of which is a column of about 12 inches diameter, and 3 feet high. General Clark,[17] who informs me of it, kindled the vapor, stayed about an hour, and left it burning.

---

[16]chalybeate: a spring with water rich in iron.

[17]George Rogers Clark (1752–1814), Revolutionary War general and native of Albemarle County, Virginia, who won important battles against British and Native forces in the Ohio country.

The mention of uncommon springs leads me to that of Syphon fountains. There is one of these near the intersection of the Lord Fairfax's boundary with the North Mountain, not far from Brock's Gap, on the stream of which is a grist mill, which grinds two bushels of grain at every flood of the spring. Another, near the Cow Pasture River, a mile and a half below its confluence with the Bull Pasture River, and 16 or 17 miles from the Hot Springs, which intermits once in every twelve hours. One also near the mouth of the North Holston.

After these may be mentioned the *Natural Well*, on the lands of a Mr. Lewis in Frederick county. It is somewhat larger than a common well: the water rises in it as near the surface of the earth as in the neighboring artificial wells, and is of a depth as yet unknown. It is said there is a current in it tending sensibly downwards. If this be true, it probably feeds some fountain, of which it is the natural reservoir, distinguished from others like that of Madison's Cave, by being accessible. It is used with a bucket and windlass, as an ordinary well.

A complete catalogue of the trees, plants, fruits, &c., is probably not desired. I will sketch out those which would principally attract notice, as being 1. Medicinal; 2. Esculent[18]; 3. Ornamental, or 4. Useful for fabrication; adding the Linnæan[19] to the popular names, as the latter might not convey precise information to a foreigner. I shall confine myself too to native plants.

[Jefferson here lists 21 medicinal plants, 34 esculent plants, 41 ornamental plants, and 27 trees useful for building. Here, as elsewhere in the text, long lists of data will be summarized.]

The following were found in Virginia when first visited by the English; but it is not said whether of spontaneous growth, or by cultivation only. Most probably they were natives of more southern climates, and handed along the continent from one nation to another of the savages.

Tobacco—Nicotiana. Maize—Zea mays. Round potatoes—Solanum tuberosum. Pumpkins—Cucurbita pepo. Cymlings—Cucurbita verrucosa. Squashes—Cucurbita melopepo.

There is an infinitude of other plants and flowers, for an enumeration and scientific description of which I must refer to the Flora Vir-

---

[18]Esculent: suitable for food.

[19]Linnæan: system of classifying plants into genus and species, based on shared characteristics, first proposed by Swedish naturalist Carolus Linnaeus in his *Systema Naturae* (1758).

ginica of our great botanist, Dr. Clayton, published by Gronovius at Leyden, in 1762. This accurate observer was a native and resident of this state, passed a long life in exploring and describing its plants, and is supposed to have enlarged the botanical catalogue as much as almost any man who has lived.

Besides these plants, which are native, our *Farms* produce wheat, rye, barley, oats, buckwheat, broom corn, and Indian corn. The climate suits rice well enough wherever the lands do. Tobacco, hemp, flax, and cotton, are staple commodities. Indigo yields two cuttings. The silk worm is a native, and the mulberry, proper for its food, grows kindly.

We cultivate also potatoes, both the long and the round, turnips, carrots, parsnips, pumpkins, and ground nuts (Arachis). Our grasses are Lucerne, St. Foin, Burnet, Timothy, ray, and orchard grass; red, white, and yellow clover; greensward, blue grass, and crab grass.

The *gardens* yield musk melons, water melons, tomatoes, ochre, pomegranates, fig, and the esculent plants of Europe.

The *orchards* produce apples, pears, cherries, quinces, peaches, nectarines, apricots, almonds, and plums.

Our quadrupeds have been mostly described by Linnæus and Mons. de Buffon. Of these the mammoth, or big buffalo, as called by the Indians, must certainly have been the largest. Their tradition is, that he was carnivorous, and still exists in the Northern parts of America. A delegation of warriors from the Delaware tribe having visited the governor of Virginia, during the present revolution, on matters of business, after these had been discussed and settled in council, the governor asked them some questions relative to their country, and, among others, what they knew or had heard of the animal whose bones were found at the Saltlicks, on the Ohio. Their chief speaker immediately put himself into an attitude of oratory, and with a pomp suited to what he conceived the elevation of his subject, informed him that it was a tradition handed down from their fathers, "That in ancient times a herd of these tremendous animals came to the Big Bone licks, and began an universal destruction of the bear, deer, elks, buffaloes, and other animals, which had been created for the use of the Indians; that the Great Man above, looking down and seeing this, was so enraged that he seized his lightning, descended on the earth, seated himself on a neighboring mountain, on a rock, of which his seat and the print of his feet are still to be seen, and hurled his bolts among them till the whole were slaughtered, except the big bull, who, presenting his forehead to the shafts, shook them off as they fell; but missing one at length, it wounded him in the side; whereon, springing round, he bounded over the Ohio, over the Wabash, the Illinois, and finally over the great lakes, where he is living at this day." It is well known that on the Ohio, and in many parts of America further North, tusks, grinders, and skeletons of unparalleled magnitude, are found in great numbers, some lying on the surface of the earth, and some a little below it. A Mr. Stanley, taken prisoner by the Indians near the mouth of the Tanissee, relates that, after being transferred through several tribes, from one to another, he was at length carried over the mountains West of the Missouri to a river which runs westwardly; that these bones abounded there; and that the natives described to him the animal to which they belonged as still existing in the northern parts of their country; from which description he judged it to be an elephant. Bones of the same kind have been lately found some feet below the surface of the earth, in salines opened on the North Holston, a branch of the Tanissee, about the latitude of 36½° North. From the accounts published in Europe, I suppose it to be decided that these are of the same kind with those found in Siberia. Instances are mentioned of like animal remains found in the more Southern climates of both hemispheres; but they are either so loosely mentioned as to leave a doubt of the fact, so inaccurately described as not to authorize the classing them with the great northern bones, or so rare as to found a suspicion that they have been carried thither as curiosities from more northern regions. So that on the whole there seem to be no certain vestiges of the existence of this animal further south than the salines last mentioned. It is remarkable that the tusks and skeleton have been ascribed by the naturalists of Europe to the elephant, while the grinders have been given to the hippopotamus, or river horse. Yet it is acknowledged that the tusks and skeletons are much larger than those of the elephant, and the grinders many times greater than those of the hippopotamus, and essentially different in form. Wherever these grinders are found, there also we find the tusks and skeleton; but no skeleton of the hippopotamus nor grinders of the elephant. It will not be said that the hippopotamus and elephant came always to the same spot, the former to deposit his grinders, and the latter his tusks and skeleton. For what became of the parts not deposited there? We must agree then that these remains belong to each other, that they are of one and the same animal, that this was not a hippopotamus, because the hippopotamus had no tusks nor such a frame, and because the grinders differ in their size as well as in the number and form of their points. That it was not an elephant, I think ascertained by proofs equally decisive. I will not avail myself of the authority of the celebrated anatomist,[20] who, from an examination of the form and structure of the tusks, has declared they were essentially different from those of the elephant, because another anatomist,[21] equally celebrated, has declared, on a like examination, that they are precisely the same. Between two such authorities I will suppose this circumstance equivocal. But, 1. The skeleton of the mammoth (for so the incognitum has been called) bespeaks an animal of six times the cubic volume of the elephant, as Mons. de Buffon has admitted. 2. The grinders are five times as large, are square, and the grinding surface studded with four or five rows of blunt points: whereas those of the elephant are broad and thin, and their grinding surface flat. 3. I have never heard an instance, and suppose there has been none, of the grinder of an elephant being found in America. 4. From the known temperature and constitution of the elephant he could never have existed in those regions where the remains of the mammoth have been found. The elephant is a native only of the torrid zone and its vicinities: if, with the assistance of warm apartments and warm clothing, he has been preserved in life in the temperate climates of Europe, it has only been for a small portion of what would have been his natural period, and no instance of his multiplication in them has ever been known. But no bones of the mammoth, as I have before observed, have been ever found further South than the salines of the Holston, and they have been found as far North as the Arctic circle. Those, therefore, who are of opinion that the elephant and mammoth are the same, must believe, 1. That the elephant known to us can exist and multiply in the frozen zone; or, 2. That an internal fire may once have warmed those regions, and since abandoned them, of which, however, the globe exhibits no unequivocal indications; or, 3. That the obliquity of the ecliptic,[22] when these elephants lived, was so great as to include within the tropics all those regions in which the bones are found; the tropics being as is before observed, the natural limits of habitation for the elephant. . . . But if it be admitted that this obliquity has really decreased, and we adopt the highest rate of decrease yet pretended, that is, of one minute in a century, to transfer the northern

---

[20] John Hunter, "Observations on the Bones Commonly Supposed to Be Elephant's Bones, Which Have Been Found Near the River Ohio, in America," Royal Society, *Transactions* 58 (1768): 34–35.

[21] Louis Jean Marie D'Aubenton, a French naturalist who collaborated with Buffon.

[22] obliquity of the ecliptic: angle or plane of the sun relative to the earth, making an eclipse possible.

tropic to the Arctic circle, would carry the existence of these supposed elephants 250,000 years back; a period far beyond our conception of the duration of animal bones left exposed to the open air, as these are in many instances. Besides, though these regions would then be supposed within the tropics, yet their winters would have been too severe for the sensibility of the elephant. They would have had too but one day and one night in the year, a circumstance to which we have no reason to suppose the nature of the elephant fitted. However, it has been demonstrated, that, if a variation of obliquity in the ecliptic takes place at all, it is vibratory, and never exceeds the limits of 9 degrees, which is not sufficient to bring these bones within the tropics. One of these hypotheses, or some other equally voluntary and inadmissible to cautious philosophy, must be adopted to support the opinion that these are the bones of the elephant. For my own part, I find it easier to believe that an animal may have existed, resembling the elephant in his tusks and general anatomy, while his nature was in other respects extremely different. From the 30th degree of South latitude to the 30th of North, are nearly the limits which nature has fixed for the existence and multiplication of the elephant known to us. Proceeding thence northwardly to 36½ degrees, we enter those assigned to the mammoth. The further we advance North, the more their vestiges multiply as far as the earth has been explored in that direction; and it is as probable as otherwise, that this progression continues to the pole itself, if land extends so far. The centre of the frozen zone then may be the acme of their vigor, as that of the torrid is of the elephant. Thus nature seems to have drawn a belt of separation between these two tremendous animals, whose breadth, indeed, is not precisely known, though at present we may suppose it about 6½ degrees of latitude; to have assigned to the elephant the regions South of these confines, and those North to the mammoth, founding the constitution of the one in her extreme of heat, and that of the other in the extreme of cold. When the Creator has therefore separated their nature as far as the extent of the scale of animal life allowed to this planet would permit, it seems perverse to declare it the same, from a partial resemblance of their tusks and bones. But to whatever animal we ascribe these remains, it is certain such a one has existed in America, and that it has been the largest of all terrestrial beings. It should have sufficed to have rescued the earth it inhabited, and the atmosphere it breathed, from the imputation of impotence in the conception and nourishment of animal life on a large scale: to have stifled in its birth the opinion of a writer, the most learned too of all others in the science of animal history, that in the new world, "La nature vivante est beaucoup moins agissante, beaucoup moins forte": that nature is less active, less energetic on one side of the globe than she is on the other. As if both sides were not warmed by the same genial sun; as if a soil of the same chemical composition was less capable of elaboration into animal nutriment; as if the fruits and grains from that soil and sun yielded a less rich chyle,[23] gave less extension to the solids and fluids of the body, or produced sooner in the cartilages, membranes, and fibres, that rigidity which restrains all further extension, and terminates animal growth. The truth is, that a pigmy and a Patagonian, a mouse and a mammoth, derive their dimensions from the same nutritive juices. The difference of increment depends on circumstances unsearchable to beings with our capacities. Every race of animals seems to have received from their Maker certain laws of extension at the time of their formation. Their elaborative organs were formed to produce this, while proper obstacles were opposed to its further progress. Below these limits they cannot fall, nor rise above them. What intermediate station they shall take may depend on soil, on climate, on food, on a careful choice of breeders. But all the manna of heaven would never raise the mouse to the bulk of the mammoth.

The opinion advanced by the Count de Buffon is, 1. That the animals, common both to the old and new world, are smaller in the latter. 2. That those peculiar to the new are on a smaller scale. 3. That those which have been domesticated in both, have degenerated in America; and, 4. That on the whole it exhibits fewer species. And the reason he thinks is, that the heats of America are less; that more waters are spread over its surface by nature, and fewer of these drained off by the hand of man. In other words, that *heat* is friendly, and *moisture* adverse to the production and development of large quadrupeds. I will not meet this hypothesis on its first doubtful ground, whether the climate of America be comparatively more humid? Because we are not furnished with observations sufficient to decide this question. And though, till it be decided, we are as free to deny, as others are to affirm the fact, yet for a moment let it be supposed. The hypothesis, after this supposition, proceeds to another; that *moisture* is unfriendly to animal growth. The truth of this is inscrutable to us by reasonings a priori. Nature has hidden from us her modus agendi. Our only appeal on such questions is to experience; and I think that experience is against the supposition. It is by the assistance of *heat* and *moisture*

[23]chyle: a fluid produced during digestion and delivered into the bloodstream.

that vegetables are elaborated from the elements of earth, air, water, and fire. We accordingly see the more humid climates produce the greater quantity of vegetables. Vegetables are mediately or immediately the food of every animal; and in proportion to the quantity of food, we see animals not only multiplied in their numbers, but improved in their bulk, as far as the laws of their nature will admit. Of this opinion is the Count de Buffon himself in another part of his work: . . . Here then a race of animals, and one of the largest two, has been increased in its dimensions by *cold* and *moisture,* in direct opposition to the hypothesis, which supposes that these two circumstances diminish animal bulk, and that it is their contraries, *heat* and *dryness,* which enlarge it. But when we appeal to experience, we are not to rest satisfied with a single fact. Let us therefore try our question on more general ground. Let us take two portions of the earth, Europe and America for instance, sufficiently extensive to give operation to general causes; let us consider the circumstances peculiar to each, and observe their effect on animal nature. America, running through the torrid as well as temperate zone, has more *heat,* collectively taken, than Europe. But Europe, according to our hypothesis, is the *dryest.* They are equally adapted then to animal productions, each being endowed with one of those causes which befriend animal growth, and with one which opposes it. If it be thought unequal to compare Europe with America, which is so much larger, I answer, not more so than to compare America with the whole world. Besides, the purpose of the comparison is to try an hypothesis, which makes the size of animals depend on the *heat* and *moisture* of climate. If therefore we take a region, so extensive as to comprehend a sensible distinction of climate, and so extensive too as that local accidents, or the intercourse of animals on its borders, may not materially affect the size of those in its interior parts, we shall comply with those conditions which the hypothesis may reasonably demand. The objection would be the weaker in the present case, because any intercourse of animals which may take place on the confines of Europe and Asia, is to the advantage of the former, Asia producing certainly larger animals than Europe. Let us then take a comparative view of the quadrupeds of Europe and America, presenting them to the eye in three different tables, in one of which shall be enumerated those found in both countries; in a second those found in one only; in a third those which have been domesticated in both. To facilitate the comparison, let those of each table be arranged in gradation according to their sizes, from the greatest to the smallest, so far as their sizes can be conjectured. The weights of the large animals shall be expressed in the English avoirdupois[24] pound and its decimals; those of the smaller in the ounce and its decimals. Those which are marked thus, * are actual weights of particular subjects, deemed among the largest of their species. Those marked thus †, are furnished by judicious persons, well acquainted with the species, and saying, from conjecture only, what the largest individual they had seen would probably have weighed. The other weights are taken from Messrs. Buffon and D'Aubenton, and are of such subjects as came casually to their hands for dissection. This circumstance must be remembered where their weights and mine stand opposed; the latter being stated, not to produce a conclusion in favor of the American species, but to justify a suspension of opinion until we are better informed, and a suspicion in the mean time that there is no uniform difference in favor of either, which is all I pretend.

I have not inserted in the first table the phoca nor leather-winged bat, because the one living half the year in the water, and the other being a winged animal, the individuals of each species may visit both continents.

Of the animals in the first table, Mons. de Buffon himself informs us, that the roe, the beaver, the otter, and shrew mouse, though of the same species, are larger in America than Europe. This should therefore have corrected the generality of his expressions that the animals common to the two countries are considerably less in America than in Europe. . . . "and that without exception." He tells us too, that on examining a bear from America, he remarked no difference. . . . But adds from Bartram's[25] journal, that an American bear weighed 400 lb English, equal to 367 lb French; whereas we find the European bear, examined by Mons. D'Aubenton, weighed but 141 lb French. That the palmated Elk is larger in America than Europe we are informed by Kalm, a Naturalist who visited the former by public appointment for the express purpose of examining the subjects of Natural history.[26] In this fact Pennant concurs with him. The same Kalm tells us that the Black Moose, or Renne of America, is as high as a tall horse; and Catesby, that it is about the bigness of a middle sized ox. The same account of their size has been given me by many who have seen them. But Mons. D'Aubenton says that the Renne of Europe is but about the size of a Red-deer. The weasel is larger in America than in Europe, as

---

[24]avoirdupois: weight as measured by the displacement of water; official British system of weights.

[25]John Bartram, pioneering American naturalist.

[26]Peter Kalm, *Travels into North America,* 3 vols. (London, 1770–71).

Figure 5. Part of table of quadrupeds from the 1787 edition of *Notes on the State of Virginia.* Benjamin Franklin Collection, Yale University Library.

[77]

A comparative View of the Quadrupeds of Europe and of America.

I. *Aboriginals of both.*

	Europe.	America.
	lb.	lb.
Mammoth		
Buffalo. Bifon		*1800
White bear. Ours blanc		
Caribou. Renne		
Bear. Ours	153.7	*410
Elk. Elan. Orignal, palmated		
Red deer. Cerf	288.8	*273
Fallow deer. Daim	167.8	
Wolf. Loup	69.8	
Roe. Chevreuil	56.7	
Glutton. Glouton. Carcajou		
Wild cat. Chat fauvage		†30
Lynx. Loup cervier	25.	
Beaver. Caftor	18.5	*45
Badger. Blaireau	13.6	
Red Fox. Renard	13.5	
Grey Fox. Ifatis		
Otter. Loutre	8.9	†12
Monax. Marmotte	6.5	
Vifon. Fouine	2.8	
Hedgehog. Heriffon	2.2	
Martin. Marte	1.9	†6
	oz.	
Water rat. Rat d'eau	7.5	
Wefel. Belette	2.2	oz.
Flying fquirrel. Polatouche	2.2	†4
Shrew moufe. Mufaraigne	1.	

may be seen by comparing its dimensions as reported by Mons. D'Aubenton and Kalm. The latter tells us that the lynx, badger, red fox, and flying squirrel, are the *same* in America as in Europe; by which expression I understand they are the same in all material circumstances, in size as well as others; for if they were smaller, they would differ from the European. Our grey fox is, by Catesby's[27] account, little different in size and shape from the European fox. I presume he means the red fox of Europe, as does Kalm, where he says,

[27] Mark Catesby, *The Natural History of Carolina, Florida, and the Bahama Islands,* 2 vols. (London, 1731–43).

[78]

II. *Aboriginals of one only.*

EUROPE.		AMERICA.	
	lb.		lb.
Sanglier. Wild boar	280.	Tapir	534.
Mouflon. Wild sheep	56.	Elk, round horned	†450.
Bouquetin. Wild goat		Puma	
Lievre. Hare	7.6	Jaguar	218.
Lapin. Rabbet	3.4	Cabiai	109.
Putois. Polecat	3.3	Tamanoir	109.
Genette	3.1	Tamandua	65.4
Desman. Muskrat	oz.	Cougar of N. Amer.	75.
Ecureuil. Squirrel	12.	Cougar of S. Amer.	59.4
Hermine. Ermin	8.2	Ocelot	
Rat. Rat	7.5	Pecari	46.3
Loirs	3.1	Jaguaret	43.6
Lerot. Dormouse	1.8	Alco	
Taupe. Mole	1.2	Lama	
Hamster	.9	Paco	
Zisel		Paca	32.7
Leming		Serval	
Souris. Mouse	.6	Sloth. Unau	27¼
		Saricovienne	
		Kincajou	
		Tatou Kabassou	21.8
		Urson. Urchin	
		Raccoon. Raton	16.5
		Coati	
		Coendou	16.3
		Sloth. Aï	13.
		Sapajou Ouarini	
		Sapajou Coaita	9.8
		Tatou Encubert	
		Tatou Apar	
		Tatou Cachica	7.
		Little Coendou	6.5
		Opossum. Sarigue	

Figure 6. Part of table of quadrupeds from the 1787 edition of *Notes on the State of Virginia.*
Benjamin Franklin Collection, Yale University Library.

that in size "they do not quite come up to our foxes." For proceeding next to the red fox of America, he says "they are entirely the same with the European sort," which shows he had in view one European sort only, which was the red. So that the result of their testimony is, that the American grey fox is somewhat less than the European red; which is equally true of the grey fox of Europe, as may be seen by comparing the measures of the Count de Buffon and Mons. D'Aubenton. The white bear of America is as large as that of Europe. The bones of the mammoth, which have been found in America, are as large as those found in the old world. It may be asked, why I insert the mammoth, as if it still existed? I ask in return why I should omit it,

Figure 7. Part of table of domesticated animals from the 1787 edition of *Notes on the State of Virginia.* Benjamin Franklin Collection, Yale University Library.

III. *Domeſticated in both.*

	Europe.	America.
	lb.	lb.
Cow	763.	*2500
Horſe		*1366
Aſs		
Hog		*1200
Sheep		*125
Goat		*80
Dog	67.6	
Cat	7.	

as if it did not exist? Such is the economy of nature, that no instance can be produced of her having permitted any one race of her animals to become extinct; of her having formed any link in her great work so weak as to be broken. To add to this, the traditionary testimony of the Indians, that this animal still exists in the northern and western parts of America, would be adding the light of a taper to that of the meridian sun. Those parts still remain in their aboriginal state, unexplored and undisturbed by us, or by others for us. He may as well exist there now, as he did formerly, where we find his bones. If he be a carnivorous animal, as some anatomists have conjectured, and the Indians affirm, his early retirement may be accounted for from the general destruction of the wild game by the Indians, which commences in the first instant of their connection with us, for the purpose of purchasing matchcoats, hatchets, and fire locks, with their skins. There remain then the renne, the buffalo, red deer, fallow deer, wolf, glutton, wild cat, monax, vison, hedgehog, martin, and water rat, of the comparative sizes of which we have not sufficient testimony. It does not appear that Messrs. de Buffon and D'Aubenton have measured, weighed, or seen those of America. It is said of some of them, by some travelers, that they are smaller than the European. But who were these travelers? Have they not been men of a very different description from those who have laid open to us the other three quarters of the world? Was natural history the object of their travels? Did they measure or weigh the animals they speak of? or did they not judge of them by sight, or perhaps even from report only? Were they acquainted with the animals of their own country, with which they undertake to compare them? Have they not been so ignorant as often to mistake the species?

A true answer to these questions would probably lighten their authority, so as to render it insufficient for the foundation of an hypothesis. How unripe we yet are, for an accurate comparison of the animals of the two countries, will appear from the work of Mons. de Buffon. The ideas we should have formed of the sizes of some animals, from the information he had received at his first publications concerning them, are very different from what his subsequent communications give us. And indeed his candor in this can never be too much praised. One sentence of his book must do him immortal honor. "I love as much a person who corrects my error, as one who teaches me a truth, because in effect an error corrected is a truth." He seems to have thought the Cabiai he first examined wanted little of its full growth. "It was not yet fully grown." Yet he weighed but 46½ lb, and he found afterwards that these animals, when full grown, weigh 100 lb. He had supposed, from the examination of a jaguar, said to be two years old, which weighed but 16 lb 12 oz., that, when he should have acquired his full growth, he would not be larger than a middle-sized dog. But a subsequent account raises his weight to 200 lb. Further information will, doubtless, produce further corrections. The wonder is, not that there is yet something in this great work to correct, but that there is so little. The result of this view then is, that of 26 quadrupeds common to both countries, 7 are said to be larger in America, 7 of equal size, and 12 not sufficiently examined. So that the first table impeaches the first member of the assertion, that of the animals common to both countries, the American are smallest, "and that without exception." It shows it not just, in all the latitude in which its author has advanced it, and probably not to such a degree as to found a distinction between the two countries.

Proceeding to the second table, which arranges the animals found in one of the two countries only, Mons. de Buffon observes that the tapir, the elephant of America, is but of the size of a small cow. To preserve our comparison, I will add that the wild boar, the elephant of Europe, is little more than half that size. I have made an elk, with round or cylindrical horns, an animal of America, and peculiar to it, because I have seen many of them myself, and more of their horns; and because I can say from the best information, that in Virginia this kind of elk has abounded much, and still exists in smaller numbers; the palmated kind is confined to the more Northern latitudes. I have made our hare or rabbit peculiar, believing it to be different from both the European animals of those denominations, and calling it therefore by its Algonquin name Whabus, to keep it distinct from these. Kalm is of the same opinion. I have enumerated the squirrels according to our own knowledge, derived from daily sight of them, because I am not able to reconcile with that the European appellations and descriptions. I have heard of other species, but they have never come within my own notice. These, I think, are the only instances in which I have departed from the authority of Mons. de Buffon in the construction of this table. I take him for my ground work, because I think him the best informed of any Naturalist who has ever written. The result is, that there are 18 quadrupeds peculiar to Europe; more than four times as many, to wit 74, peculiar to America; that the first of these 74 weighs more than the whole column of Europeans; and consequently this second table disproves the second member of the assertion, that the animals peculiar to the new world are on a smaller scale, so far as that assertion relied on European animals for support; and it is in full opposition to the theory which makes the animal volume to depend on the circumstances of *heat* and *moisture*.

The third table comprehends those quadrupeds only which are domestic in both countries. That some of these, in some parts of America, have become less than their original stock, is doubtless true; and the reason is very obvious. In a thinly peopled country, the spontaneous productions of the forests and waste fields are sufficient to support indifferently the domestic animals of the farmer, with a very little aid from him in the severest and scarcest season. He therefore finds it more convenient to receive them from the hand of nature in that indifferent state, than to keep up their size by a care and nourishment which would cost him much labor. If, on this low fare, these animals dwindle, it is no more than they do in those parts of Europe where the poverty of the soil, or poverty of the owner, reduces them to the same scanty subsistence. It is the uniform effect of one and the same cause, whether acting on this or that side of the globe. It would be erring therefore against that rule of philosophy, which teaches us to ascribe like effects to like causes, should we impute this diminution of size in America to any imbecility or want of uniformity in the operations of nature. It may be affirmed with truth that, in those countries, and with those individuals of America, where necessity or curiosity has produced equal attention as in Europe to the nourishment of animals, the horses, cattle, sheep and hogs of the one continent are as large as those of the other. There are particular instances, well attested, where individuals of this country have imported good breeders from England, and have improved their size by care in the course of some years. To make a fair comparison between the two countries, it will not answer to bring together animals of what might be deemed the middle or ordinary size of their species; because an error in judging of that middle or ordinary size would vary the result of the comparison. Thus Monsieur D'Aubenton considers a horse of 4 feet 5 inches high and 400 lb weight French, equal to 4 feet 8.6 inches, and 436 lb English, as a middle-sized horse. Such a one is deemed a small horse in America. The extremes must therefore be resorted to. The same anatomist dissected a horse of 5 feet 9 inches height, French measure, equal to 6 feet 1.7 English. This is near 6 inches higher than any horse I have seen; and could it be supposed that I had seen the largest horses in America, the conclusion would be, that ours have diminished, or that we have bred from a smaller stock. In Connecticut and Rhode Island, where the climate is favorable to the production of grass, bullocks have been slaughtered which weighed 2500, 2200, and 2100 lb nett; and those of 1800 lb have been frequent. I have seen a hog weigh 1050 lb after the blood, bowels and hair had been taken from him. Before he was killed an attempt was made to weigh him with a pair of steelyards, graduated to 1200 lb, but he weighed more. Yet this hog was probably not within fifty generations of the European stock. I am well informed of another which weighed 1100 lb gross. Asses have been still more neglected than any other domestic animal in America. They are neither fed nor housed in the most rigorous season of the year. Yet they are larger than those measured by Mons. D'Aubenton, of 3 feet 7¼ inches, 3 feet 4 inches, and 3 feet 2½ inches; the latter weighing only 215.8 lb. These sizes, I suppose, have been produced by the same negligence in Europe, which has produced a like diminution here. Where care has been taken of them on that side of the water, they have been raised to a size bordering on that of the horse; not by the *heat* and *dryness* of the climate, but by good food and shelter. Goats have been also much neglected in America. Yet they are very prolific here, bearing twice or three times a year, and from one to five kids at a birth. Mons. de Buffon has been sensible of a difference in this circumstance in favor of America. But what are their greatest weights I cannot say. A large sheep here weighs 100 lb. I observe Mons. D'Aubenton calls a ram of 62 lb one of the middle size. But to say what are the extremes of growth in these and the other domestic animals of America, would require information of which no one individual is possessed. The weights actually known and stated in the third table preceding, will suffice to shew that we may conclude, on probable grounds, that, with equal food and care, the climate of America will preserve the races of domestic animals as large as the European stock from which they are derived; and consequently that the third member of Mons. de Buffon's assertion, that the domestic animals are subject to degeneration from the climate of America, is as probably wrong as the first and second were certainly so.

That the last part of it is erroneous, which affirms that the species of American quadrupeds are comparatively few, is evident from the tables taken all together. By these it appears that there are an hundred species aboriginal of America. Mons. de Buffon supposes about double that number existing on the whole earth. Of these, Europe, Asia, and Africa, furnish suppose 126; that is, the 26 common to Europe and America, and about 100 which are not in America at all. The American species then are to those of the rest of the earth, as 100 to 126, or 4 to 5. But the residue of the earth being double the extent of America, the exact proportion would have been but as 4 to 8.

Hitherto I have considered this hypothesis as applied to brute animals only, and not in its extension to the man of America, whether aboriginal or transplanted. It is the opinion of Mons. de Buffon that the former furnishes no exception to it:

> Although the savage of the new world is about the same height as man in our world, this does not suffice for him to constitute an exception to the general fact that all living nature has become smaller on that continent. The savage is feeble, and has small organs of generation; he has neither hair nor beard, and no ardor whatever for his female; although swifter than the European because he is better accustomed to running, he is, on the other hand, less strong in body; he is also less sensitive, and yet more timid and cowardly; he has no vivacity, no activity of mind; the activity of his body is less an exercise, a voluntary motion, than a necessary action caused by want; relieve him of hunger and thirst, and you deprive him of the active principle of all his movements; he will rest stupidly upon his legs or lying down entire days. There is no need for seeking further the cause of the isolated mode of life of these savages and their repugnance for society: the most precious spark of the fire of nature has been refused to them; they lack ardor for their females, and consequently have no love for their fellow men: not knowing this strongest and most tender of all affections, their other feelings are also cold and languid; they love their parents and children but little; the most intimate of all ties, the family connection, binds them therefore but loosely together; between family and family there is no tie at all; hence they have no communion, no commonwealth, no state of society. Physical love constitutes their only morality; their heart is icy, their society cold, and their rule

harsh. They look upon their wives only as servants for all work, or as beasts of burden, which they load without consideration with the burden of their hunting, and which they compel without mercy, without gratitude, to perform tasks which are often beyond their strength. They have only few children, and they take little care of them. Everywhere the original defect appears: they are indifferent because they have little sexual capacity, and this indifference to the other sex is the fundamental defect which weakens their nature, prevents its development, and—destroying the very germs of life— uproots society at the same time. Man is here no exception to the general rule. Nature, by refusing him the power of love, has treated him worse and lowered him deeper than any animal.

An afflicting picture indeed, which, for the honor of human nature, I am glad to believe has no original. Of the Indian of South America I know nothing, for I would not honor with the appellation of knowledge what I derive from the fables published of them. These I believe to be just as true as the fables of Aesop. This belief is founded on what I have seen of man, white, red, and black, and what has been written of him by authors, enlightened themselves, and writing amidst an enlightened people. The Indian of North America being more within our reach, I can speak of him somewhat from my own knowledge, but more from the information of others better acquainted with him, and on whose truth and judgment I can rely. From these sources I am able to say, in contradiction to this representation, that he is neither more defective in ardor, nor more impotent with his female, than the white reduced to the same diet and exercise; that he is brave, when an enterprise depends on bravery; education with him making the point of honor consist in the destruction of an enemy by stratagem, and in the preservation of his own person free from injury; or perhaps this is nature; while it is education which teaches us to honor force more than finesse; that he will defend himself against an host of enemies, always choosing to be killed rather than to surrender, though it be to the whites, who he knows will treat him well; that in other situations also he meets death with more deliberation, and endures tortures with a firmness unknown almost to religious enthusiasm with us; that he is affectionate to his children, careful of them, and indulgent in the extreme; that his affections comprehend his other connections, weakening, as with us, from circle to circle, as they recede from the center; that his friendships are strong and faithful to the uttermost extremity; that his sensibility is keen, even the warriors weeping most bitterly on the loss of their children, though in general they endeavor to appear superior to human events; that his vivacity and activity of mind is equal to ours in the same situation; hence his eagerness for hunting, and for games of chance. The women are submitted to unjust drudgery. This I believe is the case with every barbarous people. With such, force is law. The stronger sex therefore imposes on the weaker. It is civilization alone which replaces women in the enjoyment of their natural equality. That first teaches us to subdue the selfish passions, and to respect those rights in others which we value in ourselves. Were we in equal barbarism, our females would be equal drudges. The man with them is less strong than with us, but their woman stronger than ours; and both for the same obvious reason; because our man and their woman is habituated to labor, and formed by it. With both races the sex which is indulged with ease is least athletic. An Indian man is small in the hand and wrist for the same reason for which a sailor is large and strong in the arms and shoulders, and a porter in the legs and thighs. They raise fewer children than we do. The causes of this are to be found, not in a difference of nature, but of circumstance. The women very frequently attending the men in their parties of war and of hunting, child-bearing becomes extremely inconvenient to them. It is said, therefore, that they have learnt the practice of procuring abortion by the use of some vegetable; and that it even extends to prevent conception for a considerable time after. During these parties they are exposed to numerous hazards, to excessive exertions, to the greatest extremities of hunger. Even at their homes the nation depends for food, through a certain part of every year, on the gleanings of the forest: that is, they experience a famine once in every year. With all animals, if the female be badly fed, or not fed at all, her young perish; and if both male and female be reduced to like want, generation becomes less active, less productive. To the obstacles then of want and hazard, which nature has opposed to the multiplication of wild animals, for the purpose of restraining their numbers within certain bounds, those of labor and of voluntary abortion are added with the Indian. No wonder then if they multiply less than we do. Where food is regularly supplied, a single farm will show more of cattle than a whole country of forests can of buffaloes. The same Indian women, when married to white traders, who feed them and their children plentifully and regularly, who exempt them from excessive drudgery, who keep them stationary and unexposed to accident, produce and raise as many children as the white women. Instances are known, under these circumstances, of their rearing a dozen children. An inhuman practice once prevailed in this country of making slaves of the Indians. This practice commenced with the Spaniards with the first discovery of America. It is a fact well known with us, that the Indian women so enslaved produced and raised as numerous families as either the whites or blacks among whom they lived.—It has been said that Indians have less hair than the whites, except on the head. But this is a fact of which fair proof can scarcely be had. With them it is disgraceful to be hairy on the body. They say it likens them to hogs. They therefore pluck the hair as fast as it appears. But the traders who marry their women, and prevail on them to discontinue this practice, say that Nature is the same with them as with the whites. Nor, if the fact be true, is the consequence necessary which has been drawn from it. Negroes have notoriously less hair than the whites; yet they are more ardent. But if cold and moisture be the agents of nature for diminishing the races of animals, how comes she all at once to suspend their operation as to the physical man of the new world, whom the Count acknowledges to be "about the same size as men in our hemisphere," and to let loose their influence on his moral faculties? How has this "combination of the elements and other physical causes, so contrary to the enlargement of animal nature in this new world, these obstacles to the developement and formation of great germs," been arrested and suspended, so as to permit the human body to acquire its just dimensions, and by what inconceivable process has their action been directed on his mind alone? To judge of the truth of this, to form a just estimate of their genius and mental powers, more facts are wanting, and great allowance to be made for those circumstances of their situation which call for a display of particular talents only. This done, we shall probably find that they are formed in mind as well as in body, on the same module with the "Homo sapiens Europaeus." The principles of their society forbidding all compulsion, they are to be led to duty and to enterprise by personal influence and persuasion. Hence eloquence in council, bravery and address in war, become the foundations of all consequence with them. To these acquirements all their faculties are directed. Of their bravery and address in war we have multiplied proofs, because we have been the subjects on which they were exercised. Of their eminence in oratory we have fewer examples, because it is displayed chiefly in their own councils. Some, however, we have of very superior lustre. I may challenge the whole orations or Demosthenes and Cicero, and of any more eminent orator, if Europe has furnished more eminent, to produce a single passage, superior to the speech of Logan, a Mingo chief, to Lord Dunmore, when Governor of this State. And, as a testimony of their talents in this line, I beg leave to introduce it, first stating the incidents necessary for understanding it. In the spring of the year 1774, a robbery and murder were committed on an inhabitant of the frontiers of Virginia, by two Indians of the Shawanee tribe. The neighboring whites, according to their custom, undertook to punish this outrage in a summary way. Col. Cresap, a man infamous for the many murders he had committed on those much-injured people, collected a party, and proceeded down the Kanhaway in quest of vengeance. Unfortunately a canoe of women and children, with one man only, was seen coming from the opposite shore, unarmed, and unsuspecting a hostile attack from the whites. Cresap and his party concealed themselves on the bank of the river, and the moment the canoe reached the shore, singled out their objects, and, at one fire, killed every person in it. This happened to be the family of Logan, who had long been distinguished as a friend of the whites. This unworthy return provoked his vengeance. He accordingly signalized himself in the war which ensued. In the autumn of the same year, a decisive battle was fought at the mouth of the Great Kanhaway, between the collected forces of the Shawanees, Mingoes, and Delawares, and a detachment of the Virginia militia. The Indians were defeated, and sued for peace. Logan however disdained to be seen among the suppliants. But, lest the sincerity of a treaty should be distrusted, from which so distinguished a chief absented himself, he sent by a messenger the following speech to be delivered to Lord Dunmore.

"I appeal to any white man to say if ever he entered Logan's cabin hungry, and he gave him not meat; if ever he came cold and naked, and he clothed him not. During the course of the last long and bloody war, Logan remained idle in his cabin, an advocate for peace. Such was my love for the whites, that my countrymen pointed as they passed, and said, 'Logan is the friend of white men.' I had even thought to have lived with you, but for the injuries of one man. Col. Cresap, the last Spring, in cold blood, and unprovoked, murdered all the relations of Logan, not sparing even my women and children. There runs not a drop of my blood in the veins of any living creature. This called on me for revenge. I have sought it: I have killed many: I have fully glutted vengeance. For my country, I rejoice at the beams of peace. But do not harbor a thought that mine is the joy of fear. Logan never felt fear. He will not turn on his heel to save his life. Who is there to mourn for Logan?—Not one."

Before we condemn the Indians of this continent as wanting genius, we must consider that letters have not yet been introduced among them. Were we to compare them in their present state with the Europeans North of the Alps, when the Roman arms and arts first crossed those mountains, the comparison would be unequal, because, at that time, those parts of Europe were swarming with numbers; because numbers produce emulation, and multiply the chances of improvement, and one improvement begets another. Yet I may safely ask, How many good poets, how many able mathematicians, how many great inventors in arts or sciences, had Europe North of the Alps then produced? And it was sixteen centuries after this before a Newton could be formed. I do not mean to deny that there are varieties in the race of man, distinguished by their powers both of body and mind. I believe there are, as I see to be the case in the races of other animals. I only mean to suggest a doubt, whether the bulk and faculties of animals depend on the side of the Atlantic on which their food happens to grow, or which furnishes the elements of which they are compounded? Whether nature has enlisted herself as a Cis or Trans-Atlantic partisan? I am induced to suspect there has been more eloquence than sound reasoning displayed in support of this theory; that it is one of those cases where the judgment has been seduced by a glowing pen; and whilst I render every tribute of honor and esteem to the celebrated Zoologist, who has added, and is still adding, so many precious things to the treasures of science, I must doubt whether in this instance he has not cherished error also, by lending her for a moment his vivid imagination and bewitching language.

So far the Count de Buffon has carried this new theory of the tendency of nature to belittle her productions on this side the Atlantic. Its application to the race of whites, transplanted from Europe, remained for the Abbé Rayanal.[28] "It is astonishing," he says, "that America has not produced a good poet, one able mathematician, one man of genius in a single art or a single science." When we shall have existed as a people as long as the Greeks did before they produced a Homer, the Romans a Virgil, the French a Racine and Voltaire, the English a Shakespeare and Milton, should this reproach be still true, we will enquire from what unfriendly causes it has proceeded, that the other countries of Europe and quarters of the earth shall not have inscribed any name in the roll of poets. But neither has America produced "one able mathematician, one man of genius in a single art or a single science." In war we have produced a Washington, whose memory

---

[28]Guillaume Thomas François Raynal, *Histoire Philosophique et Politique des Establissemens et du Commerce des Europééns dans le deux Indes,* 4 vols. (Amsterdam, 1770).

will be adored while liberty shall have votaries, whose name will triumph over time, and will in future ages assume its just station among the most celebrated worthies of the world, when that wretched philosophy shall be forgotten, which would have arranged him among the degeneracies of nature. In physics we have produced a Franklin, than whom no one of the present age has made more important discoveries, nor has enriched philosophy with more or more ingenious solutions of the phenomena of nature. We have supposed Mr. Rittenhouse[29] second to no astronomer living; that in genius he must be the first, because he is self-taught. As an artist he has exhibited as great a proof of mechanical genius as the world has ever produced. He has not indeed made a world; but he has by imitation approached nearer its Maker than any man who has lived from the creation to this day. As in philosophy and war, so in government, in oratory, in painting, in the plastic art, we might show that America, though but a child of yesterday, has already given hopeful proofs of genius, as well of the nobler kinds, which arouse the best feelings of man, which call him into action, which substantiate his freedom, and conduct him to happiness, as of the subordinate, which serve to amuse him only. We therefore suppose that this reproach is as unjust as it is unkind; and that of the geniuses which adorn the present age, America contributes its full share. For comparing it with those countries, where genius is most cultivated, where are the most excellent models for art, and scaffoldings for the attainment of science, as France and England for instance, we calculate thus. The United States contain three millions of inhabitants; France twenty millions; and the British islands ten. We produce a Washington, a Franklin, a Rittenhouse. France then should have half a dozen in each of these lines, and Great Britain half that number, equally eminent. It may be true, that France has: we are but just becoming acquainted with her, and our acquaintance so far gives us high ideas of the genius of her inhabitants. It would be injuring too many of them to name particularly a Voltaire, a Buffon, the constellation of Encyclopedists, the Abbé Raynal himself, &c., &c. We therefore have reason to believe she can produce her full quota of genius. The present war having so long cut off all communication with Great Britain, we are not able to make a fair estimate of the state of science in that country. The spirit in which she wages war is the only sample before our eyes, and that does not seem the legitimate offspring either

[29]David Rittenhouse (1732–96) instrument maker and astronomer, had fashioned a working orrery, or model of the planetary system, in 1771.

of science or of civilization. The sun of her glory is fast descending to the horizon. Her philosophy has crossed the Channel, her freedom the Atlantic, and herself seems passing to that awful dissolution, whose issue is not given human foresight to scan.*

Having given a sketch of our minerals, vegetables, and quadrupeds, and being led by a proud theory to make a comparison of the latter with those of Europe, and to extend it to the Man of America, both aboriginal and emigrant, I will proceed to the remaining articles comprehended under the present query.

Between ninety and an hundred of our birds have been described by Catesby. His drawings are better as to form and attitude, than coloring, which is generally too high. They are the following:

[Jefferson here lists 91 species of birds also listed in Linnaeus or Catesby's works, plus 33 others, ending the list with the remark: "And doubtless many others which have not yet been described and classed."]

To this catalogue of our indigenous animals, I will add a short account of an anomaly of nature, taking place sometimes in the race of negroes brought from Africa, who, though black themselves, have, in rare instances, white children, called Albinos. I have known four of these myself, and have faithful accounts of three others. The circumstances in which all the individuals agree are these. They are of a pallid cadaverous white, untinged with red, without any colored spots or seams; their hair of the same kind of white, short, coarse, and

---

*In a later edition of the Abbé Raynal's work, he has withdrawn his censure from that part of the new world inhabited by the Federo-Americans; but has left it still on the other parts. North America has always been more accessible to strangers than South. If he was mistaken then as to the former, he may be so as to the latter. The glimmerings which reach us from South America enable us only to see that its inhabitants are held under the accumulated pressure of slavery, superstition and ignorance. Whenever they shall be able to rise under this weight, and to show themselves to the rest of the world, they will probably show they are like the rest of the world. We have not yet sufficient evidence that there are more *lakes* and *fogs* in South America than in other parts of the earth. Amer. Vesp., 115. Quivi il cielo e l'aere è rare volte adombrato dalle nuvole, quasi sempre i giorni sono sereni? As little do we know what would be their operation on the mind of man. That country has been visited by Spaniards and Portuguese chiefly, and almost exclusively. These, going from a country of the old world remarkably dry in its soil and climate, fancied there were more lakes and fogs in South America than in Europe. An inhabitant of Ireland, Sweden, or Finland, would have formed the contrary opinion. Had South America then been discovered and seated by a people from a fenny country, it would probably have been represented as much drier than the old world. A patient pursuit of facts, and cautious combination and comparison of them, is the drudgery to which man is subjected by his Maker, if he wishes to attain sure knowledge. [Jefferson's note.]

curled as is that of the negro; all of them well formed, strong, healthy, perfect in their senses, except that of sight, and born of parents who had no mixture of white blood. Three of these Albinos were sisters, having two other full sisters, who were black. The youngest of the three was killed by lightning, at twelve years of age. The eldest died at about 27 years of age, in childbed, with her second child. The middle one is now alive in health, and has issue, as the eldest had, by a black man, which issue was black. They are uncommonly shrewd, quick in their apprehensions and in reply. Their eyes are in a perpetual tremulous vibration, very weak, and much affected by the sun; but they see better in the night than we do. They are of the property of Col. Skipwith, of Cumberland. The fourth is a negro woman, whose parents came from Guinea, and had three other children, who were of their own color. She is freckled, her eye sight so weak, that she is obliged to wear a bonnet in the summer; but it is better in the night than day. She had an Albino child by a black man. It died at the age of a few weeks. These were the property of Col. Carter, of Albemarle. A sixth instance is a woman of the property of Mr. Butler, near Petersburgh. She is stout and robust, has issue a daughter, jet black, by a black man. I am not informed as to her eye sight. The seventh instance is of a male belonging to a Mr. Lee, of Cumberland. His eyes are tremulous and weak. He is tall of stature, and now advanced in years. He is the only male of the Albinos which have come within my information. Whatever be the cause of the disease in the skin, or in its coloring matter, which produces this change, it seems more incident to the female than male sex. To these I may add the mention of a negro man within my own knowledge, born black, and of black parents; on whose chin, when a boy, a white spot appeared. This continued to increase till he became a man, by which time it had extended over his chin, lips, one cheek, the under jaw and neck on that side. It is of the Albino white, without any mixture of red, and has for several years been stationary. He is robust and healthy, and the change of color was not accompanied with any sensible disease, either general or topical.

Of our fish and insects there has been nothing like a full description or collection. More of them are described in Catesby than in any other work. Many also are to be found in Sir Hans Sloane's Jamaica, as being common to that and this country.[30] The honey bee is not a native of our continent. Marcgrave indeed mentions a species of

[30]Sir Hans Sloane, *A Voyage to the Islands Madera, Barbadoes, Nieves, St. Christopher's, and Jamaica,* 2 vols. (London, 1707–25).

honey bee in Brasil.[31] But this has no sting, and is therefore different from the one we have, which resembles perfectly that of Europe. The Indians concur with us in the tradition that it was brought from Europe; but when, and by whom, we know not. The bees have generally extended themselves into the country, a little in advance of the white settlers. The Indians, therefore, call them the white man's fly, and consider their approach as indicating the approach of the settlements of the whites. A question here occurs, how far northwardly have these insects been found? That they are unknown in Lapland, I infer from Scheffer's information that the Laplanders eat the pine bark, prepared in a certain way, instead of those things sweetened with sugar. Certainly, if they had honey, it would be a better substitute for sugar than any preparation of the pine bark. Kalm tells us the honey bee cannot live through the Winter in Canada. They furnish then an additional proof of the remarkable fact first observed by the Count de Buffon, and which has thrown such a blaze of light on the field of natural history, that no animals are found in both continents, but those which are able to bear the cold of those regions where they probably join.

QUERY VII: CLIMATE

A Notice of All What Can Increase the Progress of Human Knowledge?

Under the latitude of this query, I will presume it not improper nor unacceptable to furnish some data for estimating the climate of Virginia. Journals of observations on the quantity of rain, and degree of heat, being lengthy, confused, and too minute to produce general and distinct ideas, I have taken five years observations, to wit, from 1772 to 1777, made in Williamsburgh and its neighborhood, have reduced them to an average for every month in the year, and stated those averages in the following table, adding an analytical view of the winds during the same period.

The rains of every month, (as of January for instance) through the whole period of years, were added separately, and an average drawn from them. The coolest and warmest point of the same day in each year of the period were added separately, and an average of the

---

[31] Willem Piso [and Georg Margraf], *Historia Naturalis Brasilae,* 2 vols. (Leyden and Amsterdam, 1648).

	Fall of rain, &c. in inches.	Leaſt & greateſt daily heat by Farenheit's thermometer.		WINDS.								
				N.	N. E.	E.	S. E.	S.	S. W.	W.	N. W.	Total.
Jan.	3.192	$38\frac{1}{2}$ to	44	73	47	32	10	11	78	40	46	337
Feb.	2.049	41	$47\frac{1}{2}$	61	52	24	11	4	63	30	31	276
Mar.	3.95	48	$54\frac{1}{2}$	49	44	38	28	14	83	29	33	318
April	3.68	56	$62\frac{1}{2}$	35	44	54	19	9	58	18	20	257
May	2.871	63	$70\frac{1}{2}$	27	36	62	23	7	74	32	20	281
June	3.751	$71\frac{1}{2}$	$78\frac{1}{4}$	22	34	43	24	13	81	25	25	267
July	4.497	77	$82\frac{1}{2}$	41	44	75	15	7	95	32	19	328
Aug.	9.153	$76\frac{1}{4}$	81	43	52	40	30	9	103	27	30	334
Sept.	4.761	$69\frac{1}{2}$	$74\frac{1}{4}$	70	60	51	18	10	81	18	37	345
Oct.	3.633	$61\frac{1}{4}$	$66\frac{1}{2}$	52	77	64	15	6	56	23	34	327
Nov.	2.617	$47\frac{3}{4}$	$53\frac{1}{2}$	74	21	20	14	9	63	35	58	294
Dec.	2.877	43	$48\frac{3}{4}$	64	37	18	16	10	91	42	56	334
Total.	47.038	8.A.M.	4.P.M.	611	548	521	223	109	926	351	409	3698

Figure 8. Table of rainfall and temperature in Virginia from 1787 edition of *Notes on the State of Virginia.*
Benjamin Franklin Collection, Yale University Library.

greatest cold and greatest heat of that day was formed. From the averages of every day in the month, a general average for the whole month was formed. The point from which the wind blew was observed two or three times in every day. These observations, in the month of January for instance, through the whole period, amounted to 337. At 73 of these the wind was from the North; at 47 from the Northeast, &c. So that it will be easy to see in what proportion each wind usually prevails in each month; or, taking the whole year, the total of observations through the whole period having been 3698, it will be observed that 611 of them were from the North, 558 from the Northeast, &c.

Though by this table it appears we have on an average 47 inches of rain annually, which is considerably more than usually falls in Europe, yet from the information I have collected, I suppose we have a much greater proportion of sunshine here than there. Perhaps it will be found there are twice as many cloudy days in the middle parts of Europe as in the United States of America. I mention the middle parts of Europe, because my information does not extend to its northern or southern parts.

In an extensive country, it will, of course, be expected that the climate is not the same in all its parts. It is remarkable that, proceeding on the same parallel of latitude westwardly, the climate becomes colder in like manner as when you proceed northwardly. This continues to be the case till you attain the summit of the Alleghaney, which is the highest land between the ocean and the Missisipi. From thence, descending in the same latitude to the Missisipi, the change reverses; and, if we may believe travelers, it becomes warmer there than it is in the same latitude on the sea side. Their testimony is strengthened by the vegetables and animals which subsist and multiply there naturally, and do not on our sea coast. Thus Catalpas grow spontaneously on the Missisipi, as far as the latitude of 37°, and reeds as far as 38°. Perroquets even winter on the Sioto, in the 39th degree of latitude. In the Summer of 1779, when the thermometer was at 90° at Monticello, and 96 at Williamsburgh, it was 110° at Kaskaskia. Perhaps the mountain, which overhangs this village on the North side, may, by its reflection, have contributed somewhat to produce this heat. The difference of temperature of the air at the sea coast, or on Chesapeak bay, and at the Alleghaney, has not been ascertained; but contemporary observations, made at Williamsburgh; or in its neighborhood, and at Monticello, which is on the most eastern ridge of mountains, called the South West, where they are intersected by the Rivanna, have furnished a ratio by which that difference may in some degree be conjectured. These observations make the difference between Williamsburgh and the nearest mountains, at the position before mentioned, to be on an average 6⅛ degrees of Fahrenheit's thermometer. Some allowance however is to be made for the difference of latitude between these two places, the latter being 38° 8′ 17″, which is 52′ 22″ North of the former. By cotemporary observations of between five and six weeks, the averaged and almost unvaried difference of the height of mercury in the barometer, at those two places, was .784 of an inch, the atmosphere at Monticello being so much the lightest, that is to say, about 1/37 of its whole weight. It should be observed, however, that the hill of Monticello is of 500 feet perpendicular height above the river which washes its base. This position being nearly central between our northern and southern boundaries, and between the bay and Alleghaney, may be considered as furnishing the best average of the temperature of our climate. Williamsburgh is much too near the Southeastern corner to give a fair idea of our general temperature.

But a more remarkable difference is in the winds which prevail in the different parts of the country. The following table exhibits a comparative view of the winds prevailing at Williamsburgh, and at Monticello. It is formed by reducing nine months observations at Monticello to four principal points, to wit, the northeast, southeast, southwest, and northwest: these points being perpendicular to, or parallel with our coast, mountains and rivers; and by reducing, in like manner, an equal number of observations, to wit, 421, from the preceding table of winds at Williamsburgh, taking them proportionably from every point:

	N. E.	S. E.	S. W.	N. W.	Total.
Williamsburgh	127	61	132	101	421
Monticello	32	91	126	172	421

By this it may be seen that the Southwest wind prevails equally at both places; that the Northeast is, next to this, the principal wind towards the sea coast, and the Northwest is the predominant wind at the mountains. The difference between these two winds to sensation, and in fact, is very great. The Northeast is loaded with vapor, insomuch that the salt-makers have found that their crystals would not shoot while that blows; it brings a distressing chill, is heavy and oppressive to the spirits; the Northwest is dry, cooling, elastic and animating. The Eastern and Southeastern breezes come on generally in the afternoon. They have advanced into the country very sensibly within the memory of people now living. They formerly did not penetrate far above Williamsburgh. They are now frequent at Richmond, and every now and then reach the mountains. They deposit most of their moisture, however, before they get that far. As the lands become more cleared, it is probable they will extend still further westward.

Going out into the open air, in the temperate, and in the warm months of the year, we often meet with bodies of warm air, which, passing by us in two or three seconds, do not afford time to the most sensible thermometer to seize their temperature. Judging from my feelings only, I think they approach the ordinary heat of the human body. Some of them perhaps go a little beyond it. They are of about 20 or 30 feet diameter horizontally. Of their height we have no experience; but probably they are globular volumes wafted or rolled along with the wind. But whence taken, where found, or how generated? They are not to be ascribed to Volcanos, because we have none. They do not happen in the winter when the farmers kindle large fires in clearing up their grounds. They are not confined to the spring season, when we have fires which traverse whole counties, consuming the leaves which have fallen from the trees. And they are too frequent and general to be ascribed to accidental fires. I am persuaded their cause must be sought for in the atmosphere itself, to aid us in which I know but of these constant circumstances: a dry air, a temperature as warm at least as that of the spring or autumn, and a moderate current of wind. They are most frequent about sunset; rare in the middle parts of the day; and I do not recollect having ever met with them in the morning.

The variation in the weight of our atmosphere, as indicated by the barometer, is not equal to two inches of mercury. During twelve months observation at Williamsburgh, the extremes were 29, and 30.86 inches, the difference being 1.86 of an inch; and in nine months, during which the height of the mercury was noted at Monticello, the extremes were 28.48 and 29.69 inches, the variation being 1.21 of an inch. A gentleman, who has observed his barometer many years, assures me it has never varied two inches. Cotemporary observations, made at Monticello and Williamsburgh, proved the variations in the weight of air to be simultaneous and corresponding in these two places.

Our changes from heat to cold, and cold to heat, are very sudden and great. The mercury in Fahrenheit's thermometer has been known to descend from 92° to 47° in thirteen hours.

It is taken for granted, that the preceding table of averaged heat will not give a false idea on this subject, as it proposes to state only the ordinary heat and cold of each month, and not those which are extraordinary. At Williamsburgh in August, 1766, the mercury in Fahrenheit's thermometer was at 98°, corresponding with 29½ of Reaumur. At the same place in January, 1780, it was at 6°, corresponding with 11½ below 0 of Reaumur. I believe these may be considered to be nearly the extremes of heat and cold in that part of the country. The latter may most certainly, as at that time York River, at York Town, was frozen over, so that people walked across it; a circumstance which proves it to have been colder than the Winter of 1740, 1741, usually called the cold Winter, when York River did not freeze over at that place. In the same season of 1780, Chesapeak Bay was solid, from its head to the mouth of Patowmac. At Annapolis, where it is 5¼ miles over between the nearest points of land, the ice was from 5 to 7 inches thick quite across, so that loaded carriages went over on it. Those, our extremes of heat and cold, of 6° and 98° were indeed very distressing to us, and were thought to put the extent of the human constitution to considerable trial. Yet a Siberian would have considered them as scarcely a sensible variation. At Jenniseitz in that country, in latitude of 58° 27′, we are told that the cold in 1735 sunk the mercury by Fahrenheit's scale to 126° below nothing; and the inhabitants of the same country use stove rooms two or three times a week, in which they stay two hours at a time, the atmosphere of which raises the mercury to 135° above nothing. Late experiments shew that the human body will exist in rooms heated to 140° of Reaumur, equal to 347° of Farenheit, and 135° above boiling water. The hottest point of the 24 hours is about 4 o'clock, P.M. and the dawn of day the coldest.

The access of frost in Autumn, and its recess in the spring, do not seem to depend merely on the degree of cold; much less on the air's being at the freezing point. White frosts are frequent when the thermometer is at 47°, have killed young plants of Indian corn at 48°, and have been known at 54°. Black frost, and even ice, have been produced at 38½°, which is 6½ degrees above the freezing point. That other circumstances must be combined with the cold to produce frost, is evident from this also, that on the higher parts of mountains, where it is absolutely colder than in the plains on which they stand, frosts do not appear so early by a considerable space of time in autumn, and go off sooner in the Spring, than in the plains. I have known frosts so severe as to kill the hiccory trees round about Monticello, and yet not injure the tender fruit blossoms then in bloom on the top and higher parts of the mountain; and, in the course of 40 years, during which it has been settled, there have been but two instances of a general loss of fruit on it; while, in the circumjacent country, the fruit has escaped but twice in the last seven years. The plants of tobacco, which grow from the roots of those which have been cut off in the Summer, are frequently green here at Christmas. This privilege against the frost is undoubtedly combined with the want of dew on the mountains. That the dew is very rare on their higher parts I may say with certainty, from 12 years observations, having scarcely ever, during that time, seen an unequivocal proof of its existence on them at all during summer. Severe frosts in the depth of Winter prove that the region of dews extends higher in that season than the tops of the mountains; but certainly, in the summer season, the vapors, by the time they attain that height, are become so attenuated as not to subside and form a dew when the sun retires.

The weavil has not yet ascended the high mountains.

A more satisfactory estimate of our climate to some may perhaps be formed, by noting the plants which grow here, subject however to be killed by our severest colds. These are the fig, pomegranate, artichoke, and European walnut. In mild Winters lettuce and endive require no shelter; but generally they need a slight covering. I do not know that the want of long moss, reed, myrtle, swamp laurel, holly and cypress, in the upper country, proceeds from a greater degree of cold, nor that they were ever killed with any degree of cold in the lower country. The aloe lived in Williamsburgh in the open air through the severe Winter of 1779, 1780.

A change in our climate, however, is taking place very sensibly. Both heats and colds are become much more moderate within the memory even of the middle-aged. Snows are less frequent and less deep. They do not often lie below the mountains more than one, two or three days, and very rarely a week. They are remembered to have been formerly frequent, deep, and of long continuance. The elderly inform me the earth used to be covered with snow about three months in every year. The rivers, which then seldom failed to freeze over in the course of the winter, scarcely ever do so now. This change has produced an unfortunate fluctuation between heat and cold, in the spring of the year, which is very fatal to fruits. From the year 1741 to 1769, an interval of twenty-eight years, there was no instance of fruit killed by the frost in the neighborhood of Monticello. An intense cold, produced by constant snows, kept the buds locked up till the sun could obtain, in the Spring of the year, so fixed an ascendancy as to dissolve these snows, and protect the buds, during their development, from every danger of returning cold. The accumulated snows of the winter remaining to be dissolved all together in the Spring, produced those overflowings of our rivers, so frequent then, and so rare now.

Having had occasion to mention the particular situation of Monticello for other purposes, I will just take notice that its elevation affords an opportunity of seeing a phenomenon which is rare at land, though frequent at sea. The seamen call it *looming*. Philosophy is as yet in the rear of the seamen, for so far from having accounted for it, she has not given it a name. Its principal effect is to make distant objects appear larger, in opposition to the general law of vision, by which they are diminished. I knew an instance, at York town, from whence the water prospect eastwardly is without termination, wherein a canoe with three men, at a great distance, was taken for a ship with its three masts. I am little acquainted with the phenomenon as it shows itself at sea; but at Monticello it is familiar. There is a solitary mountain about 40 miles off, in the south, whose natural shape, as presented to view there, is a regular cone; but, by the effect of looming, it sometimes subsides almost totally into the horizon; sometimes it rises more acute and more elevated; sometimes it is hemispherical; and sometimes its sides are perpendicular, its top flat, and as broad as its base. In short, it assume at times the most whimsical shapes, and all these perhaps successively in the same morning. The Blue Ridge of mountains comes into view, in the Northeast, at about 100 miles distance, and, approaching in a direct line, passes by within 20 miles, and goes off to the Southwest. This phenomenon begin to show itself on these mountains, at about 50 miles distance, and continues beyond that as far as they are seen. I remark no particular state, either in the weight, moisture, or heat of the atmosphere, necessary to produce this. The only constant circumstances are, its appearance in the morning only, and on objects at least 40 or 50 miles distant. In this latter circumstance, if not in both, it differs from the looming on the water. Refraction will not account for this metamorphosis. That only changes the proportions of length and breadth, base and altitude, preserving the general outlines. Thus it may make a circle appear elliptical, raise or depress a cone, but by none of its laws, as yet developed, will it make a circle appear a square, or a cone a sphere.

QUERY VIII: POPULATION

The Number of Its Inhabitants?

The following table shows the number of persons imported for the establishment of our colony in its infant state, and the census of inhabitants at different periods, extracted from our historians and public records, as particularly as I have had opportunities and leisure to examine them. Successive lines in the same year show successive periods of time in that year. I have stated the census in two different columns, the whole inhabitants having been sometimes numbered, and sometimes the *tythes* only.[32] This term, with us, includes the free males above 16 years of age, and slaves above that age of both sexes. A further examination of our records would render this history of our population much more satisfactory and perfect, by furnishing a greater number of intermediate terms:

YEARS.	SETTLERS IMPORTED.	CENSUS OF INHABITANTS.	CENSUS OF TYTHES.
1607	100		
		40	
	120		
1608		130	
	70		
1609		490	

[32]taxable population.

YEARS.	SETTLERS IMPORTED.	CENSUS OF INHABITANTS.	CENSUS OF TYTHES.
	16		
		60	
1610	150		
		200	
1611	3 ship loads		
	300		
1612	80		
1617		400	
1618	200		
	40		
		600	
1619	1216		
1621	1300		
1622		3800	
		2500	
1628		3000	
1632			2000
1644			4822
1645			5000
1652			7000
1654			7209
1700			22,000
1748			82,100
1759			105,000
1772			153,000
1782		567,614	

Those, however, which are here stated, will enable us to calculate, with a considerable degree of precision, the rate at which we have increased. During the infancy of the colony, while numbers were small, wars, importations, and other accidental circumstances render the progression fluctuating and irregular. By the year 1654, however, it becomes tolerably uniform, importations having in a great measure ceased from the dissolution of the company, and the inhabitants become too numerous to be sensibly affected by Indian wars. Beginning at that period, therefore, we find that from thence to the year 1772, our tythes had increased from 7209 to 153,000. The whole term being of 118 years, yields a duplication once in every 27¼ years. The intermediate enumerations taken in 1700, 1748, and 1759, furnish proofs of the uniformity of this progression. Should this rate of increase continue, we shall have between six and seven millions of inhabitants within 95 years. If we suppose our country to be bounded, at some future day, by the meridian of the mouth of the Great Kanhaway, (within which it has been before conjectured, are 64,491 square miles,) there will then be 100 inhabitants for every square mile, which is nearly the state of population in the British islands.

Here I will beg leave to propose a doubt. The present desire of America is to produce rapid population by as great importations of foreigners as possible. But is this founded in good policy? The advantage proposed is the multiplication of numbers. Now let us suppose (for example only) that in this State we could double our numbers in one year by the importation of foreigners; and this is a greater accession than the most sanguine advocate for emigration has a right to expect. Then I say, beginning with a double stock, we shall attain any given degree of population only 27 years and 3 months sooner than if we proceed on our single stock. If we propose four millions and a half as a competent population for this State, we should be 54½ years attaining it, could we at once double our numbers; and 81¾ years, if we rely on natural propagation, as may be seen by the following table:

	PROCEEDING ON OUR PRESENT STOCK.	PROCEEDING ON A DOUBLE STOCK.
1781	567,614	1,135,228
1808¼	1,135,228	2,270,456
1835½	2,270,456	4,540,912
1862¾	4,450,912	

In the first column are stated periods of 27¼ years; in the second are our numbers, at each period, as they will be if we proceed on our actual stock; and in the third are what they would be, at the same periods, were we to set out from the double of our present stock. I have taken the term of four millions and a half of inhabitants for example's sake only. Yet I am persuaded it is a greater number than the country spoken of, considering how much inarable land it contains, can clothe and feed, without a material change in the quality of their diet. But are there no inconveniences to be thrown into the scale against the advantage expected from a multiplication of numbers by the importation of foreigners? It is for the happiness of those united in society to harmonize as much as possible in matters which they must of necessity transact together. Civil government being the sole object of forming societies, its administration must be conducted by common consent. Every species of government has its specific principles. Ours perhaps are more peculiar than those of any other in the universe. It is a composition of the freest principles of the English constitution, with others derived from natural right and natural reason. To these nothing can be more opposed than the maxims of absolute monarchies. Yet, from such, we are to expect the greatest number of emigrants. They will bring with them the principles of the governments they leave, imbibed in their early youth; or, if able to throw them off, it will be in exchange for an unbounded licentiousness, passing, as is usual, from one extreme to another. It would be a miracle were they to stop precisely at the point of temperate liberty. These principles, with their language, they will transmit to their children. In proportion to their numbers, they will share with us the legislation. They will infuse into it their spirit, warp and bias its direction, and render it a heterogeneous, incoherent, distracted mass. I may appeal to experience, during the present contest, for a verification of these conjectures. But, if they be not certain in event, are they not possible, are they not probable? Is it not safer to wait with patience 27 years and 3 months longer, for the attainment of any degree of population desired, or expected? May not our government be more homogeneous, more peaceable, more durable? Suppose 20 millions of republican Americans thrown all of a sudden into France, what would be the condition of that kingdom? If it would be more turbulent, less happy, less strong, we may believe that the addition of half a million of foreigners to our present numbers would produce a similar effect here. If they come of themselves, they are entitled to all the rights of citizenship; but I doubt the expediency of inviting them by extraordinary encouragements. I mean not that these doubts should be extended to the importation of useful artificers. The policy of that measure depends on very different considerations. Spare no expense in obtaining them. They will after a while go to the plough and the hoe; but, in the mean time, they will teach us something we do not know. It is not so in agriculture. The indifferent state of that among us does not proceed from a want of knowledge merely; it is from our having such quantities of land to waste as we please. In Europe the object is to make the most of their land, labor being abundant: here it is to make the most of our labor, land being abundant.

It will be proper to explain how the numbers for the year 1782 have been obtained; as it was not from a perfect census of the inhabitants.

It will at the same time develope the proportion between the free inhabitants and slaves. The following return of taxable articles for that year was given in:

53,289	free males above 21 years of age.
211,698	slaves of all ages and sexes.
238,766	not distinguished in the returns, but said to be tithe-able slaves.
195,439	horses.
609,734	cattle.
5,126	wheels of riding carriages.
191	taverns.

There were no returns from the 8 counties of Lincoln, Jefferson, Fayette, Monongalia, Yohogania, Ohio, Northampton, and York. To find the number of slaves which should have been returned instead of the 23,766 titheables, we must mention that some observations on a former census had given reason to believe that the numbers above and below 16 years of age were equal. The double of this number, therefore, to wit, 47,532 must be added to 211,698, which will give us 259,230 slaves of all ages and sexes. To find the number of free inhabitants, we must repeat the observation, that those above and below 16 are nearly equal. But as the number 53,289 omits the males between 16 and 21, we must supply them from conjecture. On a former experiment it had appeared that about one-third of our militia, that is, of the males between 16 and 50, were unmarried. Knowing how early marriage takes place here, we shall not be far wrong in supposing that the unmarried part of our militia are those between 16 and 21. If there by young men who do not marry till after 21, there are as many who marry before that age. But as the men above 50 were not included in the militia, we will suppose the unmarried, or those between 16 and 21, to be one-fourth of the whole number above 16, then we have the following calculation:

53,289	free males above 21 years of age.
17,763	free males between 16 and 21.
71,052	free males under 16.
142,104	free females of all ages.
284,208	free inhabitants of all ages.
259,230	slaves of all ages.

543,438 inhabitants, exclusive of the 8 counties from which were no returns. In these 8 counties in the years 1779 and 1780 were 3,161 militia. Say then,

3,161   free males above the age of 16.
3,161   ditto under 16.
6,322   free females.

12,644 free inhabitants in these 8 counties. To find the number of slaves, say, as 284,208 to 259,230, so is the 12,644 to 11,532. Adding the third of these numbers to the first, and the fourth to the second, we have,

296,852   free inhabitants.
270,762   slaves.

567,614 inhabitants of every age, sex, and condition. But 296,852, the number of free inhabitants, are to 270,762, the number of slaves, nearly as 11 to 10. Under the mild treatment our slaves experience, and their wholesome, though coarse food, this blot in our country increases as fast, or faster, than the whites. During the regal government, we had at one time obtained a law, which imposed such a duty on the importation of slaves as amounted nearly to a prohibition, when one inconsiderate assembly, placed under a peculiarity of circumstance, repealed the law. This repeal met a joyful sanction from the then sovereign, and no devices, no expedients, which could ever after be attempted by subsequent assemblies, and they seldom met without attempting them, could succeed in getting the royal assent to a renewal of the duty. In the very first session held under the republican government, the assembly passed a law for the perpetual prohibition of the importation of slaves. This will, in some measure, stop the increase of this great political and moral evil, while the minds of our citizens may be ripening for a complete emancipation of human nature.

QUERY IX: MILITARY FORCE

The Number and Condition of the Militia and Regular Troops, and Their Pay?

The following is a state of the militia, taken from returns of 1780 and 1781, except in those counties marked with an asterisk, the returns from which are somewhat older.

Every able-bodied freeman, between the ages of 16 and 50, is enrolled in the militia. Those of every county are formed into companies, and these again into one or more battalions, according to the numbers in the county. They are commanded by colonels, and other subordinate officers, as in the regular service. In every county is a county-lieutenant, who commands the whole militia of his county, but ranks only as a colonel in the field. We have no general officers always existing. These are appointed occasionally, when an invasion or insurrection happens, and their commission determines with the occasion. The governor is head of the military, as well as civil power. The law requires every militia-man to provide himself with the arms usual in the regular service. But this injunction was always indifferently complied with, and the arms they had have been so frequently called for to arm the regulars, that in the lower parts of the country they are entirely disarmed. In the middle country a fourth or fifth part of them may have such firelocks as they had provided to destroy the noxious animals which infest their farms; and on the western side of the Blue Ridge they are generally armed with rifles. The pay of our militia, as well as of our regulars, is that of the Continental regulars. The condition of our regulars, of whom we have none but Continentals, and part of a battalion of state troops, is so constantly on the change that a state of it at this day would not be its state a month hence. It is much the same with the condition of the other Continental troops, which is well enough known.

QUERY X: MARINE FORCE

The Marine?

Before the present invasion of this State by the British under the command of General Phillips, we had three vessels of 16 guns, one of 14, five small galleys, and two or three armed boats. They were generally so badly manned as seldom to be in condition for service. Since the perfect possession of our rivers assumed by the enemy, I believe we are left with a single armed boat only.

QUERY XI: ABORIGINES

A Description of the Indians Established in That State?

When the first effectual settlement of our Colony was made, which was in 1607, the country from the sea-coast to the mountains, and from Patowmac to the most southern waters of James river, was occupied by upwards of forty different tribes of Indians. Of these the *Powhatans,* the *Mannahoacs,* and *Monacans,* were the most powerful. Those between the sea-coast and falls of the rivers, were in amity with

Military. Qu. 9. The number & condition of the militia & regular troops, & their pay.

The following is a state of the militia taken from returns of 1780 & 1781. except in those counties marked with an asterisk. the returns from which are somewhat older. [Then follows the table.]

Situation	Counties	Militia	Situation	Counties	Militia
Westward of the Alleghaney 4468	Lincoln	800	Between James river and Carolina 6959	Greenesville	500
	Jefferson	300		Dinwiddie	*750
	Fayette	156		Chesterfield	655
	Ohio			Prince George	302
	Monongalia	*1000		Surry	380
	Washington	*929		Sussex	*700
	Montgomery	1071		Southampton	874
	Green-briar	502		Isle of Wight	*600
Between the Alleghaney and Blue-ridge 7673	Hampshire	930		Nansemond	*644
	Berkeley	*1100		Norfolk	*880
	Frederick	1143		Princess Anne	*594
	Shenando	*925	Between James and York rivers 3009	Henrico	619
	Rockingham	875		Hanover	796
	Augusta	1375		New Kent	*418
	Rockbridge	*625		Charles City	286
	Botetourt	700		James City	235
Between the Blue ridge and Tide waters 16928	Loudoun	1746		Williamsburg	129
	Fauquier	1078		York	*244
	Culpeper	1513		Warwick	*100
	Spotsylvania	480		Elizabeth city	182
	Orange	600	Between York and Rappahanock 2250	Caroline	805
	Louisa	603		King William	436
	Goochland	*550		King & Queen	*500
	Fluvanna	*296		Essex	468
	Albemarle	873		Middlesex	*210
	Amherst	896		Gloucester	850
	Buckingham	625		Fairfax	652
	Bedford	1300		Prince William	614
	Henry	1004		Stafford	*500
	Pittsylvania	*725		King George	483
	Halifax	*1129		Richmond	412
	Charlotte	612		Westmoreland	526
	Prince Edward	589		Northumberland	630
	Cumberland	408		Lancaster	302
	Powhatan	330	On the Eastern Shore 1926	Accomac	*1208
	Amelia	*1125		Northampton	*430
	Lunenburg	677	Whole militia of the State		49,971
	Mecklenburg	1100			
	Brunswic	559			

Every able bodied freeman between the ages of 16. and 50. is enrolled in the militia. those of every county are formed into companies, & these again into one or more battalions, according to the number in the county. they are commanded by colonels & other subordinate officers, as in the regular service. in every county is a county Lieutenant, who commands the whole militia of his county, but ranks only as a Colonel in the field. we have no general officers always existing. these are appointed occasionally, when an invasion or insurrection happens, & their commission determines with the occasion. the governor is head of the military as well as civil power. the law requires every militia man to provide himself with the arms usual in the regular service. but this injunction was always indifferently complied with, and the arms they had have been so frequently called for to arm the regulars, that in the lower parts of the country they are entirely disarmed. in the middle country a fourth or fifth part of them may have such firelocks as they had provided to destroy the noxious animals which infest their farms, and on the Western side of the Blue ridge they are generally armed with rifles. the pay of our militia as well as of our regulars is that of the

Figure 9. Jefferson very carefully prepared the tables for the *Notes on the State of Virginia,* as this page from one of his manuscripts reveals.
Coolidge Collection, Thomas Jefferson Papers, Massachusetts Historical Society.

one another, and attached to the *Powhatans* as their link of union. Those between the falls of the rivers and the mountains, were divided into two confederacies: the tribes inhabiting the head waters of Patowmac and Rappahanoc being attached to the *Mannahoacs,* and those on the upper parts of James River to the *Monacans.* But the *Monacans* and their friends were in amity with the *Mannahoacs* and their friends, and waged joint and perpetual war against the *Powhatans.* We are told that the *Powhatans, Mannahoacs,* and *Monacans,* spoke languages so radically different that interpreters were necessary when they transacted business. Hence we may conjecture that this was not the case between all the tribes, and probably that each spoke the language of the nation to which it was attached, which we know to have been the case in many particular instances. Very possibly there may have been anciently three different stocks, each of which multiplying in a long course of time, had separated into so many little societies. This practice results from the circumstance of their having never submitted themselves to any laws, any coercive power, any shadow of government. Their only controls are their manners, and that moral sense of right and wrong which, like the sense of tasting and feeling, in every man makes a part of his nature. An offence against these is punished by contempt, by exclusion from society, or, where the case is serious, as that of murder, by the individuals whom it concerns. Imperfect as this species of coercion may seem, crimes are very rare among them: insomuch that were it made a question, whether no law, as among the savage Americans, or too much law, as among the civilized Europeans, submits man to the greatest evil, one who has seen both conditions of existence would pronounce it to be the last, and that the sheep are happier of themselves than under care of the wolves. It will be said that great societies cannot exist without government. The savages, therefore, break them into small ones.

The territories of the *Powhatan* confederacy south of the Patowmac, comprehended about 8000 square miles, 30 tribes, and 2400 warriors. Capt. Smith tells us, that within 60 miles of Jamestown were 5000 people, of whom 1500 were warriors.[33] From this we find the proportion of their warriors to their whole inhabitants, was as 3 to 10. The *Powhatan* confederacy, then, would consist of about 8000 inhabitants, which was one for every square mile: being about the twentieth part of our present population in the same territory, and the hundredth of that of the British islands.

---

[33]John Smith, *The Generall Historie of Virginia, New-England, and the Summer Isles* (London, 1624).

EAST.

NORTH.   SOUTH.

WEST.

MANNAHOACS. / MONACANS.

Region	Tribes	Country	Chief Town	Warr's 1607	Warr's 1669
Betw'n Patowmac & Rappahanoc	Whonkenties,	Fauquier,			
	Tegninaties,	Culpeper,			
	Ontponies,	Orange,			
	Tauxitanians,	Fauquier,			
	Hassinungaes,	Culpeper,			
Betn York & York	Stegarakies,	Orange,			
	Shackakonies,	Spotsylvania,			
	Mannahoacs,	Stafford, Spotsylvania,			
Between York & James (MONACANS)	Monacans,	James River above Falls, Louisa,	Fork of Jas. River,		30
	Monasica-panoes,	Fluvanna,			
Betn Jas. & Car'lina	Monahassanoes,	Bedford,			
	Massinacacs,	Buckingham,			
	Mohemenchoes,	Cumberland, Powhatan,			

POWHATANS.

Region	Tribes	Country	Chief Town	Warriors 1607	Warriors 1669	By name
Betw'n Patowmac & Rappahanoc	Tauxenents,	Fairfax,	About General Washington's,	40		
	Patowomekes,	Stafford, King George,	Patowmac Creek,	200		By name of Matchotic, U. Matc'dic, Nanzaticos, Nanzatico, Appamatox, Matox.
	Cuttatawomans,	King George,	About Lamb Creek,	20	60	
	Pissasecs,	King George, Richmond,	Above Leedstown,	—		
	Onaumanients,	Westmoreland,	Nomony River,	100		
	Rappahanocs,	Richmond county,	Rappahanoc Creek,	100	30	By name Totuskeys.
	Moraughtacunds,	Lancaster, Richmond,	Moratico River,	80	40	
	Seeacaonies,	Northumberland,	Coan River,	30		
	Wighcocomicoes,	Northumberland,	Wicocomico River,	130	70	
	Cuttatawomans,	Lancaster,	Corotoman,	30		
Betn York & York	Nantaughtacunds,	Essex, Caroline,	Port Tobacco Creek,	150	60	
	Mattaponies,	Mattapony River,	— — — —	30	20	
	Pamunkies,	King William,	Romuncock,	300	50	
	Werowocomicos,	Gloucester,	About Rosewell,	40		
	Payankatanks,	Piarkatank River,	Turk's Ferry, Grimesby,	55		
Between York & James	Youghtanunds,	Parunky River,	— — — —	60	60	
	Chickahominies,	Chickahominy Rver,	Orapaks,	250	10	
	Powhatans,	Henrico,	Powhatan, Mayo's,	40		
	Arrowhatocs,	Henrico,	Arrohatocs,	30		
	Weanocs,	Charles City,	Weynoke,	100	15	
	Paspapheghes,	Charles City, James City,	Sandy Point,	40		
	Chiskiacs,	York,	Chiskiae,	45	15	
	Kecoughtans,	Elizabeth City,	Roscows,	20		
Betn Jas. & Car'lina	Appamattocs,	Chesterfield,	Bermuda Hundred,	60	50	1669
	Quiocohanocs,	Surry,	About Upper Chipoak,	25	3 Phics	
	Warrasqeaks,	Isle of Wght,	Warrasqueae,			Nottways, 90
	Nansamonds,	Nansamond,	About mouth of West. Branch,	200	45	Meherrics, 50
	Chesapeaks,	Princess Anne,	About Lynhaven River,	100		Tuteloes,
East'n Shore	Accohanocs,	Accomac, Northampton,	Accohannoc River,	40		
	Accomacks,	Northampton,	About Cheriton's,	80		

Besides these were the *Nottoways,* living on Nottoway River, the *Meherrins* and *Tuteloes* on Meherrin River, who were connected with the Indians of Carolina, probably with the Chowanocs.

The preceding table contains a state of these several tribes, according to their confederacies and geographical situation, with their numbers when we first became acquainted with them, where these numbers are known. The numbers of some of them are again stated as they were in the year 1669, when an attempt was made by the assembly to enumerate them. Probably the enumeration is imperfect, and in some measure conjectural, and that a further search into the records would furnish many more particulars. What would be the melancholy sequel of their history may however be augured from the census of 1669; by which we discover that the tribes therein enumerated were, in the space of 62 years, reduced to about one-third of their former numbers. Spirituous liquors, the small pox, war, and an abridgment of territory, to a people who lived principally on the spontaneous productions of nature, had committed terrible havoc among them, which generation, under the obstacles opposed to it among them, was not likely to make good. That the lands of this country were taken from them by conquest, is not so general a truth as is supposed. I find in our historians and records repeated proofs of purchase, which cover a considerable part of the lower country; and many more would doubtless be found on further search. The upper country we know has been acquired altogether by purchases made in the most unexceptionable form.

Westward of all these tribes, beyond the mountains, and extending to the great lakes, were the *Massawomecs,* a most powerful confederacy, who harrassed unremittingly the *Powhatans* and *Manahoacs.* These were probably the ancestors of the tribes known at present by the name of the *Six Nations.*[34]

Very little can now be discovered of the subsequent history of these tribes severally. The *Chickahominies* removed, about the year 1661, to Mattapony River. Their chief, with one from each of the tribes of the Pamunkies and Mattaponies, attended the treaty of Albany in 1685. This seems to have been the last chapter in their history. They retained however their separate name so late as 1705, and were at length blended with the Pamunkies and Mattaponies, and exist at present only under their names. There remain of the *Mattaponies* three or four men only, and they have more negro than Indian blood

---

[34] *Six Nations:* The Iroquois alliance, or confederacy.

in them. They have lost their language, have reduced themselves by voluntary sales to about fifty acres of land, which lie on the river of their own name, and have, from time to time, been joining the Pamunkies, from whom they are distant but 10 miles. The *Pamunkies* are reduced to about 10 or 12 men, tolerably pure from mixture with other colors. The older ones among them preserve their language in a small degree, which are the last vestiges on earth, as far as we know, of the Powhatan language. They have about 300 acres of very fertile land, on Pamunkey River, so encompassed by water that a gate shuts in the whole. Of the *Nottoways,* not a male is left. A few women constitute the remains of that tribe. They are seated on Nottoway River, in Southhampton county, on very fertile lands. At a very early period, certain lands were marked out and appropriated to these tribes, and were kept from encroachment by the authority of the laws. They have usually had trustees appointed, whose duty was to watch over their interests, and guard them from insult and injury.

The *Monacans* and their friends, better known latterly by the name of *Tuscaroras,* were probably connected with the Massawomecs, or Five Nations. For though we are told their languages were so different that the intervention of interpreters was necessary between them, yet do we also learn that the Erigas, a nation formerly inhabiting on the Ohio, were of the same original stock with the Five Nations, and that they partook also of the Tuscarora language. Their dialects might, by long separation, have become so unlike as to be unintelligible to one another. We know that in 1712 the Five Nations received the Tuscaroras into their confederacy, and made them the Sixth Nation. They received the Meherrins and Tuteloes also into their protection; and it is most probable that the remains of many other of the tribes, of whom we find no particular account, retired westwardly in like manner, and were incorporated with one or other of the western tribes.

I know of no such thing existing as an Indian monument: for I would not honor with that name arrow points, stone hatchets, stone pipes, and half-shapen images. Of labor on the large scale, I think there is no remain as respectable as would be a common ditch for the draining of lands, unless indeed it be the Barrows, of which many are to be found all over this country. These are of different sizes, some of them constructed of earth, and some of loose stones. That they were repositories of the dead has been obvious to all: but on what particular occasion constructed was matter of doubt. Some have thought they covered the bones of those who have fallen in battles fought on the spot of interment. Some ascribed them to the custom, said to prevail among the Indians, of collecting, at certain periods, the bones of all their dead, wheresoever deposited at the time of death. Others again supposed them the general sepulchres for towns, conjectured to have been on or near these grounds; and this opinion was supported by the quality of the lands in which they are found, (those constructed of earth being generally in the softest and most fertile meadow-grounds on river sides) and by a tradition, said to be handed down from the Aboriginal Indians, that, when they settled in a town, the first person who died was placed erect, and earth put about him, so as to cover and support him; that, when another died, a narrow passage was dug to the first, the second reclined against him, and the cover of earth replaced, and so on. There being one of these in my neighborhood, I wished to satisfy myself whether any, and which of these opinions were just. For this purpose I determined to open and examine it thoroughly. It was situated on the low grounds of the Rivanna, about two miles above its principal fork, and opposite to some hills, on which had been an Indian town. It was of a spheroidical form, of about 40 feet diameter at the base, and had been of about twelve feet altitude, though now reduced by the plough to seven and a half, having been under cultivation about a dozen years. Before this it was covered with trees of twelve inches diameter, and round the base was an excavation of five feet depth and width, from whence the earth had been taken of which the hillock was formed. I first dug superficially in several parts of it, and came to collections of human bones, at different depths, from six inches to three feet below the surface. These were lying in the utmost confusion, some vertical, some oblique, some horizontal, and directed to every point of the compass, entangled, and held together in clusters by the earth. Bones of the most distant parts were found together, as, for instance, the small bones of the foot in the hollow of a scull, many sculls would sometimes be in contact, lying on the face, on the side, on the back, top or bottom, so as on the whole to give the idea of bones emptied promiscuously from a bag or basket, and covered over with earth, without any attention to their order. The bones of which the greatest numbers remained were sculls, jaw bones, teeth, the bones of the arms, thighs, legs, feet, and hands. A few ribs remained, some vertebræ of the neck and spine, without their processes, and one instance only of the bone which serves as a base to the vertebral column. The sculls were so tender, that they generally fell to pieces on being touched. The other bones were stronger. There were some teeth which were judged to be smaller than those of an adult; a scull, which, on a slight view, appeared to be that of an infant, but it fell to pieces on being taken out, so as to prevent satisfactory examination; a rib, and a fragment of the under jaw of a person about half grown; another rib of an infant, and part of the jaw of a child, which had not yet cut its teeth. This last furnishing the most decisive proof of the burial of children here, I was particular in my attention to it. It was part of the right half of the under jaw. The processes, by which it was articulated to the temporal bones, were entire, and the bone itself firm to where it had been broken off, which, as nearly as I could judge, was about the place of the eye-tooth. Its upper edge, wherein would have been the sockets of the teeth, was perfectly smooth. Measuring it with that of an adult, by placing their hinder processes together, its broken end extended to the penultimate grinder of the adult. This bone was white, all the others of a sand color. The bones of infants being soft, they probably decay sooner, which might be the cause so few were found here. I proceeded then to make a perpendicular cut through the body of the barrow, that I might examine its internal structure. This passed about three feet from its centre, was opened to the former surface of the earth, and was wide enough for a man to walk through and examine its sides. At the bottom, that is, on the level of the circumjacent plain, I found bones; above these a few stones, brought from a cliff a quarter of a mile off, and from the river one-eighth of a mile off; then a large interval of earth, then a stratum of bones, and so on. At one end of the section were four strata of bones plainly distinguishable; at the other, three; the strata in one part not ranging with those in another. The bones nearest the surface were least decayed. No holes were discovered in any of them, as if made with bullets, arrows, or other weapons. I conjectured that in this barrow might have been a thousand skeletons. Every one will readily seize the circumstances above related, which militate against the opinion, that it covered the bones only of persons fallen in battle; and against the tradition also, which would make it the common sepulchre of a town, in which the bodies were placed upright, and touching each other. Appearances certainly indicate that it has derived both origin and growth from the accustomary collection of bones, and deposition of them together; that the first collection had been deposited on the common surface of the earth, a few stones put over it, and then a covering of earth, that the second had been laid on this, had covered more or less of it in proportion to the number of bones, and was then also covered with earth, and so on. The following are the particular circumstances which give it this aspect: 1. The number of bones. 2. Their confused position. 3. Their being in different strata. 4. The strata in one part having no correspondence with those in another. 5. The different states of decay in these strata, which seem to indicate a difference in the time of inhumation. 6. The existence of infant bones among them.

But on whatever occasion they may have been made, they are of considerable notoriety among the Indians: for a party passing, about thirty years ago, through the part of the country where this barrow is, went through the woods directly to it, without any instructions or enquiry, and having staid about it some time, with expressions which were construed to be those of sorrow, they returned to the high road, which they had left about half a dozen miles to pay this visit, and pursued their journey. There is another barrow, much resembling this in the low grounds of the South branch of Shenandoah, where it is crossed by the road leading from the Rockfish Gap to Staunton. Both of these have, within these dozen years, been cleared of their trees and put under cultivation, are much reduced in their height, and spread in width by the plough, and will probably disappear in time. There is another on a hill in the Blue Ridge of mountains, a few miles North of Wood's Gap, which is made up of small stones thrown together. This has been opened, and found to contain human bones, as the others do. There are also many others in other parts of the country.

Great question has arisen from whence came those aboriginal inhabitants of America. Discoveries, long ago made, were sufficient to show that a passage from Europe to America was always practicable, even to the imperfect navigation of ancient times. In going from Norway to Iceland, from Iceland to Greenland, from Greenland to Labrador, the first traject is the widest; and this having been practised from the earliest times of which we have any account of that part of the earth, it is not difficult to suppose that the subsequent trajects may have been sometimes passed. Again, the late discoveries of Captain Cook, coasting from Kamschatka to California, have proved that, if the two continents of Asia and America be separated at all, it is only by a narrow strait.[35] So that from this side also inhabitants may have passed into America; and the resemblance between the Indians of America and the Eastern inhabitants of Asia would induce us to conjecture, that the former are the descendants of the latter, or the latter of the former, excepting indeed the Eskimaux, who, from the same circumstance of resemblance, and from identity of language, must be derived from the Greenlanders, and these probably from some of the

[35]James Cook, English explorer made famous for his voyages to the north and south Pacific between 1771 and 1779 in search of a Northwest passage to the Atlantic.

northern parts of the old continent. A knowledge of their several languages would be the most certain evidence of their derivation which could be produced. In fact, it is the best proof of the affinity of nations which ever can be referred to. How many ages have elapsed since the English, the Dutch, the Germans, the Swiss, the Norwegians, Danes and Swedes have separated from their common stock? Yet how many more must elapse before the proofs of their common origin, which exist in their several languages, will disappear? It is to be lamented then, very much to be lamented, that we have suffered so many of the Indian tribes already to extinguish, without our having previously collected and deposited in the records of literature the general rudiments at least of the languages they spoke. Were vocabularies formed of all the languages spoken in North and South America, preserving their appellations of the most common objects in nature, of those which must be present to every nation, barbarous or civilized, with the inflections of their nouns and verbs, their principles of regimen and concord, and these deposited in all the public libraries, it would furnish opportunities to those skilled in the languages of the old world to compare them with these, now, or at any future time, and hence to construct the best evidence of the derivation of this part of the human race.

But imperfect as is our knowledge of the tongues spoken in America, it suffices to discover the following remarkable fact. Arranging them under the radical ones to which they may be palpably traced, and doing the same by those of the red men of Asia, there will be found probably twenty in America for one in Asia of those radical languages, so called because, if they were ever the same, they have lost all resemblance to one another. A separation into dialects may be the work of a few ages only, but for two dialects to recede from one another till they have lost all vestiges of their common origin, must require an immense course of time; perhaps not less than many people give to the age of the earth. A greater number of those radical changes of language having taken place among the red men of America, proves them of greater antiquity than those of Asia.

I will now proceed to state the nations and numbers of the Aborigines which still exist in a respectable and independent form. And as their undefined boundaries would render it difficult to specify those only which may be within any certain limits, and it may not be unacceptable to present a more general view of them, I will reduce within the form of a catalogue all those within, and circumjacent to, the United States, whose names and numbers have come to my notice.

These are taken from four different lists, the first of which was given in the year 1759 to General Stanwix by George Croghan, deputy agent for Indian affairs under Sir William Johnson; the second was drawn up by a French trader of considerable note, resident among the Indians many years, and annexed to Colonel Bouquet's[36] printed account of his expedition in 1764. The third was made out by Captain Hutchins, who visited most of the tribes by order, for the purpose of learning their numbers in 1768. And the fourth by John Dodge, an Indian trader, in 1779, except the numbers marked *, which are from other information.

[Jefferson here lists 84 tribes and their homelands.]

QUERY XII: COUNTIES AND TOWNS

A Notice of the Counties, Cities, Townships and Villages?

The counties have been enumerated under Query IX. They are 74 in number, of very unequal size and population. Of these 35 are on the tide waters, or in that parallel; 23 are in the Midlands, between the tide waters and Blue Ridge of mountains; 8 between the Blue Ridge and Alleghaney; and 8 westward of the Alleghaney.

The State, by another division, is formed into parishes, many of which are commensurate with the counties; but sometimes a county comprehends more than one parish, and sometimes a parish more than one county. This division had relation to the religion of the state, a parson of the Anglican church, with a fixed salary, having been heretofore established in each parish. The care of the poor was another object of the parochial division.

We have no townships. Our country being much intersected with navigable waters, and trade brought generally to our doors, instead of our being obliged to go in quest of it, has probably been one of the causes why we have no towns of any consequence. Williamsburgh, which, till the year 1780, was the seat of our government, never contained above 1800 inhabitants; and Norfolk, the most populous town we ever had, contained but 6000. Our towns, but more properly our villages or hamlets, are as follows:

---

[36]Henry Bouquet, *Voyage Historique et Politique, dans l'Amerique* (Paris, 1778).

On *James River* and its waters, Norfolk, Portsmouth, Hampton, Suffolk, Smithfield, Williamsburgh, Petersburg, Richmond the seat of our government, Manchester, Charlottesville, New London.

On *York River* and its waters, York, Newcastle, Hanover.

On *Rappahannoc,* Urbanna, Port Royal, Fredericksburg, Falmouth.

On *Patowmac* and its waters, Dumfries, Colchester, Alexandria, Winchester, Staunton.

On *Ohio,* Louisville.

There are other places at which, like some of the foregoing, the *laws* have said there shall be towns; but *Nature* has said there shall not, and they remain unworthy of enumeration. *Norfolk* will probably be the emporium for all the trade of the Chesapeak Bay and its waters; and a canal of 8 or 10 miles will bring to it all that of Albemarle sound and its waters. Secondary to this place are the towns at the head of the tide waters, to wit, Petersburgh on Appomattox, Richmond on James River, Newcastle on York River, Alexandria on Patowmac, and Baltimore on the Patapsco. From these the distribution will be to subordinate situations in the country. Accidental circumstances, however, may control the indications of nature, and in no instances do they do it more frequently than in the rise and fall of towns.

QUERY XIII: CONSTITUTION

The Constitution of the State and Its Several Charters?

Queen Elizabeth by her letters patent, bearing date March 25, 1584, licensed Sir Walter Raleigh to search for remote heathen lands not inhabited by Christian people, and granted to him, in fee simple, all the soil within 200 leagues of the places where his people should within 6 years make their dwellings or abidings; reserving only to herself and her successors, their allegiance, and one-fifth part of all the gold silver ore they should obtain. Sir Walter immediately sent out two ships, which visited Wococon Island, in North Carolina, and the next year dispatched seven, with 107 men, who settled in Roanoke Island, about latitude 35° 50'. Here Okisko, King of the Weopomeiocs, in a full council of his people, is said to have acknowledged himself the homager of the Queen of England, and after her of Sir Walter Raleigh. A supply of 50 men were sent in 1586, and 150 in 1587. With these last, Sir Walter sent a Governor, appointed him twelve assistants, gave them a charter of incorporation, and instructed them to settle on

Chesapeak Bay. They landed, however, at Hatorask. In 1588, when a fleet was ready to sail with a new supply of colonists and necessaries, they were detained by the Queen, to assist against the Spanish Armada. Sir Walter having now expended £40,000 in these enterprises, obstructed occasionally by the crown, without a shilling of aid from it, was under a necessity of engaging others to adventure their money. He therefore, by deed bearing date the 7th of March, 1589, by the name of Sir Walter Raleigh, Chief Governor of Assamàcomòc, (probably Acomàc), alias Wingadacoia, alias Virginia, granted to Thomas Smith and others, in consideration of their adventuring certain sums of money, liberty of trade to his new country, free from all customs and taxes for seven years, excepting the fifth part of the gold and silver ore to be obtained; and stipulated with them, and the other assistants then in Virginia, that he would confirm the deed of incorporation which he had given in 1587, with all the prerogatives, jurisdictions, royalties and privileges granted to him by the Queen. Sir Walter, at different times, sent five other adventures hither, the last of which was in 1602: for in 1603 he was attainted,[37] and put into close imprisonment, which put an end to his cares over his infant colony. What was the particular fate of the colonists he had before sent and seated has never been known: whether they were murdered, or incorporated with the savages.

Some gentlemen and merchants, supposing that by the attainder of Sir Walter Raleigh the grant to him was forfeited, not enquiring over carefully whether the sentence of an English Court could affect lands not within the jurisdiction of that court, petitioned King James for a new grant of Virginia to them. He accordingly executed a grant to Sir Thomas Gates and others, bearing date the 9th of March 1607, under which, in the same year, a settlement was effected at James–town and ever after maintained. Of this grant, however, no particular notice need be taken, as it was superseded by letters patent of the same King, of May 23, 1609, to the Earl of Salisbury and others, incorporating them by the name of "the Treasurer and Company of adventurers and planters of the City of London for the first colony in Virginia," granting to them and their successors all the lands in Virginia from Point Comfort along the sea coast to the northward 200 miles, and from the same point along the sea coast to the southward 200 miles, and all the space from this precinct on the sea coast up into the land, West and Northwest, from sea to sea, and the islands within one hun-

[37] attainted: convicted.

dred miles of it, with all the commodities, jurisdictions, royalties, privileges, franchises and pre-eminences within the same, and thereto and thereabouts, by sea and land, appertaining, in as ample manner as had before been granted to any adventurer; to be held of the King and his successors, in common soccage, yielding one-fifth part of the gold and silver ore to be therein found, for all manner of services; establishing a council in England for the direction of the enterprise, the members of which were to be chosen and displaced by the voice of the majority of the company and adventurers, and were to have the nomination and revocation of governors, officers and ministers, which by them should be thought needful for the colony, the power of establishing laws, and forms of government, and magistracy, obligatory not only within the colony, but also on the seas in going, and coming to, and from it; authorizing them to carry thither any persons who should consent to go, freeing them forever from all taxes and impositions on any goods or merchandize on importation into the colony, or exportation out of it, except the five per cent. due for custom on all goods imported into the British dominions, according to the ancient trade of merchants; which five per cent. only being paid, they might, within 13 months, reexport the same goods into foreign parts, without any custom, tax, or other duty, to the king or any of his officers or deputies; with powers of waging war against those who should annoy them; giving to the inhabitants of the colony all the rights of natural subjects, as if born and abiding in England; and declaring that these letters should be construed, in all doubtful parts, in such manner as should be most for the benefit of the grantees.

Afterwards, on the 12th of March, 1612, by other letters patent, the king added to his former grants all islands in any part of the ocean between the 30th and 41st degrees of latitude, and within 300 leagues of any of the parts before granted to the Treasurer and company, not being possessed or inhabited by any other christian prince or state, nor within the limits of the northern colony.

In pursuance of the authorities given to the company by these charters, and more especially of that part in the charter of 1609, which authorized them to establish a form of government, they on the 24th of July 1621, by charter under their common seal, declared that from thenceforward there should be two supreme councils in Virginia, the one to be called the council of state, to be placed and displaced by the treasurer, council in England, and company, from time to time, whose office was to be that of assisting and advising the governor; the other to be called the general assembly, to be convened by the governor once yearly or oftener, which was to consist of the council of state, and two burgesses out of every town, hundred, or plantation, to be respectively chosen by the inhabitants. In this all matters were to be decided by the greater part of the votes present, reserving to the governor a negative voice; and they were to have power to treat, consult, and conclude all emergent occasions concerning the public weal, and to make laws for the behoof and government of the colony, imitating and following the laws and policy of England as nearly as might be, providing that these laws should have no force till ratified in a general quarter court of the company in England, and returned under their common seal; and declaring that, after the government of the colony should be well framed and settled, no orders of the council in England should bind the colony unless ratified in the said general assembly. The king and company quarrelled, and, by a mixture of law and force, the latter were ousted of all their rights, without retribution, after having expended £100,000 in establishing the colony, without the smallest aid from government. King James suspended their powers by proclamation of July 15, 1624, and Charles I took the government into his own hands. Both sides had their partizans in the colony; but, in truth, the people of the colony in general thought themselves little concerned in the dispute. There being three parties interested in these several charters, what passed between the first and second it was thought could not affect the third. If the king seized on the powers of the company, they only passed into other hands, without increase or diminution, while the rights of the people remained as they were. But they did not remain so long. The northern parts of their country were granted away to the Lords Baltimore and Fairfax, the first of these obtaining also the rights of separate jurisdiction and government. And in 1650 the parliament, considering itself as standing in the place of their deposed king, and as having succeeded to all his powers, without as well as within the realm, began to assume a right over the colonies, passing an act for inhibiting their trade with foreign nations. This succession to the exercise of the kingly authority gave the first color for parliamentary interference with the colonies, and produced that fatal precedent which they continued to follow after they had retired, in other respects, within their proper functions. When this colony, therefore, which still maintained its opposition to Cromwell and the parliament, was induced in 1651 to lay down their arms, they previously secured their most essential rights, by a solemn convention, which having never seen in print, I will here insert literally from the records.

[Jefferson inserts the 1651 articles of governance, plus a contemporary "Act of indemnity against accusations of treason against the English parliament and commonwealth."]

The colony supposed that by this solemn convention, entered into with arms in their hands, they had secured the ancient limits of their country, its free trade, its exemption from taxation, but by their own assembly, and exclusion of military force from among them. Yet in every of these points was this convention violated by subsequent kings and parliaments, and other infractions of their constitution, equally dangerous, committed. Their General Assembly, which was composed of the council of state and burgesses, sitting together and deciding by plurality of voices, was split into two houses, by which the council obtained a separate negative on their laws. Appeals from their supreme court, which had been fixed by law in their General Assembly, were arbitrarily revoked by England, to be there heard before the king and council. Instead of four hundred miles on the sea coast, they were reduced, in the space of thirty years, to about one hundred miles. Their trade with foreigners was totally suppressed, and, when carried to Great Britain, was there loaded with imposts. It is unnecessary, however, to glean up the several instances of injury, as scattered through American and British history, and the more especially as, by passing on to the accession of the present king, we shall find specimens of them all, aggravated, multiplied and crowded within a small compass of time, so as to evince a fixed design of considering our rights natural, conventional and chartered as mere nullities. The following is an epitome of the first fifteen years of his reign.[38] The colonies were taxed internally and externally; their essential interests sacrificed to individuals in Great Britain; their legislatures suspended; charters annulled; trials by juries taken away; their persons subjected to transportation across the Atlantic, and to trial before foreign judicatories; their supplications for redress thought beneath answer; themselves published as cowards in the councils of their mother country and courts of Europe; armed troops sent among them to enforce submission to these violences; and actual hostilities commenced against them. No alternative was presented but resistance, or unconditional submission. Between these could be no hesitation. They closed in the

---

[38]George III acceded to the throne in 1760; Jefferson thus refers to the period 1760–1775.

appeal to arms. They declared themselves independent States. They confederated together into one great republic; thus securing to every State the benefit of an union of their whole force. In each state separately a new form of government was established. Of ours particularly the following are the outlines.[39] The executive powers are lodged in the hands of a governor, chosen annually, and incapable of acting more than three years in seven. He is assisted by a council of eight members. The judiciary powers are divided among several courts, as will be hereafter explained. Legislation is exercised by two houses of assembly, the one called the house of Delegates, composed of two members from each county, chosen annually by the citizens possessing an estate for life in 100 acres of uninhabited land, or 25 acres with a house on it, or in a house or lot in some town: the other called the Senate, consisting of 24 members, chosen quadrennially by the same electors, who for this purpose are distributed into 24 districts. The concurrence of both houses is necessary to the passage of a law. They have the appointment of the governor and council, the judges of the superior courts, auditors, attorney–general, treasurer, register of the land office, and delegates to congress. As the dismemberment of the State had never had its confirmation, but, on the contrary, had always been the subject of protestation and complaint, that it might never be in our own power to raise scruples on that subject, or to disturb the harmony of our new confederacy, the grants to Maryland, Pennsylvania, and the two Carolinas, were ratified.

This constitution was formed when we were new and unexperienced in the science of government. It was the first too which was formed in the whole United States. No wonder then that time and trial have discovered very capital defects in it:

1. The majority of the men in the state, who pay and fight for its support, are unrepresented in the legislature, the roll of freeholders entitled to vote, not including generally the half of those on the roll of the militia, or of the tax–gatherers.

2. Among those who share the representation, the shares are very unequal. Thus the county of Warwick, with only one hundred fighting men, has an equal representation with the county of Loudon, which has 1746. So that every man in Warwick has as much influence in the government as 17 men in Loudon. But lest it should be thought that an equal interspersion of small among large counties, through the whole State, may prevent any danger of injury to particular parts of it,

[39]The Virginia Constitution of 1776.

	SQUARE MILES.	FIGHTING MEN.	DELEGATES.	SENATORS.
Between the sea coast and falls of the rivers	11,205	19,012	71	12
Between the falls of the rivers and the Blue ridge of mountains	18,759	18,828	46	8
Between the Blue ridge and the Alleghaney	11,911	7,673	16	2
Between the Alleghaney and Ohio	79,650	4,458	16	2
Total	121,525	49,971	149	24

we will divide it into districts, and shew the proportions of land, of fighting men, and of representation in each.

An inspection of this table will supply the place of commentaries on it. It will appear at once that nineteen thousand men, living below the falls of the rivers, possess half the senate, and want four members only of possessing a majority of the house of delegates; a want more than supplied by the vicinity of their situation to the seat of government, and of course the greater degree of convenience and punctuality with which their members may and will attend in the legislature. These nineteen thousand, therefore, living in one part of the country, give law to upwards of thirty thousand, living in another, and appoint all their chief officers, executive and judiciary. From the difference of their situation and circumstances, their interests will often be very different.

3. The senate is, by its constitution, too homogeneous with the house of delegates. Being chosen by the same electors, at the same time, and out of the same subjects, the choice falls of course on men of the same description. The purpose of establishing different houses of legislation is to introduce the influence of different interests or different principles. Thus in Great Britain it is said their constitution relies on the house of commons for honesty, and the lords for wisdom, which would be a rational reliance if honesty were to be bought with money, and if wisdom were hereditary. In some of the American states the delegates and senators are so chosen, as that the first represent the persons, and the second the property of the state. But with us wealth and wisdom have equal chance for admission into both houses. We do not therefore derive from the separation of our Legislature into two houses, those benefits which a proper complication of principles is

capable of producing, and those which alone can compensate the evils which may be produced by their dissensions.

4. All the powers of government, legislative, executive and judiciary, result to the legislative body. The concentrating these in the same hands is precisely the definition of despotic government. It will be no alleviation that these powers will be exercised by a plurality of hands, and not by a single one. 173 despots would surely be as oppressive as one. Let those who doubt it turn their eyes on the republic of Venice. As little will it avail us that they are chosen by ourselves. An *elective despotism* was not the government we fought for, but one which should not only be founded on free principles, but in which the powers of government should be so divided and balanced among several bodies of magistracy, as that no one could transcend their legal limits without being effectually checked and restrained by the others. For this reason that convention, which passed the ordinance of government, laid its foundation on this basis, that the legislative, executive and judiciary departments should be separate and distinct, so that no person should exercise the powers of more than one of them at the same time. But no barrier was provided between these several powers. The judiciary and executive members were left dependent on the legislative for their subsistence in office, and some of them for their continuance in it. If therefore the legislature assumes executive and judiciary powers no opposition is likely to be made; nor if made can it be effectual, because in that case they may put their proceedings into the form of an act of assembly, which will render them obligatory on the other branches. They have accordingly, in many instances, decided rights which should have been left to judiciary controversy; and the direction of the executive, during the whole time of their session, is becoming habitual and familiar. And this is done with no ill intention. The views of the present members are perfectly upright. When they are led out of their regular province, it is by art in others, and inadvertence in themselves. And this will probably be the case for some time to come. But it will not be a very long time. Mankind soon learn to make interested uses of every right and power which they possess, or may assume. The public money and public liberty, intended to have been deposited with three branches of magistracy, but found inadvertently to be in the hands of one only, will soon be discovered to be sources of wealth and dominion to those who hold them; distinguished too by this tempting circumstance, that they are the instrument as well as the object of acquisition. With money we will get men, said Cæsar, and with men we will get money. Nor should our

assembly be deluded by the integrity of their own purposes, and conclude that these unlimited powers will never be abused, because themselves are not disposed to abuse them. They should look forward to a time, and that not a distant one, when corruption in this, as in the country from which we derive our origin, will have seized the heads of government, and be spread by them through the body of the people; when they will purchase the voices of the people, and make them pay the price. Human nature is the same on every side of the Atlantic, and will be alike influenced by the same causes. The time to guard against corruption and tyranny, is before they shall have gotten hold on us. It is better to keep the wolf out of the fold, than to trust to drawing his teeth and talons after he shall have entered. To render these considerations the more cogent, we must observe in addition,

5. That the ordinary legislature may alter the constitution itself. On the discontinuance of assemblies, it became necessary to substitute in their place some other body, competent to the ordinary business of government, and to the calling forth the powers of the State for the maintenance of our opposition to Great Britain. Conventions were therefore introduced, consisting of two delegates from each county, meeting together and forming one house, on the plan of the former house of Burgesses, to whose places they succeeded. These were at first chosen anew for every particular session. But in March, 1775, they recommended to the people to choose a convention, which should continue in office a year. This was done accordingly in April 1775, and in the July following, that convention passed an ordinance for the election of delegates in the month of April annually. It is well known, that in July 1775, a separation from Great Britain and establishment of Republican government had never yet entered into any person's mind. A convention therefore, chosen under that ordinance, cannot be said to have been chosen for purposes which certainly did not exist in the minds of those who passed it. Under this ordinance, at the annual election in April 1776, a convention for the year was chosen. Independence, and the establishment of a new form of government, were not even yet the objects of the people at large. One extract from the pamphlet called Common Sense had appeared in the Virginia papers in February, and copies of the pamphlet itself had got into a few hands. But the idea had not been opened to the mass of the people in April, much less can it be said that they had made up their minds in its favor. So that the electors of April 1776, no more than the legislators of July 1775, not thinking of independence and a permanent republic, could not mean to vest in these delegates powers of

establishing them, or any authorities other than those of the ordinary Legislature. So far as a temporary organization of government was necessary to render our opposition energetic, so far their organization was valid. But they received in their creation no powers but what were given to every legislature before and since. They could not therefore pass an act transcendent to the powers of other legislatures. If the present assembly pass any act, and declare it shall be irrevocable by subsequent assemblies, the declaration is merely void, and the act repealable, as other acts are. So far, and no farther authorized, they organized the government by the ordinance entitled a Constitution or Form of government. It pretends to no higher authority than the other ordinances of the same session; it does not say that it shall be perpetual; that it shall be unalterable by other legislatures; that it shall be transcendent above the powers of those who they knew would have equal power with themselves. Not only the silence of the instrument is a proof they thought it would be alterable, but their own practice also: for this very convention, meeting as a House of Delegates in General Assembly with the new Senate in the autumn of that year, passed acts of assembly in contradiction to their ordinance of government; and every assembly from that time to this has done the same. I am safe, therefore, in the position that the constitution itself is alterable by the ordinary legislature. Though this opinion seems founded on the first elements of common sense, yet is the contrary maintained by some persons: 1. Because, say they, the conventions were vested with every power necessary to make effectual opposition to Great Britain. But to complete this argument, they must go on, and say further, that effectual opposition could not be made to Great Britain without establishing a form of government perpetual and unalterable by the legislature, which is not true. An opposition which, at some time or other, was to come to an end, could not need a perpetual institution to carry it on; and a government, amendable as its defects should be discovered, was as likely to make effectual resistance, as one which should be unalterably wrong. Besides, the assemblies were as much vested with all powers requisite for resistance as the conventions were. If, therefore, these powers included that of modelling the form of government in the one case, they did so in the other. The assemblies then, as well as the conventions, may model the government; that is, they may alter the ordinance of government. 2. They urge that if the convention had meant that this instrument should be alterable, as their other ordinances were, they would have called it an ordinance; but they have called it a *constitution,* which, ex vi termini,[40] means "an act above the power of the ordinary Legislature." I answer, that *constitutio, constitutum, statutum, lex,* are convertible terms. . . . *Constitution* and *statute* were originally terms of the civil law, and from thence introduced by Ecclesiastics into the English law. Thus in the statute 25 Hen. 8, c. 19, § 1, *"Constitutions* and *ordinances"* are used as synonymous. The term *constitution,* has many other significations in physics and in politics; but in Jurisprudence, whenever it is applied to any act of the legislature, it invariably means a statute, law, or ordinance, which is the present case. No inference then of a different meaning can be drawn from the adoption of this title: on the contrary, we might conclude that, by their affixing to it a term synonymous with ordinance, or statute, they meant it to be an ordinance or statute. But of what consequence is their meaning, where their power is denied? If they meant to do more than they had power to do, did this give them power? It is not the name, but the authority, which renders an act obligatory. Lord Coke[41] says, "an article of the statute 11 R. 2, c. 5, that no person should attempt to revoke any ordinance then made, is repealed, for that such restraint is against the jurisdiction and power of the parliament." And again, "though divers parliaments have attempted to restrain subsequent parliaments, yet could they never effect it; for the latter parliament hath ever power to abrogate, suspend, qualify, explain, or make void the former in the whole or in any part thereof, notwithstanding any words of restraint, prohibition, or penalty, in the former; for it is a maxim in the laws of the parliament, "subsequent laws nullify earlier laws that are contrary." To get rid of the magic supposed to be in the word *constitution,* let us translate it into its definition, as given by those who think it above the power of the law; and let us suppose the convention instead of saying, "We, the ordinary legislature, establish a *constitution,*" had said, "We, the ordinary legislature, establish an act *above the power of the ordinary legislature."* Does not this expose the absurdity of the attempt? 3. But, say they, the people have acquiesced, and this has given it an authority superior to the laws. It is true, that the people did not rebel against it; and was that a time for the people to rise in rebellion? Should a prudent acquiescence, at a critical time, be construed into a confirmation of every illegal thing done during that period? Besides, why should they rebel? At an annual election they had chosen delegates for the year, to exercise the ordinary powers of legislation, and

[40]ex vi termini: by definition or implication.
[41]Lord Coke: Sir Edward Coke (1552–1634), chief justice and codifier of the laws of England.

to manage the great contest in which they were engaged. These delegates thought the contest would be best managed by an organized government. They therefore, among others, passed an ordinance of government. They did not presume to call it perpetual and unalterable. They well knew they had no power to make it so; that our choice of them had been for no such purpose, and at a time when we could have no such purpose in contemplation. Had an unalterable form of government been meditated, perhaps we should have chosen a different set of people. There was no cause then for the people to rise in rebellion. But to what dangerous lengths will this argument lead? Did the acquiescence of the colonies, under the various acts of power exercised by Great Britain in our infant state, confirm these acts, and so far invest them with the authority of the people as to render them unalterable, and our present resistance wrong? On every unauthorative exercise of power by the Legislature, must the people rise in rebellion, or their silence be construed into a surrender of that power to them? If so, how many rebellions should we have had already? One certainly for every session of assembly. The other states in the Union have been of opinion, that to render a form of government unalterable by ordinary acts of assembly, the people must delegate persons with special powers. They have accordingly chosen special conventions to form and fix their governments. The individuals then who maintain the contrary opinion in this country should have the modesty to suppose it possible that they may be wrong, and the rest of America right. But if there be only a possibility of their being wrong, if only a plausible doubt remains of the validity of the ordinance of government, is it not better to remove that doubt, by placing it on a bottom which none will dispute? If they be right, we shall only have the unnecessary trouble of meeting once in convention. If they be wrong, they expose us to the hazard of having no fundamental rights at all. True it is, this is no time for deliberating on forms of government. While an enemy is within our bowels, the first object is to expel him. But when this shall be done, when peace shall be established, and leisure given us for intrenching within good forms, the rights for which we have bled, let no man be found indolent enough to decline a little more trouble for placing them beyond the reach of question. If any thing more be requisite to produce a conviction of the expediency of calling a convention at a proper season to fix our form of government, let it be the reflection,

6. That the assembly exercises a power of determining the Quorum of their own body which may legislate for us. After the establishment

of the new form they adhered to the *Lex majoris partis,* founded in common law as well as common right. It is the natural law of every assembly of men, whose numbers are not fixed by any other law. They continued for some time to require the presence of a majority of their whole number, to pass an act. But the British parliament fixes its own quorum: our former assemblies fixed their own quorum; and one precedent in favor of power is stronger than an hundred against it. The house of delegates therefore have lately voted that, during the present dangerous invasion, forty members shall be a house to proceed to business. They have been moved to this by the fear of not being able to collect a house. But this danger could not authorize them to call that a house, which was none; and if they may fix it at one number, they may at another, till it loses its fundamental character of being a representative body. As this vote expires with the present invasion, it is probable the former rule will be permitted to revive, because at present no ill is meant. The power, however, of fixing their own quorum has been avowed, and a precedent set. From forty it may be reduced to four, and from four to one: from a house to a committee, from a committee to a chairman or speaker, and thus an oligarchy or monarchy be substituted under forms supposed to be regular.... When therefore it is considered, that there is no legal obstacle to the assumption by the assembly of all the powers legislative, executive, and judiciary, and that these may come to the hands of the smallest rag of delegation, surely the people will say, and their representatives, while yet they have honest representatives, will advise them to say, that they will not acknowledge as laws any acts not considered and assented to by the major part of their delegates.

In enumerating the defects of the constitution, it would be wrong to count among them what is only the error of particular persons. In December 1776, our circumstances being much distressed, it was proposed in the House of Delegates to create a *dictator,* invested with every power legislative, executive, and judiciary, civil and military, of life and of death, over our persons and over our properties; and in June 1781, again under calamity, the same proposition as repeated, and wanted a few votes only of being passed. One who entered into this contest from a pure love of liberty, and a sense of injured rights, who determined to make every sacrifice, and to meet every danger, for the re-establishment of those rights on a firm basis, who did not mean to expend his blood and substance for the wretched purpose of changing this master for that, but to place the powers of governing him in a plurality of hands of his own choice, so that the corrupt will of no one man might in future oppress him, must stand confounded and dismayed when he is told that a considerable portion of that plurality had meditated the surrender of them into a single hand, and, in lieu of a limited monarch, to deliver him over to a despotic one! How must we find his efforts and sacrifices abused and baffled, if he may still by a single vote be laid prostrate at the feet of one man! In God's name, from whence have they derived this power? Is it from our ancient laws? None such can be produced. Is it from any principle in our new constitution, expressed or implied? Every lineament of that, expressed or implied, is in full opposition to it. Its fundamental principle is, that the state shall be governed as a commonwealth. It provides a republican organization, proscribes under the name of *prerogative* the exercise of all powers undefined by the laws; places on this basis the whole system of our laws; and, by consolidating them together, chooses that they shall be left to stand or fall together, never providing for any circumstances, nor admitting that such could arise, wherein either should be suspended, no, not for a moment. Our ancient laws expressly declare, that those who are but delegates themselves shall not delegate to others powers which require judgment and integrity in their exercise.—Or was this proposition moved on a supposed right in the movers of abandoning their posts in a moment of distress? The same laws forbid the abandonment of that post, even on ordinary occasions; and much more a transfer of their powers into other hands and other forms, without consulting the people. They never admit the idea that these, like sheep or cattle, may be given from hand to hand without an appeal to their own will.—Was it from the necessity of the case? Necessities which dissolve a government, do not convey its authority to an oligarchy or a monarchy. They throw back, into the hands of the people, the powers they had delegated, and leave them as individuals to shift for themselves. A leader may offer, but not impose himself, nor be imposed on them. Much less can their necks be submitted to his sword, their breath be held at his will or caprice. The necessity which should operate these tremendous effects should at least be palpable and irresistible. Yet in both instances where it is feared, or pretended with us, it was belied by the event. It was belied too by the preceding experience of our sister states, several of whom had grappled through greater difficulties without abandoning their forms of government. When the proposition was first made, Massachusetts had found even the government of committees sufficient to carry them through an invasion. But we at the time of that proposition were under no invasion. When the second was made, there had been added to this example those of Rhode Island, New York, New Jersey, and Pennsylvania, in all of which the republican form had been found equal to the task of carrying them through the severest trials. In this state alone did there exist so little virtue, that fear was to be fixed in the hearts of the people, and to become the motive of their exertions and the principle of their government? The very thought alone was treason against the people; was treason against mankind in general; as rivetting forever the chains which bow down their necks, by giving to their oppressor a proof, which they would have trumpeted through the universe, of the imbecility of republican government, in times of pressing danger, to shield them from harm. Those who assume the right of giving away the reins of government in any case, must be sure that the herd, whom they hand on to the rods and hatchet of the dictator, will lay their necks on the block when he shall nod to them. But if our assemblies supposed such a resignation in the people, I hope they mistook their character. I am of opinion that the government, instead of being braced and invigo rated for greater exertions under their difficulties, would have been thrown back upon the bungling machinery of county committees for administration, till a convention could have been called, and its wheels again set into regular motion. What a cruel moment was this for creating such an embarrassment, for putting to the proof the attachment of our countrymen to republican government! Those who meant well of the advocates for this measure, (and most of them meant well, for I know them personally, had been their fellow laborers in the common cause, and had often proved the purity of their principles), had been seduced in their judgment by the example of an ancient republic, whose constitution and circumstances were fundamentally different. They had sought this precedent in the history of Rome, where alone it was to be found, and here at length too it had proved fatal. They had taken it from a republic, rent by the most bitter factions and tumults, where the government was of a heavy-handed unfeeling aristocracy, over a people ferocious, and rendered desperate by poverty and wretchedness; tumults which could not be allayed under the most trying circumstances, but by the omnipotent hand of a single despot. Their constitution, therefore, allowed a temporary tyrant to be erected, under the name of a Dictator; and that temporary tyrant, after a few examples, became perpetual. They misapplied this precedent to a people, mild in their dispositions, patient under their trial, united for the public liberty, and affectionate to their leaders. But if from the constitution of the Roman Government there resulted to their Senate a power of submitting all their rights to the will of one man, does it follow that the assembly of Virginia have the same authority? What clause in our constitution has substituted that of Rome, by way of residuary provision, for all cases not otherwise provided for? Or if they may step as they wish, into any other form of government for precedents to rule us by, for what oppression may not a precedent be found in this world of the war of all against all?—Searching for the foundations of this proposition, I can find none which may pretend a color of right or reason, but the defect before developed, that there being no barrier between the legislative, executive, and judiciary departments, the Legislature may seize the whole; that having seized it, and possessing a right to fix their own quorum, they may reduce that quorum to one, whom they may call a chairman, speaker, dictator, or by any other name they please.—Our situation is indeed perilous, and I hope my countrymen will be sensible of it, and will apply at a proper season the proper remedy; which is a convention to fix the constitution, to amend its defects, to bind up the several branches of government by certain laws, which when they transgress their acts shall become nullities; to render unnecessary an appeal to the people, or in other words a rebellion, on every infraction of their rights, on the peril that their acquiescence shall be construed into an intention to surrender those rights.

QUERY XIV: LAWS

The Administration of Justice and Description of the Laws?

The state is divided into counties. In every county are appointed magistrates, called justices of the peace, usually from eight, to thirty or forty in number, in proportion to the size of the county, of the most discreet and honest inhabitants. They are nominated by their fellows, but commissioned by the governor, and act without reward. These magistrates have jurisdiction, both criminal and civil. If the question before them be a question of law only, they decide on it themselves; but if it be of fact, or of fact and law combined, it must be referred to a jury. In the latter case, of a combination of law and fact, it is usual for the jurors to decide the fact, and to refer the law arising on it to the decision of the judges. But this division of the subject lies with their discretion only. And if the question relate to any point of public liberty, or if it be one of those in which the judges may be suspected of bias, the jury undertake to decide both law and fact. If they be mistaken, a decision against right, which is casual only, is less dangerous to the state, and less afflicting to the loser, than one which makes part of a regular and uniform system. In truth, it is better to toss up cross and pile in a cause, than to refer it to a judge whose mind is warped by any motive whatever, in that particular case. But the common sense of twelve honest men gives still a better chance of just decision, than the hazard of cross and pile. These judges execute their process by the sheriff or coroner of the county, or by constables of their own appointment. If any free person commit an offence against the commonwealth, if it be below the degree of felony, he is bound by a justice to appear before their court, to answer it on indictment or information. If it amount to felony, he is committed to jail, a court of these justices is called; if they on examination think him guilty, they send him to the jail of the general court, before which court he is to be tried first by a grand jury of 24, of whom 13 must concur in opinion; if they find him guilty, he is then tried by a jury of 12 men of the county where the offence was committed, and by their verdict, which must be unanimous, he is acquitted or condemned without appeal. If the criminal be a slave, the trial by the county court is final. In every case however, except that of high treason, there resides in the governor a power of pardon. In high treason, the pardon can only flow from the general assembly. In civil matters these justices have jurisdiction in all cases of whatever value, not appertaining to the department of the admiralty. This jurisdiction is two fold. If the matter in dispute be of less value than 4⅙ dollars, a single member may try it at any time and place within his county, and may award execution on the goods of the party cast. If it be of that or greater value, it is determinable before the county court, which consists of four at the least of those justices, and assembles at the court house of the county on a certain day in every month. From their determination, if the matter be of the value of ten pounds sterling, or concern the title or bounds of lands, an appeal lies to one of the superior courts.

There are three superior courts, to wit, the high court of chancery, the general court, and court of admiralty. The first and second of these receive appeals from the county courts, and also have original jurisdiction where the subject of controversy is of the value of ten pounds sterling, or where it concerns the title or bounds of land. The jurisdiction of the admiralty is original altogether. The high court of chancery is composed of three judges, the General Court of five, and the court of admiralty of three. The two first hold their sessions at Richmond at stated times, the chancery twice in the year, and the

General Court twice for business civil and criminal, and twice more for criminal only. The court of admiralty sits at Williamsburgh whenever a controversy arises.

There is one supreme court, called the court of appeals, composed of the judges of the three superior courts, assembling twice a year at stated times at Richmond. This court receives appeals in all civil cases from each of the superior courts, and determines them finally. But it has no original jurisdiction.

If a controversy arise between two foreigners of a nation in alliance with the United States, it is decided by the Consul for their State, or, if both parties choose it, by the ordinary courts of justice. If one of the parties only be such a foreigner, it is triable before the courts of justice of the country. But if it shall have been instituted in a county court, the foreigner may remove it into the general court, or court of chancery, who are to determine it at their first sessions, as they must also do if it be originally commenced before them. In cases of life and death, such foreigners have a right to be tried by a jury, the one-half foreigners the other natives.

All public accounts are settled with a board of auditors, consisting of three members, appointed by the general assembly, any two of whom may act. But an individual, dissatisfied with the determination of that board, may carry his case into the proper superior court.

A description of the laws:

The general assembly was constituted, as has been already shown, by letters patent of March 9th, 1607, in the 4th year of the reign of James the First. The laws of England seem to have been adopted by consent of the settlers, which might easily enough be done whilst they were few and living altogether. Of such adoption, however, we have no other proof than their practice, till the year 1661, when they were expressly adopted by an act of the assembly, except so far as "a difference of condition" rendered them inapplicable. Under this adoption, the rule, in our courts of judicature was, that the common law of England, and the general statutes previous to the fourth of James, were in force here; but that no subsequent statutes were, *unless we were named in them,* said the judges and other partisans of the crown, but *named or not named,* said those who reflected freely. It will be unnecessary to attempt a description of the laws of England, as that may be found in English publications. To those which were established here, by the adoption of the legislature, have been since added a number of acts of assembly passed during the monarchy, and ordinances of convention and acts of assembly enacted since the establishment of the republic. The following variations from the British model are perhaps worthy of being specified.

Debtors unable to pay their debts, and making faithful delivery of their whole effects, are released from confinement, and their persons forever discharged from restraint for such previous debts; but any property they may afterwards acquire will be subject to their creditors.

The poor, unable to support themselves, are maintained by an assessment on the titheable persons in their parish. This assessment is levied and administered by twelve persons in each parish, called vestrymen, originally chosen by the housekeepers of the parish, but afterwards filling vacancies in their own body by their own choice. These are usually the most discreet farmers, so distributed through their parish, that every part of it may be under the immediate eye of some one of them. They are well acquainted with the details and economy of private life, and they find sufficient inducements to execute their charge well, in their philanthrophy, in the approbation of their neighbors, and the distinction which that gives them. The poor who have neither property, friends, nor strength to labor, are boarded in the houses of good farmers, to whom a stipulated sum is annually paid. To those who are able to help themselves a little, or have friends from whom they derive some succors, inadequate however to their full maintenance, supplementary aids are given, which enable them to live comfortably in their own houses, or in the houses of their friends. Vagabonds, without visible property or vocation, are placed in workhouses, where they are well clothed, fed, lodged, and made to labor. Nearly the same method of providing for the poor prevails through all our states; and from Savannah to Portsmouth you will seldom meet a beggar. In the larger towns, indeed, they sometimes present themselves. These are usually foreigners, who have never obtained a settlement in any parish. I never yet saw a native American begging in the streets or highways. A subsistence is easily gained here; and if by misfortunes they are thrown on the charities of the world, those provided by their own country are so comfortable and so certain, that they never think of relinquishing them to become strolling beggars. Their situation too, when sick, in the family of a good farmer, where every member is emulous to do them kind offices, where they are visited by all the neighbors, who bring them the little rarities which their sickly appetites may crave, and who take by rotation the nightly watch over them, when their condition requires it, is, without comparison, better than in a general hospital, where the sick, the dying, and the dead are crammed together in the same rooms, and often in the same beds. The disadvantages, inseparable from general hospitals, are such as can never be counterpoised by all the regularities of medicine and regimen. Nature and kind nursing save a much greater proportion in our plain way, at a smaller expense, and with less abuse. One branch only of hospital institution is wanting with us; that is, a general establishment for those laboring under difficult cases of chirurgery.[42] The aids of this art are not equivocal. But an able chirurgeon cannot be had in every parish. Such a receptacle should, therefore, be provided for those patients; but no others should be admitted.

Marriages must be solemnized either on special license, granted by the first magistrate of the county, on proof of the consent of the parent or guardian of either party under age, or after solemn publication, on three several Sundays, at some place of religious worship, in the parishes where the parties reside. The act of solemnization may be by the minister of any society of Christians, who shall have been previously licensed for this purpose by the court of the county. Quakers and Menonists, however, are exempted from all these conditions, and marriage among them is to be solemnized by the society itself.

A foreigner of any nation, not in open war with us, becomes naturalized by removing to the state to reside, and taking an oath of fidelity; and, thereupon, acquires every right of a native citizen; and citizens may divest themselves of that character, by declaring by solemn deed, or in open court, that they mean to expatriate themselves, and no longer to be citizens of this state.

Conveyances of land must be registered in the court of the county wherein they lie, or in the general court, or they are void as to creditors and subsequent purchasers.

Slaves pass by descent and dower as lands do. Where the descent is from a parent, the heir is bound to pay an equal share of their value in money to each of his brothers and sisters.

Slaves, as well as lands, were entailable during the monarchy; but, by an act of the first republican assembly, all donees in tail, present and future, were vested with the absolute dominion of the entailed subject.[43]

Bills of exchange being protested, carry 10 per cent. interest from their date.

---

[42] chirurgery: surgery.

[43] The law of entail kept landed estates entirely with one descendant, usually the eldest. The change in laws, which Jefferson supported enthusiastically, permitted the current holder of entail to dispose of property however he wished.

No person is allowed, in any other case, to take more than five per cent. per annum simple interest, for the loan of moneys.

Gaming debts are made void, and moneys actually paid to discharge such debts (if they exceeded 40 shillings) may be recovered by the payer within three months, or by any other person afterwards.

Tobacco, flour, beef, pork, tar, pitch, and turpentine, must be inspected by persons publicly appointed, before they can be exported.

The erecting iron works and mills is encouraged by many privileges, with necessary cautions, however, to prevent their dams from obstructing the navigation of the water courses. The general assembly have on several occasions shewn a great desire to encourage the opening the great falls of James and Patowmac rivers. As yet, however, neither of these have been effected.

The laws have also descended to the preservation and improvement of the races of useful animals, such as horses, cattle, deer; to the extirpation of those which are noxious, as wolves, squirrels, crows, blackbirds; and to the guarding our citizens against infectious disorders, by obliging suspected vessels coming into the state, to perform quarantine, and by regulating the conduct of persons having such disorders within the state.

The mode of acquiring lands, in the earliest times of our settlement, was by petition to the general assembly. If the lands prayed for were already cleared of the Indian title, and the assembly thought the prayer reasonable, they passed the property by their vote to the petitioner. But if they had not yet been ceded by the Indians, it was necessary that the petitioner should previously purchase their right. This purchase the assembly verified, by enquiries of the Indian proprietors; and being satisfied of its reality and fairness, proceeded further to examine the reasonableness of the petition, and its consistence with policy; and, according to the result, either granted or rejected the petition. The company also sometimes, though very rarely, granted lands, independently of the General Assembly. As the colony increased, and individual applications for land multiplied, it was found to give too much occupation to the general assembly to enquire into and execute the grant in every special case. They therefore thought it better to establish general rules, according to which all grants should be made, and to leave to the governor the execution of them under these rules. This they did by what have been usually called the land laws, amending them from time to time, as their defects were developed. According to these laws, when an individual wished a portion of unappropriated land, he was to locate and survey it by a public officer, appointed for that purpose; its breadth was to bear a certain proportion to its length; the grant was to be executed by the governor; and the lands were to be improved in a certain manner within a given time. From these regulations there resulted to the state a sole and exclusive power of taking conveyances of the Indian right of soil: since, according to them, an Indian conveyance alone could give no right to an individual, which the laws would acknowledge. The state, or the crown thereafter, made general purchases of the Indians from time to time, and the Governor parcelled them out by special grants, conformed to the rules before described, which it was not in his power, or in that of the crown, to dispense with. Grants, unaccompanied by their proper legal circumstances, were set aside regularly by *scire facias,* or by bill in Chancery. Since the establishment of our new government, this order of things is but little changed. An individual, wishing to appropriate to himself lands still unappropriated by any other, pays to the public treasurer a sum of money proportioned to the quantity he wants. He carries the treasurer's receipt to the auditors of public accounts, who thereupon debit the treasurer with the sum, and order the register of the land office to give the party a warrant for his land. With this warrant from the register, he goes to the surveyor of the county where the land lies on which he has cast his eye. The surveyor lays it off for him, gives him its exact description, in the form of a certificate, which certificate he returns to the land office, where a grant is made out, and is signed by the governor. This vests in him a perfect dominion in his lands, transmissible to whom he pleases by deed or will, or by descent to his heirs if he die intestate.

Many of the laws which were in force during the monarchy being relative merely to that form of government, or inculcating principles inconsistent with republicanism, the first assembly which met after the establishment of the Commonwealth, appointed a committee to revise the whole code, to reduce it into proper form and volume, and report it to the assembly. This work has been executed by three gentlemen, and reported; but probably will not be taken up till a restoration of peace shall leave to the Legislature leisure to go through such a work.[44]

The plan of the revisal was this: The common law of England, by which is meant that part of the English law which was anterior to the date of the oldest statutes extant, is made the basis of the work. It was

[44]The committee of revisors consisted of Jefferson, George Wythe, and Edmund Pendleton. It submitted a lengthy report in June 1779; some of its recommendations were subsequently made law in Virginia.

thought dangerous to attempt to reduce it to a text: it was therefore left to be collected from the usual monuments of it. Necessary alterations in that, and so much of the whole body of the British statutes, and acts of assembly, as were thought proper to be retained, were digested into 126 new acts, in which simplicity of style was aimed at, as far as was safe. The following are the most remarkable alterations proposed:

To change the rules of descent, so as that the lands of any person dying intestate shall be divisible equally among all his children, or other representatives, in equal degree.

To make slaves distributable among the next of kin, as other moveables.

To have all public expenses, whether of the general treasury, or of a parish or county, (as for the maintenance of the poor, building bridges, court houses, &c.) supplied by assessments on the citizens, in proportion to their property.

To hire undertakers for keeping the public roads in repair, and indemnify individuals through whose lands new roads shall be opened.

To define with precision the rules whereby aliens should become citizens, and citizens make themselves aliens.

To establish religious freedom on the broadest bottom.

To emancipate all slaves born after passing the act. The bill reported by the revisors does not itself contain this proposition; but an amendment containing it was prepared, to be offered to the legislature whenever the bill should be taken up, and further directing that they should continue with their parents to a certain age, then be brought up, at the public expense, to tillage, arts or sciences, according to their geniuses, till the females should be eighteen, and the males twenty-one years of age, when they should be colonized to such place as the circumstances of the time should render most proper, sending them out with arms, implements of household and of the handicraft arts, seeds, pairs of the useful domestic animals, &c. to declare them a free and independent people, and extend to them our alliance and protection, till they shall have acquired strength; and to send vessels at the same time to other parts of the world for an equal number of white inhabitants; to induce whom to migrate hither, proper encouragements were to be proposed. It will probably be asked, Why not retain and incorporate the blacks into the state, and thus save the expense of supplying, by importation of white settlers, the vacancies they will leave? Deep-rooted prejudices entertained by the whites; ten thousand recollections, by the blacks, of the injuries they have sustained; new provocations; the real distinctions which nature has made; and many other circumstances, will divide us into parties, and produce convulsions which will probably never end but in the extermination of the one or the other race.—To these objections, which are political, may be added others, which are physical and moral. The first difference which strikes us is that of color. Whether the black of the negro resides in the reticular membrane between the skin and scarf–skin, or in the scarf–skin itself; whether it proceeds from the color of the blood, the color of the bile, or from that of some other secretion, the difference is fixed in nature, and is real as if its seat and cause were better known to us. And is this difference of no importance? Is it not the foundation of a greater or less share of beauty in the two races? Are not the fine mixtures of red and white, the expressions of every passion by greater or less suffusions of color in the one, preferable to that eternal monotony which reigns in the countenances, that immovable veil of black which covers all the emotions of the other race? Add to these flowing hair, a more elegant symmetry of form, their own judgment in favor of the whites, declared by their preference of them, as uniformly as is the preference of the Oranootan for the black women over those of his own species. The circumstance of superior beauty is thought worthy attention in the propagation of our horses, dogs, and other domestic animals; why not in that of man? Besides those of color, figure and hair, there are other physical distinctions proving a difference of race. They have less hair on the face and body. They secrete less by the kidneys, and more by the glands of the skin, which gives them a very strong and disagreeable odor. This greater degree of transpiration renders them more tolerant of heat, and less so of cold, than the whites. Perhaps, too, a difference of structure in the pulmonary apparatus, which a late ingenious experimentalist has discovered to be the principal regulator of animal heat, may have disabled them from extricating, in the act of inspiration, so much of that fluid from the outer air, or obliged them in expiration, to part with more of it. They seem to require less sleep. A black, after hard labor through the day, will be induced by the slightest amusements to sit up till midnight, or later, though knowing he must be out with the first dawn of the morning. They are at least as brave, and more adventuresome. But this may perhaps proceed from a want of forethought, which prevents their seeing a danger till it be present. When present, they do not go through it with more coolness or steadiness than the whites. They are more ardent after their female; but love seems with them to be more an eager desire, than a tender delicate mixture of sentiment and sensation. Their griefs are transient. Those numberless afflictions, which render it doubtful whether Heaven has given life to us in mercy or in wrath, are less felt, and sooner forgotten with them. In general, their existence appears to participate more of sensation than reflection. To this must be ascribed their disposition to sleep when abstracted from their diversions, and unemployed in labor. An animal whose body is at rest, and who does not reflect, must be disposed to sleep of course. Comparing them by their faculties of memory, reason, and imagination, it appears to me that in memory they are equal to the whites; in reason much inferior, as I think one could scarcely be found capable of tracing and comprehending the investigations of Euclid; and that in imagination they are dull, tasteless and anomalous. It would be unfair to follow them to Africa for this investigation. We will consider them here on the same stage with the whites, and where the facts are not apocryphal on which a judgment is to be formed. It will be right to make great allowances for the difference of condition, of education, of conversation, of the sphere in which they move. Many millions of them have been brought to, and born in America. Most of them, indeed, have been confined to tillage, to their own homes, and their own society; yet many have been so situated, that they might have availed themselves of the conversation of their masters; many have been brought up to the handicraft arts, and from that circumstance have always been associated with the whites. Some have been liberally educated, and all have lived in countries where the arts and sciences are cultivated to a considerable degree, and have had before their eyes samples of the best works from abroad. The Indians, with no advantages of this kind, will often carve figures on their pipes not destitute of design and merit. They will crayon out an animal, a plant, or a country, so as to prove the existence of a germ in their minds which only wants cultivation. They astonish you with strokes of the most sublime oratory; such as prove their reason and sentiment strong, their imagination glowing and elevated. But never yet could I find that a black had uttered a thought above the level of plain narration; never seen even an elementary trait of painting or sculpture. In music they are more generally gifted than the whites with accurate ears for tune and time, and they have been found capable of imagining a small catch.* Whether they will be equal to the composition of a more extensive run of melody, or of complicated harmony, is yet to be proved. Misery is often the parent of the most

---

*The instrument proper to them is the banjo, which they brought hither from Africa, and which is the original of the guitar, its chords being precisely the four lower chords of the guitar. [Jefferson's note.]

affecting touches in poetry.—Among the blacks is misery enough, God knows, but no poetry. Love is the peculiar œstrum of the poet. Their love is ardent, but it kindles the senses only, not the imagination. Religion, indeed, has produced a Phyllis Whately; but it could not produce a poet.[45] The compositions published under her name are below the dignity of criticism. The heroes of the Dunciad are to her as Hercules to the author of that poem. Ignatius Sancho has approached nearer to merit in composition; yet his letters do more honor to the heart than the head.[46] They breathe the purest effusions of friendship and general philanthropy, and shew how great a degree of the latter may be compounded with strong religious zeal. He is often happy in the turn of his compliments, and his style is easy and familiar, except when he affects a Shandean fabrication of words.[47] But his imagination is wild and extravagant, escapes incessantly from every restraint of reason and taste, and, in the course of its vagaries, leaves a tract of thought as incoherent and eccentric as is the course of a meteor through the sky. His subjects should often have led him to a process of sober reasoning: yet we find him always substituting sentiment for demonstration. Upon the whole, though we admit him to the first place among those of his own color who have presented themselves to the public judgment, yet when we compare him with the writers of the race among whom he lived, and particularly with the epistolary class, in which he has taken his own stand, we are compelled to enroll him at the bottom of the column. This criticism supposes the letters published under his name to be genuine, and to have received amendment from no other hand; points which would not be of easy investigation. The improvement of the blacks in body and mind, in the first instance of their mixture with the whites, has been observed by every one, and proves that their inferiority is not the effect merely of their condition of life. We know that among the Romans, about the Augustan age especially, the condition of their slaves was much more deplorable than that of the blacks on the continent of America. The two sexes were confined in separate apartments, because to raise a child cost the master more than to buy one. Cato, for a very restricted indulgence to his slaves in this particular, took from them a certain

---

[45]Phillis Wheatley, a Massachusetts slave born in Africa, author of *Poems on Various Subjects, Religious and Moral* (London, 1773).

[46]Alexander Pope, *The Dunciad* (London, 1728); Ignatius Sancho, *Letters of Ignatius Sancho*, 2 vols. (London, 1782).

[47]Laurence Sterne, *The Life and Opinions of Tristram Shandy, Gentleman* (London, 1757–71).

price. But in this country the slaves multiply as fast as the free inhabitants. Their situation and manners place the commerce between the
two sexes almost without restraint.—The same Cato, on a principle of
economy, always sold his sick and superannuated slaves. He gives it
as a standing precept to a master visiting his farm, to sell his old oxen,
old wagons, old tools, old and diseased servants, and every thing else
become useless. . . . The American slaves cannot enumerate this
among the injuries and insults they receive. It was the common practice to expose in the island of Aesculapius, in the Tyber, diseased
slaves, whose cure was like to become tedious. The Emperor Claudius
by an edict gave freedom to such of them as should recover, and first
declared, that if any person chose to kill rather than to expose them, it
should be deemed homicide. The exposing them is a crime, of which
no instance has existed with us; and were it to be followed by death, it
would be punished capitally. We are told of a certain Vedius Pollio,
who, in the presence of Augustus, would have given a slave as food to
his fish, for having broken a glass. With the Romans, the regular
method of taking the evidence of their slaves was under torture. Here
it has been thought better never to resort to their evidence. When a
master was murdered, all his slaves in the same house, or within hearing, were condemned to death. Here punishment falls on the guilty
only, and as precise proof is required against him as against a freeman. Yet notwithstanding these and other discouraging circumstances
among the Romans, their slaves were often their rarest artists. They
excelled, too, in science, insomuch as to be usually employed as tutors
to their master's children. Epictetus, Diogenes, Phaedon, Terence,
and Phædrus, were slaves. But they were of the race of whites. It is
not their condition then, but nature, which has produced the distinction.—Whether further observation will or will not verify the conjecture, that nature has been less bountiful to them in the endowments of
the head, I believe that in those of the heart she will be found to have
done them justice. That disposition to theft with which they have been
branded, must be ascribed to their situation, and not to any depravity
of the moral sense. The man, in whose favor no laws of property exist,
probably feels himself less bound to respect those made in favor of
others. When arguing for ourselves, we lay it down as a fundamental,
that laws, to be just, must give a reciprocation of right: that, without
this, they are mere arbitrary rules of conduct, founded in force, and
not in conscience; and it is a problem which I give to the master to
solve, whether the religious precepts against the violation of property
were not framed for him as well as his slave? And whether the slave

may not as justifiably take a little from one who has taken all from him, as he may slay one who would slay him? That a change in the relations in which a man is placed should change his ideas of moral right and wrong, is neither new nor peculiar to the color of the blacks. Homer tells us it was so 2600 years ago:

Jove fix'd it certain, that whatever day
Makes man a slave, takes half his worth away.

But the slaves of which Homer speaks were whites. Notwithstanding these considerations, which must weaken their respect for the laws of property, we find among them numerous instances of the most rigid integrity, and as many as among their better instructed masters, of benevolence, gratitude, and unshaken fidelity.—The opinion that they are inferior in the faculties of reason and imagination, must be hazarded with great diffidence. To justify a general conclusion, requires many observations, even where the subject may be submitted to the Anatomical knife, to Optical glasses, to analysis by fire, or by solvents. How much more then where it is a faculty, not a substance, we are examining; where it eludes the research of all the senses; where the conditions of its existence are various, and variously combined; where the effects of those which are present or absent bid defiance to calculation; let me add too, as a circumstance of great tenderness, where our conclusion would degrade a whole race of men from the rank in the scale of beings which their Creator may perhaps have given them. To our reproach it must be said, that though for a century and a half we have had under our eyes the races of black and of red men, they have never yet been viewed by us as subjects of natural history. I advance it therefore as a suspicion only, that the blacks, whether originally a distinct race, or made distinct by time and circumstances, are inferior to the whites in the endowments both of body and mind. It is not against experience to suppose that different species of the same genus, or varieties of the same species, may possess different qualifications. Will not a lover of natural history then, one who views the gradations in all the races of animals with the eye of philosophy, excuse an effort to keep those in the department of man as distinct as nature has formed them? This unfortunate difference of color, and perhaps of faculty, is a powerful obstacle to the emancipation of these people. Many of their advocates, while they wish to vindicate the liberty of human nature, are anxious also to preserve its dignity and beauty. Some of these, embarrassed by the question, "What further is to be done with them?" join themselves in opposition with those who are actuated by sordid avarice only. Among the Romans emancipation required but one effort. The slave, when made free, might mix with, without staining the blood of his master. But with us a second is necessary, unknown to history. When freed, he is to be removed beyond the reach of mixture.

The revised code further proposes to proportion crimes and punishments. This is attempted on the following scale:

I. *Crimes whose punishment extends to Life:*
    1. High treason. Death by hanging. Forfeiture of lands and goods to the Commonwealth.
    2. Petty treason. Death by hanging. Dissection. Forfeiture of half the lands and goods to the representatives of the party slain.
    3. Murder.
        1. By poison. Death by poison. Forfeiture of one-half as before.
        2. In Duel. Death by hanging. Gibbeting, if the challenger. Forfeiture of one-half as before, unless it be the party challenged, then the forfeiture is to the Commonwealth.
        3. In any other way. Death by hanging. Forfeiture of one-half as before.
    4. Manslaughter. The second offence is murder.
II. *Crimes whose punishment goes to Limb:*
    1. Rape. ⎫
    2. Sodomy. ⎭ Dismemberment.
    3. Maiming. ⎫ Retaliation, and the forfeiture of half the
    4. Disfiguring. ⎭ lands and goods to the sufferer.
III. *Crimes punishable by Labor:*
    1. Manslaughter, 1st offence. Labor 7 years for the public. Forfeiture of half as in murder.
    2. Counterfeiting money. Labor 6 years. Forfeiture of lands and goods to the Commonwealth.
    3. Arson. ⎫ Labor 5 years. Reparation
    4. Asportation of vessels. ⎭ three-fold.
    5. Robbery. ⎫ Labour 4 years. Reparation double.
    6. Burglary. ⎭
    7. House-breaking. ⎫ Labor 3 years. Reparation.
    8. Horse-stealing. ⎭
    9. Grand Larceny. Labor 2 years. Reparation. Pillory.
    10. Petty Larceny. Labor 1 year. Reparation. Pillory.

11. Pretensions to witchcraft, &c. Ducking. Stripes.

12. Excusable homicide.

13. Suicide.   } To be pitied, not punished.

14. Apostacy. Heresy.

Pardon and privilege of clergy are proposed to be abolished; but if the verdict be against the defendant, the court, in their discretion, may allow a new trial. No attainder to cause a corruption of blood,[48] or forfeiture of dower. Slaves guilty of offences punishable in others by labor, to be transported to Africa, or elsewhere, as the circumstances of the time admit, there to be continued in slavery. A rigorous regimen proposed for those condemned to labor.

Another object of the revisal is, to diffuse knowledge more generally through the mass of the people. This bill proposes to lay off every county into small districts of five or six miles square, called hundreds, and in each of them to establish a school for teaching reading, writing, and arithmetic. The tutor to be supported by the hundred, and every person in it entitled to send their children three years gratis, and as much longer as they please, paying for it. These schools to be under a visitor, who is annually to choose the boy, of best genius in the school, of those whose parents are too poor to give them further education, and to send him forward to one of the grammar schools, of which twenty are proposed to be erected in different parts of the country, for teaching Greek, Latin, geography, and the higher branches of numerical arithmetic. Of the boys thus sent in any one year, trial is to be made at the grammar schools one or two years, and the best genius of the whole selected, and continued six years, and the residue dismissed. By this means twenty of the best geniuses will be raked from the rubbish annually, and be instructed, at the public expense, so far as the grammar schools go. At the end of six years' instruction, one-half are to be discontinued, (from among whom the grammar schools will probably be supplied with future masters); and the other half, who are to be chosen for the superiority of their parts and disposition, are to be sent and continued three years in the study of such sciences as they shall choose, at William and Mary college, the plan of which is proposed to be enlarged, as will be hereafter explained, and extended to all the useful sciences. The ultimate result of the whole scheme of education would be the teaching all the children of the state reading, writing, and common arithmetic; turning out ten annually of superior

---

[48]corruption of blood: loss of hereditary title, as well as landowning and inheritance rights.

genius, well taught in Greek, Latin, geography, and the higher branches of arithmetic; turning out ten others annually of still superior parts, who, to those branches of learning, shall have added such of the sciences as their genius shall have led them to; the furnishing to the wealthier part of the people convenient schools, at which their children may be educated, at their own expense.—The general objects of this law are to provide an education adapted to the years, to the capacity, and the condition of every one, and directed to their freedom and happiness. Specific details were not proper for the law. These must be the business of the visitors entrusted with its execution. The first stage of this education being the schools of the hundreds, wherein the great mass of the people will receive their instruction, the principal foundations of future order will be laid here. Instead, therefore, of putting the Bible and Testament into the hands of the children, at an age when their judgments are not sufficiently matured for religious enquiries, their memories may here be stored with the most useful facts from Grecian, Roman, European, and American history. The first elements of morality too may be instilled into their minds: such as, when further developed as their judgments advance in strength, may teach them how to work out their own greatest happiness, by showing them that it does not depend on the condition of life in which chance has placed them, but is always the result of a good conscience, good health, occupation, and freedom in all just pursuits.—Those whom either the wealth of their parents or the adoption of the state shall destine to higher degrees of learning, will go on to the grammar schools, which constitute the next stage, there to be instructed in the languages. The learning Greek and Latin, I am told, is going into disuse in Europe. I know not what their manners and occupations may call for, but it would be very ill-judged in us to follow their example in this instance. There is a certain period of life, say from eight to fifteen or sixteen years of age, when the mind, like the body, is not yet firm enough for laborious and close operations. If applied to such, it falls an early victim to premature exertion; exhibiting, indeed, at first, in these young and tender subjects, the flattering appearance of their being men while they are yet children, but ending in reducing them to be children when they should be men. The memory is then most susceptible and tenacious of impressions; and the learning of languages being chiefly a work of memory, it seems precisely fitted to the powers of this period, which is long enough, too, for acquiring the most useful languages, ancient and modern. I do not pretend that language is science. It is only an instrument for the attainment of science. But that time is not lost which is employed in providing tools for future operation: more especially as in this case the books put into the hands of the youth for this purpose may be such as will at the same time impress their minds with useful facts and good principles. If this period be suffered to pass in idleness, the mind becomes lethargic and impotent, as would the body it inhabits if unexercised during the same time. The sympathy between body and mind during their rise, progress, and decline, is too strict and obvious to endanger our being misled while we reason from the one to the other.—As soon as they are of sufficient age, it is supposed they will be sent on from the grammar schools to the university, which constitutes our third and last stage, there to study those sciences which may be adapted to their views.—By that part of our plan which prescribes the selection of the youths of genius from among the classes of the poor, we hope to avail the State of those talents which nature has sown as liberally among the poor as the rich, but which perish without use if not sought for and cultivated.—But of all the views of this law, none is more important, none more legitimate, than that of rendering the people the safe, as they are the ultimate, guardians of their own liberty. For this purpose the reading in the first stage, where *they* will receive their whole education, is proposed, as has been said, to be chiefly historical. History, by apprising them of the past, will enable them to judge of the future; it will avail them of the experience of other times, and other nations; it will qualify them as judges of the actions and designs of men; it will enable them to know ambition under every disguise it may assume: and knowing it, to defeat its views. In every government on earth is some trace of human weakness, some germ of corruption and degeneracy, which cunning will discover, and wickedness insensibly open, cultivate, and improve. Every government degenerates when trusted to the rulers of the people alone. The people themselves therefore are its only safe depositories. And to render even them safe their minds must be improved to a certain degree. This, indeed, is not all that is necessary, though it be essentially necessary. An amendment of our constitution must here come in aid of the public education. The influence over government must be shared among all the people. If every individual which composes their mass participates of the ultimate authority, the government will be safe; because the corrupting the whole mass will exceed any private resources of wealth: and public ones cannot be provided but by levies on the people. In this case every man would have to pay his own price. The government of Great Britain has been corrupted, because but one man in ten has a right to vote for members of parliament. The sellers of the government, therefore, get nine-tenths of their price clear. It has been thought that corruption is restrained by confining the right of suffrage to a few of the wealthier of the people: but it would be more effectually restrained by an extension of that right to such numbers as would bid defiance to the means of corruption.

Lastly, it is proposed, by a bill in this revisal, to begin a public library and gallery, by laying out a certain sum annually in books, paintings, and statues.

QUERY XV: COLLEGES, BUILDINGS, AND ROADS

The Colleges and Public Establishments, the Roads, Buildings, &c.?

The College of William and Mary is the only public seminary of learning in this state. It was founded in the time of king William and queen Mary, who granted to it 20,000 acres of land, and a penny a pound duty on certain tobaccos exported from Virginia and Maryland, which had been levied by the statute of 25 Car. 2. The Assembly also gave it, by temporary laws, a duty on liquors imported, and skins and furs exported. From these resources it received upwards of £3,000 annually. The buildings are of brick, sufficient for an indifferent accommodation of perhaps an hundred students. By its charter it was to be under the government of twenty visitors, who were to be its legislators, and to have a president and six professors, who were incorporated. It was allowed a representative in the general assembly. Under this charter, a professorship of the Greek and Latin languages, a professorship of mathematics, one of moral philosophy, and two of divinity, were established. To these were annexed, for a sixth professorship, a considerable donation by Mr. Boyle of England, for the instruction of the Indians, and their conversion to Christianity.[49] This was called the professorship of Brafferton, from an estate of that name in England, purchased with the moneys given. The admission of the learners of Latin and Greek filled the college with children. This rendering it disagreeable and degrading to young gentlemen already prepared for entering on the sciences, they were discouraged from resorting to it, and thus the schools for mathematics and moral

---

[49]Robert Boyle (1627–91), English scientist and philanthropist renowned for his experiments in chemistry.

philosophy, which might have been of some service, became of very little. The revenues, too, were exhausted in accommodating those who came only to acquire the rudiments of science. After the present revolution, the visitors, having no power to change those circumstances in the constitution of the college which were fixed by the charter, and being therefore confined in the number of professorships, undertook to change the objects of the professorships. They excluded the two schools for divinity, and that for the Greek and Latin languages, and substituted others; so that at present they stand thus:

A Professorship for Law and Police;
        for Anatomy and Medicine;
        for Natural Philosophy and Mathematics;
        for Moral Philosophy, the Law of Nature and
           Nations, the Fine Arts;
        for Modern Languages;
        for the Brafferton.

And it is proposed, so soon as the Legislature shall have leisure to take up this subject, to desire authority from them to increase the number of professorships, as well for the purpose of subdividing those already instituted as of adding others for other branches of science. To the professorships usually established in the universities of Europe, it would seem proper to add one for the ancient languages and literature of the North, on account of their connection with our own language, laws, customs, and history. The purposes of the Brafferton Institution would be better answered by maintaining a perpetual mission among the Indian tribes, the object of which, besides instructing them in the principles of Christianity, as the founder requires, should be to collect their traditions, laws, customs, languages, and other circumstances which might lead to a discovery of their relation with one another, or descent from other nations. When these objects are accomplished with one tribe, the missionary might pass on to another.

The roads are under the government of the county courts, subject to be controlled by the general court. They order new roads to be opened wherever they think them necessary. The inhabitants of the county are by them laid off into precincts, to each of which they allot a convenient portion of the public roads to be kept in repair. Such bridges as may be built without the assistance of artificers, they are to build. If the stream be such as to require a bridge of regular workmanship, the court employs workmen to build it, at the expense of the whole county. If it be too great for the county, application is made to the general assembly, who authorize individuals to build it, and to take a fixed toll from all passengers, or give sanction to such other proposition as to them appears reasonable.

Ferries are admitted only at such places as are particularly pointed out by law, and the rates of ferriage are fixed.

Taverns are licensed by the courts, who fix their rates from time to time.

The private buildings are very rarely constructed of stone or brick; much the greatest proportion being of scantling and boards, plastered with lime. It is impossible to devise things more ugly, uncomfortable, and happily more perishable. There are two or three plans, on one of which, according to its size, most of the houses in the state are built. The poorest people build huts of logs, laid horizontally in pens, stopping the interstices with mud. These are warmer in winter, and cooler in summer, than the more expensive constructions of scantling and plank. The wealthy are attentive to the raising of vegetables, but very little so to fruits. The poor people attend to neither, living principally on milk and animal diet. This is the more inexcusable, as the climate requires indispensably a free use of vegetable food for health as well as comfort, and is very friendly to the raising of fruits.—The only public buildings worthy of mention are the Capitol, the Palace, the College, and the Hospital for Lunatics, all of them in Williamsburg, heretofore the seat of our government. The Capitol is a light and airy structure, with a portico in front of two orders, the lower of which, being Doric, is tolerably just in its proportions and ornaments, save only that the intercolonnations are too large. The upper is Ionic, much too small for that on which it is mounted, its ornaments not proper to the order, nor proportioned within themselves. It is crowned with a pediment, which is too high for its span. Yet, on the whole, it is the most pleasing piece of architecture we have. The Palace is not handsome without, but it is spacious and commodious within, is prettily situated, and, with the grounds annexed to it, is capable of being made an elegant seat. The College and Hospital are rude misshapen piles, which, but that they have roofs, would be taken for brick-kilns. There are no other public buildings but churches and court houses, in which no attempts are made at elegance. Indeed it would not be easy to execute such an attempt, as a workman could scarcely be found here capable of drawing an order. The genius of architecture seems to have shed its maledictions over this land. Buildings are often erected, by individuals, of considerable expense. To give these symmetry and

taste would not increase their cost. It would only change the arrangement of the materials, the form and combination of the members. This
would often cost less than the burthen of barbarous ornaments with
which these buildings are sometimes charged. But the first principles
of the art are unknown, and there exists scarcely a model among us
sufficiently chaste to give an idea of them. Architecture being one of
the fine arts, and as such within the department of a professor of the
college, according to the new arrangement, perhaps a spark may fall
on some young subjects of natural taste, kindle up their genius, and
produce a reformation in this elegant and useful art. But all we shall
do in this way will produce no permanent improvement to our country, while the unhappy prejudice prevails that houses of brick or stone
are less wholesome than those of wood. A dew is often observed on
the walls of the former in rainy weather, and the most obvious solution
is, that the rain has penetrated through these walls. The following
facts, however, are sufficient to prove the error of this solution: 1. This
dew on the walls appears when there is no rain, if the state of the
atmosphere be moist. 2. It appears on the partition as well as the exterior walls. 3. So also on pavements of brick or stone. 4. It is more copi-
ous in proportion as the walls are thicker; the reverse of which ought
to be the case, if this hypothesis were just. If cold water be poured
into a vessel of stone, or glass, a dew forms instantly on the outside;
but if it be poured into a vessel of wood, there is no such appearance.
It is not supposed, in the first case, that the water has exuded through
the glass, but that it is precipitated from the circumambient air; as the
humid particles of vapor, passing from the boiler of an alembic
through its refrigerant, are precipitated from the air, in which they
were suspended, on the internal surface of the refrigerant. Walls of
brick or stone act as the refrigerant in this instance. They are sufficiently cold to condense and precipitate the moisture suspended in the
air of the room, when it is heavily charged therewith. But walls of
wood are not so. The question then is, whether air in which this moisture is left floating, or that which is deprived of it, be most wholesome? In both cases the remedy is easy. A little fire kindled in the
room, whenever the air is damp, prevents the precipitation on the
walls: and this practice, found healthy in the warmest as well as
coolest seasons, is as necessary in a wooden as in a stone or a brick
house. I do not mean to say that the rain never penetrates through
walls of brick. On the contrary, I have seen instances of it. But with us
it is only through the northern and eastern walls of the house, after a

northeasterly storm, these being the only ones which continue long enough to force through the walls. This however happens too rarely to give a just character of unwholesomeness to such houses. In a house, the walls of which are of well-burnt brick and good mortar, I have seen the rain penetrate through but twice in a dozen or fifteen years. The inhabitants of Europe, who dwell chiefly in houses of stone or brick, are surely as healthy as those of Virginia. These houses have the advantage too of being warmer in winter and cooler in summer than those of wood; of being cheaper in their first construction, where lime is convenient, and infinitely more durable. The latter consideration renders it of great importance to eradicate this prejudice from the minds of our countrymen. A country, whose buildings are of wood, can never increase in its improvements to any considerable degree. Their duration is highly estimated at 50 years. Every half century then our country becomes a tabula rasa, whereon we have to set out anew, as in the first moment of seating it. Whereas when buildings are of durable materials, every new edifice is an actual and permanent acquisition to the state, adding to its value as well as to its ornament.

QUERY XVI: PROCEEDINGS AS TO TORIES

The Measures Taken with Regard of the Estates and Possessions of the Rebels, Commonly Called Tories?

A Tory has been properly defined to be a traitor in thought, but not in deed. The only description by which the laws have endeavored to come at them, was that of non-jurors, or persons refusing to take the oath of fidelity to the state. Persons of this description were at one time subjected to double taxation, at another to treble, and lastly were allowed retribution, and placed on a level with good citizens. It may be mentioned as a proof both of the lenity of our government and unanimity of its inhabitants, that though this war has now raged near seven years, not a single execution for treason has taken place.

Under this query I will state the measures which have been adopted as to British property, the owners of which stand on a much fairer footing than the Tories. By our laws, the same as the English in this respect, no alien can hold lands, nor alien enemy maintain an action for money or other movable thing. Lands acquired or held by aliens become forfeited to the state; and, on an action by an alien enemy to recover money, or other movable property, the defendant may plead that he is an alien enemy. This extinguishes his right in the hands of the debtor or holder of his movable property. By our separation from Great Britain, British subjects became aliens, and, being at war, they were alien enemies. Their lands were of course forfeited, and their debts irrecoverable. The assembly, however, passed laws, at various times, for saving their property. They first sequestered their land, slaves, and other property on their farms, in the hands of commissioners, who were mostly the confidential friends or agents of the owners, and directed their clear profits to be paid into the treasury; and they gave leave to all persons owing debts to British subjects to pay them also into the treasury. The moneys so to be brought in were declared to remain the property of the British subject, and, if used by the State, were to be re-paid, unless an improper conduct in Great Britain should render a detention of it reasonable. Depreciation had at that time, though unacknowledged and unperceived by the Whigs, begun in some small degree. Great sums of money were paid in by debtors. At a later period the assembly, adhering to the political principles which forbid an alien to hold lands in the state, ordered all British property to be sold: and, become sensible of the real progress of depreciation, and of the losses which would thence occur, if not guarded against, they ordered that the proceeds of the sales should be converted into their then worth in tobacco, subject to the future direction of the legislature. This act has left the question of retribution more problematical. In May 1780 another act took away the permission to pay into the public treasury debts due to British subjects.

QUERY XVII: RELIGION

The Different Religions Received into That State?

The first settlers in this country were emigrants from England, of the English Church, just at a point of time when it was flushed with complete victory over the religious of all other persuasions. Possessed as they became of the power of making, administering, and executing the laws, they showed equal intolerance in this country with their Presbyterian brethren, who had emigrated to the northern government. The poor Quakers were flying from persecution in England. They cast their eyes on these new countries as asylums of civil and religious freedom; but they found them free only for the reigning sect. Several acts of the Virginia Assembly of 1659, 1662, and 1693, had made it penal in parents to refuse to have their children baptized; had prohibited the unlawful assembling of Quakers; had made it penal for any master of a vessel to bring a Quaker into the state; had ordered those already here, and such as should come thereafter, to be imprisoned till they should abjure the country; provided a milder punishment for their first and second return, but death for their third; had inhibited all persons from suffering their meetings in or near their houses, entertaining them individually, or disposing of books which supported their tenets. If no capital execution took place here, as did in New England, it was not owing to the moderation of the church, or spirit of the legislature, as may be inferred from the law itself; but to historical circumstances which have not been handed down to us. The Anglicans retained full possession of the country about a century. Other opinions began then to creep in, and the great care of the government to support their own church, having begotten an equal degree of indolence in its clergy, two-thirds of the people had become dissenters at the commencement of the present revolution. The laws indeed were still oppressive on them, but the spirit of the one party had subsided into moderation, and of the other had risen to a degree of determination which commanded respect.

The present state of our laws on the subject of religion is this. The convention of May 1776, in their declaration of rights, declared it to be a truth, and a natural right, that the exercise of religion should be free; but when they proceeded to form on that declaration the ordinance of government, instead of taking up every principle declared in the bill of rights, and guarding it by legislative sanction, they passed over that which asserted our religious rights, leaving them as they found them. The same convention, however, when they met as a member of the general assembly in October 1776, repealed all *acts of parliament* which had rendered criminal the maintaining any opinions in matters of religion, the forbearing to repair to church, and the exercising any mode of worship; and suspended the laws giving salaries to the clergy, which suspension was made perpetual in October 1779. Statutory oppressions in religion being thus wiped away, we remain at present under those only imposed by the common law, or by our own acts of assembly. At the common law, *heresy* was a capital offence, punishable by burning. Its definition was left to the ecclesiastical judges, before whom the conviction was, till the statute of the first year of Queen Elizabeth's reign, circumscribed it, by declaring that nothing should be deemed heresy, but what had been so determined by authority of the canonical Scriptures, or by one of the four first general councils, or by some other council having for the grounds of their declaration the express and plain words of the scriptures. Heresy, thus circumscribed, being an offence at the common law, our act of assembly of October, 1777, gives cognizance of it to the general court, by declaring that the jurisdiction of that court shall be general in all matters at the common law. The execution is by the writ *De hœretico comburendo*. By our own act of assembly of 1705, if a person brought up in the Christian religion denies the being of a God, or the Trinity, or asserts there are more Gods than one, or denies the Christian religion to be true, or the scriptures to be of divine authority, he is punishable on the first offence by incapacity to hold any office or employment ecclesiastical, civil or military; on the second by disability to sue, to take any gift or legacy, to be guardian, executor, or administrator, and by three years imprisonment, without bail. A father's right to the custody of his own children being founded in law on his right of guardianship, this being taken away, they may of course be severed from him, and put, by the authority of court, into more orthodox hands. This is a summary view of that religious slavery, under which a people have been willing to remain, who have lavished their lives and fortunes for the establishment of their civil freedom. The error seems not sufficiently eradicated, that the operations of the mind, as well as the acts of the body, are subject to the coercion of the laws. But our rulers can have authority over such natural rights only as we have submitted to them. The rights of conscience we never submitted, we could not submit. We are answerable for them to our God. The legitimate powers of government extend to such acts only as are injurious to others. But it does me no injury for my neighbor to say there are twenty Gods, or no God. It neither picks my pocket nor breaks my leg. If it be said his testimony in a court of justice cannot be relied on, reject it then, and be the stigma on him. Constraint may make him worse by making him a hypocrite, but it will never make him a truer man. It may fix him obstinately in his errors, but will not cure them. Reason and free enquiry are the only effectual agents against error. Give a loose to them, they will support the true religion, by bringing every false one to their tribunal, to the test of their investigation. They are the natural enemies of error, and of error only. Had not the Roman government permitted free enquiry, Christianity could never have been introduced. Had not free enquiry been indulged, at the era of the reformation, the corruptions of Christianity could not have been purged away. If it be restrained now, the present corruptions will be protected, and new ones encouraged. Was the government to prescribe to us our medicine and diet, our bodies would be in such keeping as our souls are now. Thus in France the emetic was once forbidden as a medicine, and the potato as an article of food. Government is just as infallible too when it fixes systems in physics. Galileo was sent to the inquisition for affirming that the earth was a sphere; the government had declared it to be as flat as a trencher, and Galileo was obliged to abjure his error. This error, however, at length prevailed, the earth became a globe, and Descartes declared it was whirled round its axis by a vortex. The government in which he lived was wise enough to see that this was no question of civil jurisdiction, or we should all have been involved by authority in vortices. In fact, the vortices have been exploded, and the Newtonian principle of gravitation is now more firmly established on the basis of reason, than it would be were the government to step in and to make it an article of necessary faith. Reason and experiment have been indulged, and error has fled before them. It is error alone which needs the support of government. Truth can stand by itself. Subject opinion to coercion: whom will you make your inquisitors? Fallible men, men governed by bad passions, by private as well as public reasons. And why subject it to coercion? To produce uniformity. But is uniformity of opinion desirable? No more than of face and stature. Introduce the bed of Procrustes then, and as there is danger that the large men may beat the small, make us all of a size, by lopping the former and stretching the latter. Difference of opinion is advantageous in religion. The several sects perform the office of a censor morum[50] over each other. Is uniformity attainable? Millions of innocent men, women and children, since the introduction of Christianity, have been burnt, tortured, fined, imprisoned; yet we have not advanced one inch towards uniformity. What has been the effect of coercion? To make one-half the world fools, and the other half hypocrites. To support roguery and error all over the earth. Let us reflect that it is inhabited by a thousand millions of people. That these profess probably a thousand different systems of religion. That ours is but one of that thousand. That if there be but one right, and ours that one, we should wish

---

[50]censor morum: moral censor.

to see the 999 wandering sects gathered into the fold of truth. But against such a majority we cannot effect this by force. Reason and persuasion are the only practicable instruments. To make way for these, free enquiry must be indulged; and how can we wish others to indulge it while we refuse it ourselves. But every state, says an inquisitor, has established some religion. No two, say I, have established the same. Is this a proof of the infallibility of establishments? Our sister states of Pennsylvania and New York, however, have long subsisted without any establishment at all. The experiment was new and doubtful when they made it. It has answered beyond conception. They flourish infinitely. Religion is well supported; of various kinds, indeed, but all good enough; all sufficient to preserve peace and order: or if a sect arises, whose tenets would subvert morals, good sense has fair play, and reasons and laughs it out of doors, without suffering the state to be troubled with it. They do not hang more malefactors than we do. They are not more disturbed with religious dissensions. On the contrary, their harmony is unparalleled, and can be ascribed to nothing but their unbounded tolerance, because there is no other circumstance in which they differ from every nation on earth. They have made the happy discovery, that the way to silence religious disputes is to take no notice of them. Let us, too, give this experiment fair play, and get rid, while we may, of those tyrannical laws. It is true, we are as yet secured against them by the spirit of the times. I doubt whether the people of this country would suffer an execution for heresy, or a three years imprisonment for not comprehending the mysteries of the Trinity. But is the spirit of the people an infallible, a permanent reliance? Is it government? Is this the kind of protection we receive in return for the rights we give up? Besides, the spirit of the times may alter, will alter. Our rulers will become corrupt, our people careless. A single zealot may commence persecutor, and better men be his victims. It can never be too often repeated, that the time for fixing every essential right on a legal basis is while our rulers are honest, and ourselves united. From the conclusion of this war we shall be going down hill. It will not then be necessary to resort every moment to the people for support. They will be forgotten, therefore, and their rights disregarded. They will forget themselves, but in the sole faculty of making money, and will never think of uniting to effect a due respect for their rights. The shackles, therefore, which shall not be knocked off at the conclusion of this war, will remain on us long, will be made heavier and heavier, till our rights shall revive or expire in a convulsion.

QUERY XVIII: MANNERS

The Particular Customs and Manners That May Happen to Be Received in That State?

It is difficult to determine on the standard by which the manners of a nation may be tried, whether *catholic,* or *particular.* It is more difficult for a native to bring to that standard the manners of his own nation, familiarized to him by habit. There must doubtless be an unhappy influence on the manners of our people produced by the existence of slavery among us. The whole commerce between master and slave is a perpetual exercise of the most boisterous passions, the most unremitting despotism on the one part, and degrading submissions on the other. Our children see this, and learn to imitate it; for man is an imitative animal. This quality is the germ of all education in him. From his cradle to his grave he is learning to do what he sees others do. If a parent could find no motive either in his philanthropy or his self-love, for restraining the intemperance of passion towards his slave, it should always be a sufficient one that his child is present. But generally it is not sufficient. The parent storms, the child looks on, catches the lineaments of wrath, puts on the same airs in the circle of smaller slaves, gives a loose to his worst of passions, and thus nursed, educated, and daily exercised in tyranny, cannot but be stamped by it with odious peculiarities. The man must be a prodigy who can retain his manners and morals undepraved by such circumstances. And with what execration should the statesman be loaded, who permitting one-half the citizens thus to trample on the rights of the other, transforms those into despots, and these into enemies, destroys the morals of the one part, and the amor patriæ of the other. For if a slave can have a country in this world, it must be any other in preference to that in which he is born to live and labor for another: in which he must lock up the faculties of his nature, contribute as far as depends on his individual endeavors to the evanishment of the human race, or entail his own miserable condition on the endless generations proceeding from him. With the morals of the people their industry also is destroyed. For in a warm climate no man will labor for himself who can make another labor for him. This is so true, that of the proprietors of slaves a very small proportion indeed are ever seen to labor. And can the liberties of a nation be thought secure when we have removed their only firm basis, a conviction in the minds of the people that these liberties are of the gift of God? That they are not to be violated but with his wrath? Indeed I tremble for my country when I reflect that God is just;

that his justice cannot sleep forever; that considering numbers, nature and natural means only, a revolution of the wheel of fortune, an exchange of situation is among possible events; that it may become probable by supernatural interference! The Almighty has no attribute which can take side with us in such a contest.—But it is impossible to be temperate, and to pursue this subject through the various considerations of policy, of morals, of history, natural and civil. We must be contented to hope they will force their way into every one's mind. I think a change already perceptible, since the origin of the present revolution. The spirit of the master is abating, that of the slave rising from the dust, his condition mollifying, the way I hope preparing, under the auspices of heaven, for a total emancipation, and that this is disposed, in the order of events, to be with the consent of the masters, rather than by their extirpation.

QUERY XIX: MANUFACTURES

The Present State of Manufactures, Commerce, Interior and Exterior Trade?

We never had an interior trade of any importance. Our exterior commerce has suffered very much from the beginning of the present contest. During this time we have manufactured within our families the most necessary articles of clothing. Those of cotton will bear some comparison with the same kinds of manufacture in Europe; but those of wool, flax and hemp, are very coarse, unsightly and unpleasant; and such is our attachment to agriculture, and such our preference for foreign manufactures, that be it wise or unwise, our people will certainly return as soon as they can to the raising raw materials, and exchanging them for finer manufactures than they are able to execute themselves.

The political economists of Europe have established it as a principle that every State should endeavor to manufacture for itself; and this principle, like many others, we transfer to America, without calculating the difference of circumstance which should often produce a difference of result. In Europe the lands are either cultivated, or locked up against the cultivator. Manufacture must therefore be resorted to of necessity, not of choice, to support the surplus of their people. But we have an immensity of land courting the industry of the husbandman. Is it best then that all our citizens should be employed in its improvement, or that one-half should be called off from that to exercise manufactures and handicraft arts for the other? Those who labor in the earth are the chosen people of God, if ever he had a chosen people, whose breasts he has made his peculiar deposit for substantial and genuine virtue. It is the focus in which he keeps alive that sacred fire, which otherwise might escape from the face of the earth. Corruption of morals in the mass of cultivators is a phenomenon of which no age nor nation has furnished an example. It is the mark set on those, who not looking up to heaven, to their own soil and industry, as does the husbandman, for their subsistence, depend for it on the casualties and caprice of customers. Dependence begets subservience and venality, suffocates the germ of virtue, and prepares fit tools for the designs of ambition. This, the natural progress and consequence of the arts, has sometimes perhaps been retarded by accidental circumstances; but, generally speaking, the proportion which the aggregate of the other classes of citizens bears in any state to that of its husbandmen, is the proportion of its unsound to its healthy parts, and is a good enough barometer whereby to measure its degree of corruption. While we have land to labor then, let us never wish to see our citizens occupied at a work bench, or twirling a distaff. Carpenters, masons, smiths, are wanting in husbandry; but, for the general operations of manufacture, let our work shops remain in Europe. It is better to carry provisions and materials to workmen there, than bring them to the provisions and materials, and with them their manners and principles. The loss by the transportation of commodities across the Atlantic will be made up in happiness and permanence of government. The mobs of great cities add just so much to the support of pure government, as sores do to the strength of the human body. It is the manners and spirit of a people which preserve a republic in vigor. A degeneracy in these is a canker, which soon eats to the heart of its laws and constitution.

QUERY XX: SUBJECTS OF COMMERCE

A Notice of the Commercial Productions Particular to the State, and of Those Objects Which the Inhabitants Are Obliged to Get from Europe and from Other Parts of the World?

Before the present war we exported, each year, according to the best information I can get, nearly as follows:

ARTICLES	QUANTITY	PRICE IN DOLLARS	AMOUNT IN DOLLARS
Tobacco,	55,000 hhds. of 1,000 lb.	at 30 d. per hhd.	$1,650,000
Wheat,	800,000 bushels.	at ⅝ d. per bushel.	666,666⅔
Indian corn,	600,000 bushels.	at ⅓ d. per bushel.	200,000
Shipping,	—	—	100,000
Masts, planks, scantling, shingles, staves, tar, pitch, turpentine,	—	—	66,666⅔
Peltry, viz: skins of deer, beavers, otters, muskrats, raccoons, foxes,	30,000 barrels.	at 1⅓ d. per barrel.	40,000
	180 hhds. of 660 lb.	at 5/12 d. per lb.	42,000
Pork,	4,000 barrels.	at 10 d. per barrel.	40,000
Flax seed, hemp, cotton,	—	—	8,000
Pit coal, Pig iron,	—	—	6,666⅔
Peas,	5,000 bushels.	at ⅔ d. per bushel.	3,333⅓
Beef,	1,000 barrels.	at 3⅓ d. per barrel.	3,333⅓
Sturgeon, white shad, herring,	—	—	3,333⅓
Brandy from peaches and apples, and whiskey,	—	—	1,666⅔
Horses,	—	—	1,666⅔
This sum is equal to £850,000 Virginia money, 607,142 guineas.			**$2,833,333⅓**

In the year 1758 we exported seventy thousand hogsheads of tobacco, which was the greatest quantity ever produced in this country in one year. But its culture was fast declining at the commencement of this war, and that of wheat taking its place; and it must continue to decline on the return of peace. I suspect that the change in the temperature of our climate has become sensible to that plant, which, to be good, requires an extraordinary degree of heat. But it requires still more indispensably an uncommon fertility of soil; and the price which it commands at market will not enable the planter to produce this by manure. Was the supply still to depend on Virginia and Maryland alone, as its culture becomes more difficult, the price would rise, so as to enable the planter to surmount those difficulties and to live. But the Western country on the Missisipi, and the midlands of Georgia, having fresh and fertile lands in abundance, and a hotter sun, will be able to undersell these two states, and will oblige them to abandon the raising tobacco altogether. And a happy obligation for them it will be. It is a culture productive of infinite wretchedness. Those employed in it are in a continued state of exertion beyond the powers of nature to support. Little food of any kind is raised by them, so that the men and animals on these farms are badly fed, and the earth is rapidly impoverished. The cultivation of wheat is the reverse in every circumstance. Besides clothing the earth with herbage, and preserving its fertility, it feeds the laborers plentifully, requires from them only a moderate toil, except in the season of harvest, raises great numbers of animals for food and service, and diffuses plenty and happiness among the whole. We find it easier to make an hundred bushels of wheat than a thousand weight of tobacco, and they are worth more when made. The weevil indeed is a formidable obstacle to the cultivation of this grain with us. But principles are already known which must lead to a remedy. Thus a certain degree of heat, to wit, that of the common air in summer, is necessary to hatch the egg. If subterranean granaries, or others, therefore, can be contrived below that temperature, the evil will be cured by cold. A degree of heat, beyond that which hatches the egg, we know will kill it. But in aiming at this we easily run into that which produces putrefaction. To produce putrefaction, however, three agents are requisite: heat, moisture, and the external air. If the absence of any one of these be secured, the other two may safely be admitted. Heat is the one we want. Moisture then, or external air, must be excluded. The former has been done by exposing the grain in kilns to the action of fire, which produces heat, and extracts moisture at the same time: the latter, by putting the grain into hogsheads, covering it with a coat of lime, and heading it up. In this situation its bulk produces a heat sufficient to kill the egg; the moisture is suffered to remain indeed, but the external air is excluded. A nice operation yet has been attempted: that is, to produce an intermediate temperature of heat between that which kills the egg, and that which produces putrefaction. The threshing the grain as soon as it is cut, and laying it in its chaff, in large heaps, has been found very nearly to hit this temperature, though not perfectly, nor always. The heap generates heat sufficient to kill most of the eggs, whilst the chaff commonly restrains it from rising into putrefaction. But all these methods abridge too much the quantity which the farmer can manage, and enable other countries to undersell him which are not infested with this insect. There is still a desideratum then to give with us decisive triumph to this branch of agriculture over that of tobacco.—The culture of wheat, by enlarging our pasture, will render the Arabian horse an article of very considerable profit. Experience has shown that ours is the particular climate of America where he may be raised without degeneracy. Southwardly the heat of the sun occasions a deficiency of pasture, and northwardly the winters are too cold for the short and fine hair, the particular sensibility and constitution of that race. Animals, transplanted into unfriendly climates, either change their nature and acquire new fences against the new difficulties in which they are placed, or they multiply poorly and become extinct. A good foundation is laid for their propagation here by our possessing already great numbers of horses of that blood, and by a decided taste and preference for them established among the people. Their patience of heat without injury, their superior wind, fit them better in this and the more southern climates even for the drudgeries of the plough and wagon. Northwardly they will become an object only to persons of taste and fortune, for the saddle and light carriages. To these, and for these uses, their fleetness and beauty sill recommend them.—Besides these there will be other valuable substitutes when the cultivation of tobacco shall be discontinued, such as cotton in the eastern parts of the state, and hemp and flax in the western.

It is not easy to say what are the articles either of necessity, comfort, or luxury, which we cannot raise, and which we, therefore, shall be under a necessity of importing from abroad, as everything hardier than the olive, and as hardy as the fig, may be raised here in the open air. Sugar, coffee and tea, indeed, are not between these limits; and habit having placed them among the necessaries of life with the wealthy part of our citizens, as long as these habits remain, we must go for them to those countries which are able to furnish them.

QUERY XXI: WEIGHTS, MEASURES, AND MONEY

The Weights, Measures, and the Currency of the Hard Money? Some Details Relating to the Exchange with Europe?

Our weights and measures are the same which are fixed by acts of parliament in England.—How it has happened that in this as well as the other American states the nominal value of coin was made to differ from what it was in the country we had left, and to differ among ourselves too, I am not able to say with certainty. I find that in 1631 our house of burgesses desired of the privy council in England a coin debased to twenty-five per cent.; that, in 1645, they forbid dealing by barter for tobacco, and established the Spanish piece of eight at six shillings, as the standard of their currency; that, in 1655, they changed it to five shillings sterling. In 1680 they sent an address to the king, in consequence of which, by proclamation in 1683, he fixed the value of French crowns, rixdollars, and pieces of eight at six shillings, and the coin of New England at one shilling. That in 1710, 1714, 1727, and 1762, other regulations were made, which will be better presented to the eye, stated in the form of a table, as follows:

	1710	1714	1727	1762
Guineas	—	26s.		
British gold coin not milled, coined gold of Spain and France, chequins,	—	5s. the dwt.		
Arabian gold, moidores of Portugal,				
Coined gold of the empire,	—	5s. the dwt.	—	4s. 3d. the dwt.
English milled silver money, in proportion to the crown, at	—	5s. 10d.	6s.3d.	

(continued)

	1710	1714	1727	1762
Pieces of eight of Mexico, Seville, and Pillar, ducatoons of Flanders, French ecus, or silver Louis, crusados of Portugal,	3¾ d. the dwt.	—	4d. the dwt.	
Peru pieces, cross dollars, and old rixdollars of the Empire,	3½ d. the dwt.	—	3¾ d. the dwt.	
Old British silver coin not milled,	—	3¾ d. the dwt.		

Note: s. = shillings, dwt. = penny weight, d. = pence

The first symptom of the depreciation of our present paper money was that of silver dollars selling at six shillings, which had before been worth but five shillings and ninepence. The assembly thereupon raised them by law to six shillings. As the dollar is now likely to become the money unit of America, as it passes at this rate in some of our sister states, and as it facilitates their computation in pounds and shillings, and vice versa, this seems to be more convenient than its former denomination. But as this particular coin now stands higher than any other in the proportion of 133⅓ to 125, or 16 to 15, it will be necessary to raise the others in the same proportion.

QUERY XXII: PUBLIC REVENUE AND EXPENSES

The Public Income and Expenses?

The nominal amount of these varying constantly and rapidly, with the constant and rapid depreciation of our paper money, it becomes impracticable to say what they are. We find ourselves cheated in every essay by the depreciation intervening between the declaration of the tax and its actual receipt. It will therefore be more satisfactory to consider what our income may be when we shall find means of collecting what the people may spare. I should estimate the whole taxable property of this state at an hundred millions of dollars, or thirty millions of pounds our money. One per cent. on this, compared with any thing we ever yet paid, would be deemed a very heavy tax. Yet I think that those who manage well, and use reasonable economy, could pay one and a half per cent, and maintain their household comfortably in the mean time, without aliening any part of their principal, and that the people would submit to this willingly for the purpose of supporting their present contest. We may say, then, that we could raise, and ought to raise, from one million to one million and a half of dollars annually, that is from three hundred to four hundred and fifty thousand pounds, Virginia money.

Of our expenses it is equally difficult to give an exact state, and for the same reason. They are mostly stated in paper money, which varying continually, the legislature endeavors at every session, by new corrections, to adapt the nominal sums to the value it is wished they should bear. I will state them, therefore, in real coin, at the point at which they endeavor to keep them:

The annual expenses of the general assembly are about	$20,000
The governor	3,333⅓
The council of state	10,666⅔
Their clerks	1,166⅔
Eleven judges	11,000
The clerk of the chancery	666⅔
The attorney general	1,000
Three auditors and a solicitor	5,333⅓
Their clerks	2,000
The treasurer	2,000
His clerks	2,000
The keeper of the public jail	1,000
The public printer	1,666⅔
Clerks of the inferior courts	43,333⅓
Public levy: this is chiefly for the expenses of criminal justice	40,000
County levy, for bridges, court houses, prisons, &c.	40,000
Members of congress	7,000
Quota of the Federal civil list, supposed ⅙ of about 78,000	13,000
Expenses of collection, 6 per cent. on the above	12,310
The clergy receive only voluntary contributions: suppose them on an average ⅛ of a dollar a tythe on 200,000 tythes	25,000
Contingencies, to make round numbers not far from truth	7,523⅓
	250,000

Dollars, or 53,571 guineas. This estimate is exclusive of the military expense. That varies with the force actually employed, and in time of peace will probably be little or nothing. It is exclusive also of the public debts, which are growing while I am writing, and cannot therefore be now fixed. So it is of the maintenance of the poor, which being merely a matter of charity, cannot be deemed expended in the administration of government. And if we strike out the 25,000 dollars for the services of the clergy, which neither makes part of that administration, more than what is paid to physicians or lawyers, and being voluntary, is either much or nothing, as every one pleases, it leaves 225,000 dollars, equal to 48,208 guineas, the real cost of the apparatus of government with us. This, divided among the actual inhabitants of our country, comes to about two-fifths of a dollar, 21d. sterling, or 42 sols, the price which each pays annually for the protection of the residue of his property, that of his person, and the other advantages of a free government. The public revenues of Great Britain divided in like manner on its inhabitants would be sixteen times greater. Deducting even the double of the expenses of government, as before estimated, from the million and a half of dollars which we before supposed might be annually paid without distress, we may conclude that this state can contribute one million of dollars annually towards supporting the federal army, paying the federal debt, building a federal navy, or opening roads, clearing rivers, forming safe ports, and other useful works.

To this estimate of our abilities, let me add a word as to the application of them, if, when cleared of the present contest, and of the debts with which that will charge us, we come to measure force hereafter with any European power. Such events are devoutly to be deprecated. Young as we are, and with such a country before us to fill with people and with happiness, we should point in that direction the whole generative force of nature, wasting none of it in efforts of mutual destruction. It should be our endeavor to cultivate the peace and friendship of every nation, even of that which has injured us most, when we shall have carried our point against her. Our interest will be to throw open the doors of commerce, and to knock off all its shackles, giving perfect freedom to all persons for the vent[51] of whatever they may choose to bring into our ports, and asking the same in theirs. Never was so much false arithmetic employed on any subject, as that which has been employed to persuade nations that it is their interest to go to war. Were the money which it has cost to gain, at the close of a long

[51]vent: sale.

war, a little town, or a little territory, the right to cut wood here, or to catch fish there, expended in improving what they already possess, in making roads, opening rivers, building ports, improving the arts, and finding employment for their idle poor, it would render them much stronger, much wealthier and happier. This I hope will be our wisdom. And, perhaps, to remove as much as possible the occasions of making war, it might be better for us to abandon the ocean altogether, that being the element whereon we shall be principally exposed to jostle with other nations: to leave to others to bring what we shall want, and to carry what we can spare. This would make us invulnerable to Europe, by offering none of our property to their prize, and would turn all our citizens to the cultivation of the earth; and, I repeat it again, cultivators of the earth are the most virtuous and independent citizens. It might be time enough to seek employment for them at sea, when the land no longer offers it. But the actual habits of our country-men attach them to commerce. They will exercise it for themselves. Wars then must sometimes be our lot; and all the wise can do, will be to avoid that half of them which would be produced by our own follies, and our own acts of injustice; and to make for the other half the best preparations we can. Of what nature should these be? A land army would be useless for offence, and not the best nor safest instrument of defence. For either of these purposes, the sea is the field on which we should meet an European enemy. On that element it is necessary we should possess some power. To aim at such a navy as the greater nations of Europe possess, would be a foolish and wicked waste of the energies of our countrymen. It would be to pull on our own heads that load of military expense, which makes the European laborer go supperless to bed, and moistens his bread with the sweat of his brows. It will be enough if we enable ourselves to prevent insults from those nations of Europe which are weak on the sea, because circumstances exist, which render even the stronger ones weak as to us. Providence has placed their richest and most defenceless possessions at our door; has obliged their most precious commerce to pass as it were in review before us. To protect this, or to assail us, a small part only of their naval force will ever be risked across the Atlantic. The dangers to which the elements expose them here are too well known, and the greater dangers to which they would be exposed at home, were any general calamity to involve their whole fleet. They can attack us by detachment only; and it will suffice to make ourselves equal to what they may detach. Even a smaller force than they may detach will be rendered equal or superior by the quickness with which any check may be repaired with us, while losses with them will be irreparable till too late. A small naval force then is sufficient for us, and a small one is necessary. What this should be, I will not undertake to say. I will only say, it should by no means be so great as we are able to make it. Suppose the million of dollars, or three hundred thousand pounds, which Virginia could annually spare without distress, to be applied to the creating a navy. A single year's contribution would build, equip, man, and send to sea a force which should carry 300 guns. The rest of the confederacy, exerting themselves in the same proportion, would equip in the same time 1500 guns more. So that one year's contributions would set up a navy of 1800 guns. The British ships of the line average 76 guns; their frigates 38. 1800 guns then would form a fleet of 30 ships, 18 of which might be of the line, and 12 frigates. Allowing 8 men, the British average, for every gun, their annual expense, including subsistence, clothing, pay, and ordinary repairs, would be about 1280 dollars for every gun, or 2,304,000 dollars for the whole. I state this only as one year's possible exertion, without deciding whether more or less than a year's exertion should be thus applied.

The value of our lands and slaves, taken conjunctly, doubles in about twenty years. This arises from the multiplication of our slaves, from the extension of culture, and increased demand for lands. The amount of what may be raised will of course rise in the same proportion.

QUERY XXIII: HISTORIES, MEMORIALS, AND STATE-PAPERS

The Histories of the State, the Memorials Published in Its Name in the Time of Its Being a Colony, and the Pamphlets Relating to Its Interior or Exterior Affairs, Present or Ancient?

Captain Smith, who next to Sir Walter Raleigh, may be considered as the founder of our colony, has written its history from the first adventures to it till the year 1624. He was a member of the council, and afterwards president of the colony; and to his efforts principally may be ascribed its support against the opposition of the natives. He was honest, sensible, and well informed; but his style is barbarous and uncouth. His history, however, is almost the only source from which we derive any knowledge of the infancy of our state.

The Rev. William Stith, a native of Virginia, and president of its college, has also written the history of the same period, in a large octavo volume of small print. He was a man of classical learning, and very exact, but of no taste in style. He is inelegant, therefore, and his details often too minute to be tolerable, even to a native of the country whose history he writes.[52]

Beverley, a native also, has run into the other extreme: he has comprised our history, from the first propositions of Sir Walter Raleigh to the year 1700, in the hundredth part of the space which Stith employs for the fourth part of the period.[53]

Sir William Keith has taken it up at its earliest period, and continued it to the year 1725. He is agreeable enough in style, and passes over events of little importance. Of course he is short, and would be preferred by a foreigner.[54]

During the regal government, some contest arose on the exaction of an illegal fee by governor Dinwiddie, and doubtless there were others on other occasions not at present recollected. It is supposed that these are not sufficiently interesting to a foreigner to merit a detail.

The petition of the Council and Burgesses of Virginia to the king, their memorial to the lords, and remonstrance to the Commons in the year 1764, began the present contest: and these having proved ineffectual to prevent the passage of the stamp act, the resolutions of the house of burgesses of 1765 were passed, declaring the independence of the people of Virginia on the parliament of Great Britain, in matters of taxation. From that time till the declaration of independence by congress in 1776, their journals are filled with assertions of the public rights.

The pamphlets published in this State on the controverted question were:

1766. An Enquiry into the Rights of the British Colonies, by Richard Bland.
1769. The Monitor's Letters, by Dr. Arthur Lee.
1774. A summary View of the Rights of British America.*
——— Considerations, &c., by Robert Carter Nicholas.

Since the Declaration of Independence this State has had no controversy with any other, except with that of Pennsylvania, on their

---

[52]William Stith, *The History of the First Discovery and Settlement of Virginia* (Williamsburg, 1747).
[53]Robert Beverly, *The History and Present State of Virginia* (1705).
[54]William Keith, *The History of the British Plantations in America* (London, 1738).
*By the author of these notes.

common boundary. Some papers on this subject passed between the executive and legislative bodies of the two states, the result of which was a happy accommodation of their rights.

To this account of our historians, memorials, and pamphlets, it may not be unuseful to add a chronological catalogue of American state-papers, as far as I have been able to collect their titles. It is far from being either complete or correct. Where the title alone, and not the paper itself, has come under my observation, I cannot answer for the exactness of the date. Sometimes I have not been able to find any date at all, and sometimes have not been satisfied that such a paper exists. An extensive collection of papers of this description has been for some time in a course of preparation by a gentleman fully equal to the task, and from whom, therefore, we may hope ere long to receive it. In the mean time accept this as the result of my labors, and as closing the tedious detail which you have so undesignedly drawn upon yourself.

[Jefferson lists 243 documents dating from 1496 to 1768.]

13

BENJAMIN BANNEKER AND THOMAS JEFFERSON

Letters

August 19, 1791, and August 30, 1791

Benjamin Banneker (1731–1806), a free black who lived in Maryland, was a farmer with a passionate interest in astronomy. In 1790, he executed the astronomical calculations for an almanac—a small annual calendar that helped farmers by predicting the times of sunrise and sunset, the weather, the tides, and other useful information. When friends helped him publish the almanac he wasted no time in sending Jefferson, now secretary of state, a copy with the following letter.

Banneker's letter refers directly to Jefferson's thesis in Notes on the State of Virginia *that Africans in America had shown no signs of*

Copy of a Letter from Benjamin Banneker to the Secretary of State, with His Answer (Philadelphia: Daniel Lawrence, 1792).

"genius." Banneker's almanac was part of the antislavery effort to argue otherwise: the almanac, like Phillis Wheatley's book of poems, appeared with an engraving of the author opposite the title page, so that the public would realize that they were, in fact, of African descent. Banneker politely suggests that Jefferson would agree with him about slavery; less humbly, he goes on to quote the words of the Declaration of Independence right back to Jefferson, and expresses shock that the author of these words would hypocritically continue to hold slaves. While not the first surviving black literary response to Jefferson's egalitarianism (the soldier and later minister Lemuel Haynes wrote an essay titled "Liberty Further Extended" just a month after the Declaration of Independence was published), Banneker's letter originated the African American intellectual tradition of responding directly to Jefferson's words to argue publicly against slavery and for civil rights. William Wells Brown, the fugitive slave and antislavery activist, wrote the first African American novel on the subject of an allegedly enslaved daughter of Jefferson (Clotel; or, the President's Daughter *[1853]*).

Banneker published his letter along with Jefferson's careful but complimentary response in 1792.

To Thomas Jefferson

MARYLAND, BALTIMORE COUNTY, AUGUST 19, 1791

SIR,

I am fully sensible of the greatness of that freedom, which I take with you on the present.occasion; a liberty which seemed to me scarcely allowable, when I reflected on that distinguished and dignified station in which you stand, and the almost general prejudice and prepossession, which is so prevalent in the world against those of my complexion.

I suppose it is a truth too well attested to you, to need a proof here, that we are a race of beings, who have long labored under the abuse and censure of the world; that we have long been looked upon with an eye of contempt; and that we have long been considered rather as brutish than human, and scarcely capable of mental endowments.

Sir, I hope I may safely admit, in consequence of that report which hath reached me, that you are a man far less inflexible in sentiments of this nature, than many others; that you are measurably friendly, and well disposed towards us; and that you are willing and ready to lend your aid and assistance to our relief, from those many distresses, and numerous calamities, to which we are reduced.

Now Sir, if this is founded in truth, I apprehend you will embrace every opportunity, to eradicate that train of absurd and false ideas and opinions, which so generally prevails with respect to us; and that your sentiments are concurrent with mine, which are, that one universal Father hath given being to us all; and that he hath not only made us all of one flesh, but that he hath also, without partiality, afforded us all the same sensations and endowed us all with the same faculties; and that however variable we may be in society or religion, however diversified in situation or color, we are all of the same family, and stand in the same relation to him.

Sir, if these are sentiments of which you are fully persuaded, I hope you cannot but acknowledge, that it is the indispensible duty of those, who maintain for themselves the rights of human nature, and who possess the obligations of Christianity, to extend their power and influence to the relief of every part of the human race, from whatever burden or oppression they may unjustly labor under; and this, I apprehend, a full conviction of the truth and obligation of these principles should lead all to.

Sir, I have long been convinced, that if your love for yourselves, and for those inestimable laws, which preserved to you the rights of human nature, was founded on sincerity, you could not but be solicitous, that every individual, of whatever rank or distinction, might with you equally enjoy the blessings thereof; neither could you rest satisfied short of the most active effusion of your exertions, in order to their promotion from any state of degradation, to which the unjustifiable cruelty and barbarism of men may have reduced them.

Sir, I freely and cheerfully acknowledge, that I am of the African race, and in that color which is natural to them of the deepest dye; and it is under a sense of the most profound gratitude to the Supreme Ruler of the Universe, that I now confess to you, that I am not under that state of tyrannical thraldom, and inhuman captivity, to which too many of my brethren are doomed, but that I have abundantly tasted of the fruition of those blessings, which proceed from that free and unequalled liberty with which you are favored; and which, I hope, you will willingly allow you have mercifully received, from the immediate hand of that Being, from whom proceedeth every good and perfect Gift.

Sir, suffer me to recal[l] to your mind that time, in which the arms and tyranny of the British crown were exerted, with every powerful effort, in order to reduce you to a state of servitude: look back, I entreat you, on the variety of dangers to which you were exposed; reflect on that time, in which every human aid appeared unavailable, and in which even hope and fortitude wore the aspect of inability to the conflict, and you cannot but be led to a serious and grateful sense of your miraculous and providential preservation; you cannot but acknowledge, that the present freedom and tranquility which you enjoy you have mercifully received, and that it is the peculiar blessing of Heaven.

This, Sir, was a time when you clear[l]y saw into the injustice of a state of slavery, and in which you had just apprehensions of the horrors of its condition. It was now that your abhorrence thereof was so excited, that you publicly held forth this true and invaluable doctrine, which is worthy to be recorded and remembered in all succeeding ages: "We hold these truths to be self-evident, that all men are created equal; that they are endowed by their Creator with certain unalienable rights, and that among these are, life, liberty, and the pursuit of happiness."

Here was a time, in which your tender feelings for yourselves had engaged you thus to declare, you were then impressed with proper ideas of the great violation of liberty, and the free possession of those blessings, to which you were entitled by nature; but, Sir, how pitiable is it to reflect, that although you were so fully convinced of the benevolence of the Father of Mankind, and of his equal and impartial distribution of these rights and privileges, which he hath conferred upon them, that you should at the same time counteract his mercies, in detaining by fraud and violence so numerous a part of my brethren, under groaning captivity and cruel oppression, that you should at the same time be found guilty of that most criminal act, which you professedly detested in others, with respect to yourselves.

I suppose that your knowledge of the situation of my brethren, is too extensive to need a recital here; neither shall I presume to prescribe methods by which they may be relieved, otherwise than by recommending to you and all others, to wean yourselves from those narrow prejudices which you have imbibed with respect to them, and as Job proposed to his friends, "put your soul in their souls' stead," thus shall your hearts be enlarged with kindness and benevolence towards them; and thus shall you need neither the direction of myself or others, in what manner to proceed herein.

And now, Sir, although my sympathy and affection for my brethren hath caused my enlargement thus far, I ardently hope, that your candor and generosity will plead with you in my behalf, when I make known to you, that it was not originally my design; but having taken up my pen in order to direct to you, as a present, a copy of an Almanac, which I have calculated for the succeeding year, I was unexpectedly and unavoidably led thereto.

This calculation is the production of my arduous study, in this my advanced stage of life; for having long had unbounded desires to become acquainted with the secrets of nature, I have had to gratify my curiosity herein, through my own assiduous application to Astronomical Study, in which I need not recount to you the many difficulties and disadvantages, which I have had to encounter.

And although I had almost declined to make my calculation for the ensuing year, in consequence of that time which I had allotted therefor, being taken up at the Federal Territory, by the request of Mr. Andrew Ellicott,[1] yet finding myself under several engagements to Printers of this state, to whom I had communicated my design, on my return to my place of residence, I industriously applied myself thereto, which I hope I have accomplished with correctness and accuracy; a copy of which I have taken the liberty to direct to you, and which I humbly request you will favorably receive; and although you may have the opportunity of perusing it after its publication, yet I choose to send it to you in manuscript previous thereto, that thereby you might not only have an earlier inspection, but that you might also view it in my own hand writing.

And now, Sir, I shall conclude, and subscribe myself, with the most profound respect,

Your most obedient humble servant,
BENJAMIN BANNEKER

To Benjamin Banneker

PHILADELPHIA, AUGUST 30, 1791.

SIR,

I thank you, sincerely, for your letter of the 19th instant, and for the Almanac it contained. No body wishes more than I do, to see such proofs as you exhibit, that nature has given to our black brethren talents equal to those of the other colors of men; and that the appearance of the want of them, is owing merely to the degraded condition of

---

[1]Mr. Andrew Ellicott: A surveyor and astronomer who hired Banneker to assist him in laying out the District of Columbia in 1791.

their existence, both in Africa and America. I can add with truth, that no body wishes more ardently to see a good system commenced, for raising the condition, both of their body and mind, to what it ought to be, as far as the imbecility of their present existence, and other circumstances, which cannot be neglected, will admit.

I have taken the liberty of sending your Almanac to Monsieur de Condozett, Secretary of the Academy of Sciences at Paris, and Member of the Philanthropic Society, because I considered it as a document, to which your whole color had a right for their justification, against the doubts which have been entertained of them.

> I am with great esteem, Sir,
> Your most obedient
> Humble Servant,
> THOMAS JEFFERSON

A Thomas Jefferson Chronology
(1743–1826)

1743 Born April 13 at Shadwell, Albemarle County, Virginia, to Jane Randolph, member of one of Virginia's most established families, and Peter Jefferson, a planter and surveyor.

1757 Peter Jefferson dies.

1758–60 Studies at boarding school of Rev. James Maury in Fredericksville, Virginia.

1760–62 Enrolled in College of William and Mary, Williamsburg, Virginia.

1762–65 Studies law with George Wythe.

1763 Treaty of Paris ends the Seven Years' War, between Great Britain and France, with various native nations allied with each side.

1764 Inherits 2,750 acres of land from his father's estate upon reaching the age of twenty-one.

1769 Begins building Monticello, a neoclassical mansion, on a mountaintop in Charlottesville, Virginia. Serves his first term in the Virginia House of Burgesses, or provincial assembly. Quickly emerges as an opponent of British imperial policy.

1772 Marries Martha Wayles Skelton, a widow and daughter of the very wealthy landowner John Wayles, on January 1. Martha (Patsy) Jefferson, their first daughter, born September 27.

1773 Inherits land, slaves, and debt upon the death of his father-in-law, John Wayles.

1774 Drafts instructions for Virginia delegates to the Continental Congress, published as *A Summary View of the Rights of British America*.

1775–76 Serves in the Second Continental Congress. Lord Dunmore threatens to liberate slaves, pushing Virginia further toward independence. Drafts the Declaration of Independence and a proposed new constitution for Virginia, which was rejected by the assembly.

1777 Maria (Polly) Jefferson born, the only other of Thomas and Martha's six children to survive into adulthood.

1779 Elected governor of Virginia on June 1. Reelected a year later.

1780 British forces invade Virginia on December 29.

1781 Driven from Monticello by British raids on June 4. House of Delegates investigates Jefferson's conduct as governor; Jefferson cleared of wrongdoing after a brief investigation. Sends first set of answers to queries proposed by François Marbois, secretary to the French ministry in America, on December 20.

1782 Martha Jefferson dies September 6. Accepts appointment as peace commissioner, but bad weather prevents him from getting to England before a provisional treaty was signed.

1784 Serves in the Congress of the United States under the Articles of Confederation. Drafts plans for government in the western territories. Appointed as minister plenipotentiary to negotiate treaties of amity and commerce; arrives in France on July 30.

1785 Succeeds Benjamin Franklin as U.S. minister to France. Publishes English-language edition of *Notes on the State of Virginia* in Paris.

1786 Authors Virginia's Statute for Religious Freedom. Publishes French edition of *Notes on the State of Virginia.*

1787 Publishes English edition of *Notes on the State of Virginia* in London.

1788 Publishes *Notes on the State of Virginia* in Philadelphia.

1789 Observes the series of events leading to the French Revolution. Aids reformers and eventually supports the legitimacy of mob violence. Leaves Paris in September for Virginia, accompanied by daughter Polly and one of his slaves, Sally Hemings, who is pregnant.

1790 Accepts appointment as secretary of state under President George Washington.

1791 Disagrees with Secretary of the Treasury Alexander Hamilton on a number of pressing public issues, including the formation of a national bank. Begins to encourage the development of an opposition party, eventually known as the Democratic Republicans, who opposed the Federalists.

1793–94 Resigns as secretary of state in December, citing differences in the Washington cabinet and weariness; returns to Monticello and begins plans to expand the estate buildings.

1796 Runs for president against John Adams but comes in second and is elected vice-president, according to the rules of the electoral college at that time.

1798–99   Partisan controversy rocks the nation as a diplomatic crisis with France further divides Federalists and Democratic Republicans. Jefferson drafts Kentucky Resolutions opposing the Alien and Sedition Acts, which were intended to silence the opposition movement Federalists perceived as dangerous and disloyal.

1800–01   Publishes appendix to *Notes on the State of Virginia,* defending his account of the murder of Logan's family by frontier settlers. Runs for president and wins the popular vote, but a tie in the electoral college sends the election to the House of Representatives, where Jefferson eventually prevails over his running mate, Aaron Burr.

1802   James Thomson Callendar publishes accounts of Jefferson's affair with Sally Hemings.

1803   Succeeds in acquiring the Louisiana territory from France, more than doubling the size of the nation. Sponsors Lewis and Clark's exploratory expedition into the far western portions of the continent.

1804   Reelected president.

1807–09   Pursues controversial embargo policy, officially suspending foreign trade until Britain and France, at war with each other, recognize American neutral shipping rights.

1817–25   Plans and oversees construction of the University of Virginia.

1820   Denounces Missouri Compromise, insisting that the federal government cannot legislate against slavery, which he depicts as a matter for states to decide.

1821   Writes unfinished Autobiography.

1822   Sells his library and many of his collections at Monticello but fails to eradicate substantial debts.

1826   Frees five of his 135 slaves in his will; Sally Hemings and her four children remain at the estate. Dies July 4, the fiftieth anniversary of American independence. Buried at Monticello under a tombstone celebrating only his authorship of the Declaration of Independence, the Virginia Statute for Religious Freedom, and his founding of the University of Virginia.

Questions for Consideration

1. How did Jefferson's experience as a Virginian shape his views?
2. How did slavery affect the course of the American Revolution in Virginia?
3. Did the American Revolution change Jefferson's attitudes toward slavery and African Americans?
4. What are the important features of Jefferson's political theory or of his beliefs about the nature and practice of government?
5. What are Jefferson's opinions about nature in America? With what other beliefs about America did he contend?
6. What were Jefferson's opinions and policy recommendations concerning Native Americans during the 1780s?
7. How did Jefferson describe Native Americans and African Americans in the *Notes on the State of Virginia*?
8. What were Jefferson's views on American economic development after the American Revolution?
9. Why did Jefferson grant such importance to religious liberty?
10. Should current acceptance of Jefferson's relationship with Sally Hemings change the way we see him? Should it change the way we interpret *Notes on the State of Virginia*?

Selected Bibliography

Boyd, Julian P., Charles T. Cullen, and John Catanzariti, eds. *The Papers of Thomas Jefferson,* 28 vols. to date. Princeton, N.J., 1950–.

Cunningham, Noble E., Jr. *In Pursuit of Reason: The Life of Thomas Jefferson.* Baton Rouge, La., 1987.

Davis, David Brion. *The Problem of Slavery in the Age of Revolution, 1770–1823.* Ithaca, N.Y., 1975.

Ellis, Joseph J. *American Sphinx: The Character of Thomas Jefferson.* New York, 1997.

Engemann, Thomas, ed. *Thomas Jefferson and the Politics of Nature.* Notre Dame, Ind., 2000.

Gordon-Reed, Annette. *Thomas Jefferson and Sally Hemings: An American Controversy.* Charlottesville, Va., 1997.

Holton, Woody. *Forced Founders: Indians, Debtors, Slaves, and the Making of the American Revolution in Virginia.* Chapel Hill, 1999.

Isaac, Rhys. *The Transformation of Virginia, 1740–1790.* Chapel Hill, 1982.

Jordan, Winthrop D. *White Over Black: American Attitudes Toward the Negro, 1550–1812.* Chapel Hill, 1968.

Lewis, Jan Ellen, and Peter S. Onuf, eds. *Sally Hemings and Thomas Jefferson: History, Memory, and Civic Culture.* Charlottesville, Va., 1999.

Malone, Dumas. *Jefferson and His Time.* 6 vols. Boston, 1948–81.

McLaughlin, Jack. *Jefferson and Monticello: The Biography of a Builder.* New York, 1988.

Miller, Charles A. *Jefferson and Nature: An Interpretation.* Baltimore, 1988.

Miller, John Chester. *The Wolf by the Ears: Thomas Jefferson and Slavery.* New York, 1977.

Morgan, Edmund S. *American Slavery—American Freedom: The Ordeal of Colonial Virginia.* New York, 1976.

Onuf, Peter S. *Jefferson's Empire: The Language of American Nationhood.* Charlottesville, Va., 2000.

———, ed. *Jeffersonian Legacies.* Charlottesville, Va., 1993.

Peterson, Merrill D. *Thomas Jefferson and the New Nation.* New York, 1970.

————. ed. *Thomas Jefferson: Writings*. New York, 1984.

Sloan, Herbert E. *Principle and Interest: Thomas Jefferson and the Problem of Debt*. New York, 1995.

Wallace, Anthony F.C. *Thomas Jefferson and the Indians: The Tragic Story of the First Americans*. Cambridge, Mass., 1999.

Index